One of Geoff's books.
James Cameron was an old
friend & colleague.

D + Hunter,

sent 640

CAL

# THE NIGHT BATTLE

# THE NIGHT BATTLE

*Essays*

by

J. M. CAMERON

Controversy, at least in this age, does not lie between the hosts of heaven, Michael and his Angels on the one side, and the powers of evil on the other; but it is a sort of night battle, where each fights for himself, and friend and foe stand together.

"Faith and Reason, contrasted as Habits of Mind",
in John Henry Newman, *Sermons, chiefly on the
Theory of Religious Belief, preached before the
University of Oxford* (1843).

LONDON
BURNS & OATES

PRINTED AND BOUND IN GREAT BRITAIN BY
HAZELL WATSON AND VINEY LTD
AYLESBURY AND SLOUGH
FOR BURNS AND OATES LIMITED
25 ASHLEY PLACE, LONDON, S.W.1

# Contents

# Preface

WHEN it was suggested to me that I should select for publication some of my occasional writings of the past ten years, I was at first inclined to demur. Looking through them has been something of a penitential exercise. All the same, I have in the end been persuaded to make such a selection; and I wish to say something here to explain why these twelve essays may be thought to have some claim to be given a second life.

Few philosophers at best, in any generation, make a decisive break-through in philosophy itself. A Frege or a Husserl or a Wittgenstein is a rare genius with something of the child's eye for seeing that the emperor, praised with such unanimity for his splendid robes, is in fact naked. What the rest of us can do, with here and there some degree of success, is either to do minute work on small problems, using methods we owe to the masters, or to use the tools of the philosopher to analyse problems thrown up by the sciences or by the arts or by the political and moral articulations of human life. All these essays, except "Words and Things" which has to do with Mr. Gellner's recent attack upon linguistic philosophy, are of the latter kind: they are concerned with politics, literature and religion.

The political scene changes so rapidly that I have had to ask myself if there is anything in the political essays I would now wish to withdraw. The oldest of them, "Problems of Communist Language", I should no doubt wish to phrase somewhat differently if I were to write it again, though the analysis there given still seems to me in principle correct.

vii

Now that we see the fuller consequences of the death of Stalin and of the consequent liberalization, in some degree, of Soviet society, we may be inclined to think that I all the same underestimated the attachment of the Soviet leaders to the theory of Marxism. In an affable and ebullient moment Mr. Khrushchev confessed to the belief that he would "bury us". Such a remark certainly denotes great confidence in something, but it can scarcely be confidence in the theory of Marxism, for the reasons I give in my essay. It is rather confidence in his régime and in its attractive power. It would be rash to suppose that his confidence has no grounds. Soviet society has proved itself both tougher and more flexible than an impartial observer would have thought fifteen years ago. Its prescription for enabling a primitive society swiftly to acquire the bases of civilization seems more plausible than anything the West has to offer at the moment. No one can doubt that if the economic resources poured into South-east Asia by the United States had been deployed under Soviet auspices, there would have been more to show for the expenditure. This is not a decisive argument for preferring Soviet methods; for these are successful because the landlords, generals and members of the comprador class, to whose fingers the dollars stick and who are thereby encouraged to push their countries into absurd adventures, would be liquidated or reduced to slavery or sent into exile under Soviet rule; and this would be the prelude to a long purgatorial period of forced saving, under the tyrannical rule of party bosses, for the common people. All the same, an Asian or an African, or a worker or peasant in Central or South America, facing (or believing himself to be facing) a choice between a stagnant and corrupt régime under which men have neither political freedom nor a materially decent life and an iron age under the rule of the party, might rationally prefer the latter; for he might argue with some sense that the iron age will anyway come in the end and that it might be as well to get it over as soon as possible.

In this respect the moral balance, though still (I would argue) tilted on the side of the West, is by no means so clearly tilted as we in the West are hubristically inclined to suppose. In Africa Britain and France have on the whole done remarkably well; but the scene in South-east Asia and in Central and South America is still a painful one. In another respect the Soviet Union and the West are morally on a basis of absolute equality : they are equally committed to the use, in some circumstances, of nuclear weapons against centres of population. This is the gravest issue of the period; and although there is no essay specifically devoted to this topic, the reader will readily perceive that it is my view that a fundamental analysis of the moral position to which Catholics are committed makes it plain that in conscience Catholics are bound not to co-operate in the defence policies of the Great Powers, not on account of any foreseeable consequences, good or bad, of the use of nuclear weapons, but because their use against centres of population (and it is just false that it is still uncertain that the Powers have in mind such uses for their weapons) would be gravely sinful.

From this, and from other evidence in the following essays, it will be rightly inferred that I am what is sometimes called a "Catholic of the left". This is not so fabulous a creature as many English and American Catholics are inclined to believe; and the attitude has a respectable though somewhat troubled ancestry. What does greatly concern me as a Catholic is the extent to which Catholics are inclined to be the devotees of what I have elsewhere called "political fetishism". This fetishism "gives to the commands of the state, notably where matters of war and peace are in question, a sacred and unchallengeable character, with the result that in this area of political life there is a tacit understanding that traditional moral principles are not to be applied . . . where the security of the state is held to be in question (held to be in question, that is, by the political authorities themselves), too often a guilty silence descends. General principles may still be enunciated, but awkward or potentially treasonable applications are avoided." [1] This fetishism shows itself as well in our enchantment by the supreme political commonplaces of *les bien pensants* of every country. It is this more than anything else that has stood in the way of a sober and objective study of Communism. Thus, the remarkable changes, not all of them encouraging, that have overcome the Communist world since the death of Stalin are still not studied for what they are in themselves, but are compulsively interpreted as the deceptive camouflage of an unchanging and satanic conspiracy. That Communists are men like ourselves (indeed, in such countries as Italy and France they are our most commonplace neighbours and *pères de famille*), and not demons from the pit, is a concession many Catholic commentators are reluctant to make. Of course, it is true that the *père de famille* is capable of everything; but this excellent observation applies universally. At any rate, I hope that my essays on aspects of Communism and left-wing politics in general, slight in themselves, may serve as specimens of a more rational approach to these problems.

When I was appointed to the Chair of Philosophy in the University of Leeds an early duty, and a pleasant one, was to write my inaugural lecture. In choosing as my subject "Poetry and Dialectic" (it is here reprinted shorn of those remarks that belong uniquely to the occasion) I hoped to succeed in saying something on a theme interesting to others and of deep significance to me personally. The practice of poetry, reflection upon it and upon its connections with other disciplines and with the whole business of human life, these things, with —and in the end not separately from—my religion and my love for my family, my colleagues, my pupils and my friends, have been at the centre of my life; and it seemed therefore inescapable that I should set myself the task of saying as concisely as I could what a philosopher today might think of

1. "Obedience to Political Authority", in John M. Todd (Editor), *Problems of Authority*, Baltimore and London, 1962, pp. 212, 213.

those noble fictions without which it is hard to think of human life as tolerable. With what success I have done this is a matter to be left to the reader. The two pieces on Pope are written from the standpoint of one who is, as a philosopher, necessarily concerned with the history of ideas. I hope the polemical tone of "Mr. Tillotson and Mr. Pope" may be forgiven. As I explain, my differences from Professor Tillotson are a function of my admiration for his work; and my concern with the subject springs from my belief that the history of ideas is a desirable part of the academic study of literature as well as of philosophy.

The last two essays in this collection attempt to elucidate those aspects of the thought of John Henry Newman which seem to me of great contemporary interest. He is a theologian who asks questions and sets problems that are central for the present age. It is of some importance for English Catholics in particular that he comes from a background quite unlike the scholastic background of most modern Catholic theologians. Philosophically he is a child, as I try to show in the last essay, of the empiricist tradition; theologically his roots are Biblical and patristic. In both respects he vibrates sympathetically to the resonances of our day and is uniquely qualified—this is more readily recognized in France and Germany than in his own country—to indicate those problems in the philosophy of religion—the role of natural theology, the logical grammar of theological statements, the historical element in the religious consciousness—that press hardly upon us today. I hope some time to have an opportunity to write more systematically upon the thought of this remarkable man who, for all his own dialectical subtlety, loved to make his own the thought of St. Ambrose, a thought which philosophers especially should always keep before them: *Non in dialectica complacuit Deo salvum facere populum suum.*

J. M. CAMERON

*Leeds, March 1962*

# Acknowledgments

ACKNOWLEDGMENTS are due to the editors and proprietors of the following periodicals in which these essays first appeared: *Blackfriars, The Listener, Philosophical Studies* (Maynooth), the *Dublin Review, The Times Literary Supplement, Victorian Studies* (Indiana); and to the following for permission to reprint material: Mr. Rupert Hart-Davis, the Aristotelian Society, the Leeds University Press. It would be invidious to single out the many colleagues, friends and pupils to whom I am in one way and another indebted; but I should like to express my thanks to my secretary, Miss Dorothy Raper, for services rendered with so much patience and good nature. I must also offer my warmest thanks to Mr. T. F. Burns for his constant encouragement. What I owe to my wife will best be understood by the wives of other academic persons.

# 1
# Catholicism and Political Mythology

IN OUR day the Church is present, as it were, only on the
margin of politics. Even in those countries, such as Ireland
and Spain, where the Church is in one sense an obvious power
in politics, the action of the Church is still marginal; for the
substance of politics, however it may be constituted and
whatever analysis of it we may offer, is what it is by reason
of those secular forces which determine the character of
politics in other states where the Church institutionally is of
little or no account; and the fundamental decisions of the
political authorities are always in the last resort swayed by
secular considerations of precisely the same kind as those
operative in non-Catholic societies. There is, outside the
Soviet Union, the popular democracies and China, a common
social pattern, diversified in appearance and in its degree of
maturity and in the political superstructure it bears, but still
a common pattern: that of the capitalism of the mid-
twentieth century. It is a capitalism distinguished by vast
technical achievements, a steady flow of consumers' goods
in the more advanced countries and the promise of similar
bounty in the backward countries if only—no doubt this is
a very large if—the problems of investment and population
increase can be solved. It seems obvious to many that the
masses in at least the United States, Great Britain, Western
Germany, Scandinavia and similar countries, have "never had
it so good". That it is nevertheless a sad society is reflected in
its characteristic art. That it is an immoral society is made
plain, not so much by the sexual licence, the passion for
gambling, the violence so characteristic of its great cities, all
the things that attract the ready censure of the moralist in

I

and out of the pulpit, but rather by the way it spends its vast resources. Schools, hospitals, decent houses, handsome towns, the care of the old, the feeding of the hungry in the backward countries, these are obvious priorities in so rich a society; but they are commonly secondary to quite other concerns: advertising, palaces for oil companies, banks and pornographic newspapers; and—above all—defence, and a defence that is no defence but a threat to annihilate others a few minutes before or after we are ourselves annihilated.

This is a highly schematic and in detail unjust account of mid-century capitalism. But, despite all that is richly human within these societies, all that toughly struggles with the trivialities of the admass society, all that responds with generosity to the claims of the weak and the oppressed, it is no further from the truth than is a telling caricature from its original. We live in a corrupt society, quite possibly in a doomed society, and one doomed, not by the political conflicts within it, but by its incapacity to free itself from the demons released when the first atomic bombs were dropped upon Hiroshima and Nagasaki.

It would be unfair, but not so unfair as all that, to say that Catholics have very little to offer in face of this situation. Much moralizing goes on, it is true, rather in the style of M.R.A. (Indeed, it is alarming to find a certain rapprochement between prominent Catholic figures and this dubious movement.) There is much mulling over an ill-defined body of doctrine sometimes known as "the social teaching of the Church", a mulling over which has no political consequences whatever, for the doctrines considered remain at a high level of generality, so that often quite opposite lines of policy seem equally compatible with them (contrast, for example, the savagely competitive societies of the United States and Western Germany with the apparent paternalism of Spain and Portugal, both of them equally approved by some Catholic publicists), and a good deal of what is said on such topics as private property and nationalization is calculated to comfort those who are satisfied with things as they are. In Britain and the United States there are tiny groups—the group round Dorothy Day, for example—more or less at odds with things as they are; in France such groups are much bigger and much more important—and for this reason France is, of all the western countries, the one where the critically minded Catholic (cleric or layman) feels less stifled than elsewhere. But the general picture is one in which Catholics, both the masses and the *élites*, are, except in certain specific fields such as those of education and sexual morality, content with mid-century capitalism and prepared to defend it as a way of life against what is held to be the relentless and unceasing threat of world Communism to subvert it.

The comparative absence of the Church from the life of politics is not something peculiarly characteristic of the twentieth century. The rise of industrialism overtook a largely somnolent Christendom odiously content with the division of powers and of spheres of influence between throne and altar. The middle-class revolution and modern capitalism overcame a world wrapped in dreams of a social order, hierarchical and sanctified by the decencies of religious observance, the substance of which had dwindled to nothing. The terrible fractures of the shell of this order, from 1789 onwards, were put down to the machinations of a handful of agitators and *illuminati*. The true state of affairs was very different and corresponded with fair accuracy to that described by Marx and Engels in *The Communist Manifesto*. The middle-class revolution and the growth of industrialism were two aspects of a single process which had shattered the old social order beyond all possibility of reconstruction. The social ties of pre-capitalist society, between man and man, class and class, had been replaced by the cash nexus. Society seemed to be driving towards the point where it would be polarized between the owners of the means of production and a vast proletariat. The conflict between classes was not a fiction invented by Marx and Engels and put about

3

by agitators: it was the plainest of facts in the England of Chartism or the Europe of 1848. And the response of the proletariat to the pressures of capitalism, the creation of the labour movement—trade unions, co-operative societies, political parties—is one of the great human achievements, an achievement rich in moral significance, for it represented much more than a merely defensive movement concerned with economic interests. It was in part a reconstitution of the human community fragmented by the rise of capitalism; and it created an entire world within which the politically conscious working man enjoyed a community of moral values and a community of aspiration. It is the immense *seriousness* of the world of the labour movement, its richness and humanity, that middle-class commentators, the Catholics among them even more than the others, have failed to grasp; and because they have failed to grasp this seriousness, they have failed equally to measure the tragedy of the corruption and decline of this movement in our own day.

Of course, in ultimate terms, for the believer, for the Church, which lives by the divine promises, the failure of the Church to be visibly present in the midst of great developments of the human spirit is not tragic. We live by faith, not by sight. The implication of the Church with the world is at all periods a trial of faith. One thinks of the degradation of the Papacy in the darkness of the tenth century, of Renaissance Rome, of the blood and agony of the seventeenth century the wounds of which are as yet scarcely crusted over. And yet it is important to put aside the temptation to quietism, a relapse into a peace which is quite other than the peace of Christ. "All will be well", no doubt. To believe otherwise would be to lose one's faith. But there is a kind of peace of mind which is bought too cheaply, which represents not the victory of faith but a retreat into blindness and complacency. If in our own day there are those who (for example) treat, when faced with the problem of nuclear warfare in relation to questions of "defence", the entire

Catholic moral tradition as of no account, as irrelevant to the conflict between Russia and the West—for is this not a conflict between Christianity and atheism, between the cause of God and the cause of the Devil?—this is a peace of mind bought too cheaply. Strangers and pilgrims we may be; but unless we are to relapse into a neo-Augustinian politics of a Lutheran type—and this would be to neglect the medieval and the modern political experience—we have to face the contemporary world of politics as that world within which Providence has placed us for purposes that we can, at least in part, hope to understand.

If the Church (in the sense of the actual historical community of the faithful) is, and has been throughout the era of the middle-class revolution, present only on the margin of politics, this is not a state of affairs to be altered by a simple decision. For one thing, this does not altogether depend upon Catholics, nor has it ever done so. We rightly feel as shameful those deficiencies in us which are in part responsible for this state of affairs. But the world necessarily resists the mind of the Church, and this is, and will be, just as true of a "Catholic" régime as of any other. The Emperor Frederick II, Philip the Fair, Henry VIII, were products of a culture permeated by Catholicism, as are the Italian Communists of today. What has first to be done is something simpler and more humble: to understand how the present situation has come about; to understand our own society; to free ourselves from the major deformations that have overcome much Catholic social thinking; and patiently to explain to others how we see the tasks of Catholics today. The present writer would not wish to suggest that there is in the political field *one* saving truth which all Catholics of goodwill may be brought to accept; rather, that there is a multitude of obstacles to our thinking intelligently and responsibly about political matters. These have to be removed before we can even begin to do the job.

We are imprisoned within a number of political myths,

forms of "false consciousness", to use the Marxian-Hegelian terminology, that are demonstrably false but are nevertheless deeply rooted and hard to shift. This is almost a part of the definition of "myth" in politics: a demonstrably false picture which is all the same cherished with affection and tenacity from motives which the cherishers are unwilling to recognize. This is clear enough if we take one of the great fundamental myths of our age, one with a wider influence than we commonly allow, and one which (scandalously) is not without influence upon sections of Catholic opinion: the myth of the Jewish world conspiracy. This myth is farcically absurd; its absurdity is demonstrable; but it is alive and vigorous in the minds of many otherwise rational people. Other myths which enchant Catholics—though not Catholics only —are of a more complex order; and they are entertained with varying degrees of seriousness. I want to examine a particular instance; and then to examine the more generalized form of which this is a particular instance.

The Spanish Civil War was for European and American Catholics, as for liberals and socialists, a traumatic experience; and in both cases the war itself was transformed by mythical thinking into something that it never even remotely resembled. Here I am concerned only with the mythical thinking of Catholics. The Catholic account, set out in the Catholic press at the time, still present in the minds of the general run of Catholic publicists, is roughly as follows. The Spanish Civil War was a revolutionary attempt on the part of the Communist International to set up a Soviet State in Spain. The revolution was marked from the beginning by atrocities which revealed by their nature—the burning of churches, the murder of priests and religious, the prohibition of Catholic public worship—that a fundamental feature of Communist strategy was the destruction of the Christian religion. The attempt to set up a Soviet State was thwarted by a popular defence of the Church by Spanish Catholics under the leadership of General Franco, with the aid (it is grudgingly admitted) of Italian and German troops and war material, aid which was only solicited after the vast scale of Soviet intervention had become known.

Such is the popular Catholic account. It is false, and known to be false by many of those who nevertheless propagate the account.

The Spanish Communist party was of little importance at the beginning of the war. The major parties—and they were certainly in favour of using the war as a means of social revolution—in the Republican coalition in its first stages were the Socialists and the Anarchists, with their associated trade union organizations, and, in Catalonia, the P.O.U.M., a semi-Trotskyist workers' party. It was these parties, and these parties alone, that were responsible for the anti-clerical atrocities that marked the first stages of the war. (It is worth noting that the burning of churches and the murder of priests are not *new* phenomena in Spanish history.) The rise of the Communist party to a position, first of influence, and in the later, hopeless stages of the war, of nearly supreme power, was a consequence and a condition of the reception of military aid (material, pilots, specialists and—above all—G.P.U. men) from the Soviet Union. The Spanish Communist party, and the synthetic sister party set up in Catalonia, had no roots in the Spanish working class and was above all a party of the white-collar workers and even of sections of the bourgeoisie (e.g. the orange-growers of Valencia). Its close allies in the Republican coalition were the Basque Catholics. (These latter, many of whose leaders, priests and laymen, are still in prison or in exile, are an awkwardness for the myth-mongers, more especially as the Basque country was one of the few areas of Spain where there was evident Catholic devotion before the Civil War, where, for example, mature males of the working class or the peasantry were to be seen at Mass on Sunday.) The Communists were throughout the war a counter-revolutionary force, strangling, when and in so far as they had enough power, the incipient social revolution, partly by their influence within the Republican coalition, an influence which sprang entirely from the carefully apportioned Soviet aid (aid which, incidentally, was paid for out of the gold reserves of the Bank of Spain), partly by the use of police terror under the leadership of the G.P.U. agents that entered Spain along with the tanks and the aeroplanes. (It is a macabre and appalling postscript to the war that most of the Soviet military specialists were liquidated in the later stages of the Great Purge on their return to the Soviet Union.) The scale of Soviet aid, always far less than that of the Italians and the Germans, was never considerable enough to give the Republicans a decisive advantage; it was enough to keep the war going until Stalin decided that Spain was expendable in the interests of his grand strategy. By the end of the war, if not before, an alliance with the Germans was becoming a genuine possibility. These are the principal facts denied by the standard Catholic myth. Naturally, the myth is used in various ways and in various forms. For example, the extent of Communist terrorism against the other parties of the Republican coalition is sometimes brought out in order to magnify the role of the Communists. But in general there is no serious attempt to see the facts of the Spanish situation in all their complexity. Everything is simplified and distorted in the interests of a prefabricated picture of base Communists engaged in an anti-religious war against single-minded defenders of the Faith. It is true, the counter-myth of constitutionally minded liberals and social democrats attacked without provocation by a Fascist counter-revolution is almost as distant from the facts, though it has greater surface plausibility.

I have already said that the myth of the Spanish Civil War is a particular instance of a more general myth. This myth I will now try to describe. It is the myth of the world conflict between the Church and Communism understood as being roughly conterminous with the conflict between the western Powers and the Powers of the Soviet bloc. Of course, that these two conflicts exist, and that there are connections of a kind between them, no one would wish to deny; nor would I wish to deny that it is the steady policy of all the Communist states at best to hamper and at worst to destroy the influence of the Catholic Church and, though with less consistency, of other Christian bodies. The facts of a savage persecution in, say, Czechoslovakia, Hungary and China are plain enough. It is also plain that the Communists, in so far as we assume that what is put out for public consumption represents what they think, are also imprisoned within a myth which is the exact reverse of the Catholic myth: the view that the Pope, the Chinese bishops, indeed, all devout and active Catholics, are agents of "western imperialism" and spies for Britain and the United States.

An anecdote (a true story) well illustrates the dangers of the Catholic myth. During the war a Swiss priest was asked what he would do if there should be either a Soviet conquest of Switzerland or a Nazi conquest. He replied: "If the Communists were to come, I would stay with my people, for I know I should be faced with an anti-Christian power. If the Nazis were to come, I would try to escape abroad; *for I fear I should deceive myself.*" That we should deceive ourselves: this is what we risk as we dwell within the myth. The western world has already passed judgment upon itself. The publication of the judgment is to be found in the explicit values of the affluent society and in the accepted concept of defence (the preparation of total war with nuclear weapons). Provided we do not quarrel seriously with this judgment, we are not only tolerated within western society; we are even given a place of honour, as front-rank fighters in the struggle against Communism, as indispensable providers of moral backing for the policies of N.A.T.O. Of course, the Church as such is not sucked into the myth. The utterances of popes, of individual moral theologians and of particular national hierarchies, the witness of lay groups throughout the Catholic world, all these show an independence of the myth and are signs that the

divine origin and mission of the Church are never permitted
to be completely hidden. But if we take the Catholic masses,
in so far as they are deployed politically through the Christian Democratic parties and the Democratic and Republican
parties in the United States and receive their political forma-
tion through much of the Catholic press—notably that of the
United States—then the situation is very different; for here
the enchantment of the myth is virtually complete.[1]

The bad consequences of imprisonment within the myth
are many. The following may be singled out. First, there is a
turning away from serious political analysis to a form of
thinking which is paranoid and thus quasi-automatic.
Secondly, there is a total lack of interest in the *truth* of
political statements; [2] what are thought to matter are the
supposed interests and intentions of those who make the
statements (in this as in other matters there is a striking
parallel with the vulgar Marxism of the Communists).
Thirdly, there is a gross confusion, which is a betrayal by
Catholics of their apostolic responsibility, between the
Church and those political orders that are taken to be the
institutional defences of the Church in the present situation.

The turning away from serious political analysis may be
illustrated by the phenomenon of McCarthyism in the United
States and by the reluctance to engage in a serious examination of Communism, especially since the death of Stalin. It
would be idle to deny that the Catholic masses in the United
States were largely convinced of the truth of McCarthy's
picture of American and world politics; indeed, this picture
is still widely entertained by those influenced by such power-

1. Not all sections of the Christian Democratic parties are imprisoned
within the myth. The French M.R.P. and the left wing of the Italian
Christian Democrats are notably independent in their thinking.

2. A striking instance of this disregard of truth is to be found in a
broadcast talk delivered over the Nairobi (Kenya) Radio by the Reverend
E. Colleton, c.s.sp. "At the very beginning of the Russian Revolution a
decree was passed declaring that all women between the ages of seven-
teen and thirty-two were the property of the State." Thus Father Colleton.
It is many years since we came across this fabrication. The talk is reprinted in *Christian Order*, Vol. I, No. 1, January 1960, edited by Paul
Crane, s.j.

ful organs of Catholic opinion as the Brooklyn *Tablet*. That this picture is a form of mythical thinking need not be demonstrated in detail. McCarthy himself was always clear that the touch of fact would have disintegrated the picture; and although his allegations—that he had in his hand the names of so and so many card-carrying Communists in the employ of the State Department, and so on—were always given a factual *form*, the factual backing was never produced; in a sense—and this is the mark of mythical thinking —the question as to whether or not there *was* factual backing for these statements was profoundly uninteresting. In the same way, anti-Semites have no interest in the factual truth of allegations of ritual murder or in the provenance of the Protocols of the Elders of Zion. These matters have the same role in political discourse as magical explanations of natural processes in the natural sciences.

The failure to engage in a serious examination of Communism is more important, for it is characteristic of many intelligent Catholics who were never absorbed by the delusions of McCarthyism. Fundamentally, it springs from the desire that there should be, as it were, a counter-Church; and from this desire there springs the belief that Communism *is* this counter-Church. Further, just as in this form of thinking Communism is disengaged from the historical actualities in which it is embodied, so, too, with the Church; the Church implicated in the world, with all the ambiguities and imperfections this involves, is refined into the shining and integrated enemy of a clinically pure Communism.

Communism is as much an historical phenomenon as Jacobinism. In both cases there is a revolutionary doctrine, extremely complex in its origins, which is caught up into a great political enterprise and becomes identified with a system of states. In both cases the original dynamism of the doctrine is modified by the necessary political concerns of those who both hold the doctrine and occupy positions of power, positions which make their own demands, demands that cannot always be reconciled with what were originally taken to be the implications of the doctrine. In both cases it is hard to say at what point the doctrine changes from a genuine belief to a manipulated ideology, useful as a means of bringing about political consequences desired for reasons quite unconnected with the doctrine, and from an ideology to a form of ritual speech no longer taken seriously by those who use it. It is easy enough to see that in the case of Jacobinism the change from revolutionary doctrine to manipulated ideology is as early as Thermidor, if not earlier. It is not much more difficult to see that the Bolshevism of as early as 1921 is already beginning to change its form under the pressure of the exigencies of the situation of the young Soviet state.

It is reasonable to believe that with the death of Stalin Communism began to pass through yet another mutation. The entire period of Stalinism was in violent contrast with the critical and iconoclastic tradition of Bolshevism; and it was too profound and irreversible a social experience for it to be possible, even had such typical products of the Stalinist machine as Malenkov and Khrushchev desired it, to return to the earlier doctrine of Bolshevism. What is dead as doctrine may survive as ideology and as ritual speech.[3] But the empirical and pragmatic character of latter-day Bolshevism is revealed in a hundred ways: the compromise between the old Stalinists of the apparatus, the pitiful remnants of the opposition and the new middle class of technocrats, scientists and administrators (in itself a considerable political achievement represented by the ending of the terror and the breaking of the independent power of the political police) has already produced consequences both within the Soviet bloc and in the relations between this bloc and other states the depth and importance of which it is easy to underestimate. In any case, no political analysis which sees Mr. Khrushchev and his lieu-

3. I discuss this question in "Problems of Communist Language" on pp. 34 ff. below.

tenants as the general staff of the world revolution has much relation to the complexities of the Communist world.

Many Catholic commentators are reluctant to admit this. It is as though the picture of a bloc of states every feature of whose policy may be interpreted in relation to the strategy of world revolution *must* remain a fixed point upon which to orientate oneself. Otherwise one would be lost, one would not know where to go or what to say. Politics as a spectacle would then be infinitely complicated, infinitely baffling, a vast maze in which one cannot hope to chance upon the guiding thread; in which all judgments are judgments of, at best, probabilities, in which cautious decisions have to be taken in the twilight of opinion, not the glare of knowledge; above all, it would follow from the very uncertainties of politics that the fixed point for the Catholic would be his own moral tradition, not the delusion of the great Communist world conspiracy which provides a justification for the abandonment of this tradition; for in the apocalyptic struggle against the Communist antichrist everything (so it is supposed)—lies, hatred, slander, mass murder—is allowed. It is easier to accept a world in which the Devil is external to ourselves, is embodied in an institution, than to face the presence of evil within ourselves; and so the fixed point has to remain.

If we really are, as I have argued, faced with a form of social consciousness that is in its fundamental features delusory, then it would be wrong to suppose that it will be overcome by intellectual criticism. Paranoia is not cured by argument. Nor is there on the social level any therapy corresponding to that from which something may be expected at the level of the individual. Social delusions are destroyed by forces that one cannot anticipate and by the relentless pressure of facts, a pressure that is in the end effective. Think, for example, of the horrid prevalence of the belief in witchcraft from the fifteenth to the seventeenth centuries; or of the short nightmare during which the delusions of National Socialism overcame the German nation. In terms, then, of political argument we cannot hope to achieve more than small and isolated successes, and that with individuals whose thinking is delusory in only the most superficial sense.

The really hopeful feature of our situation lies not so much in the growing signs here and there of political sanity among Catholics (here again, in relation to such a question as the war in Algeria, the French have offered us a splendid example), signs of an increasing disposition patiently to examine the political experience of our century and to draw the necessary conclusions, though many examples could be cited, as in that profound renewal of the Church which is becoming manifest in our day. The plainest sign of this renewal is the gradual restoration of the Liturgy to the people. A change in modes of worship, and one moreover which is the fruit of the labours of scholars and antiquaries, how can this (some may ask) be a sign of a profound renewal of the life of the Church? How can a change in modes of worship affect the social role of the Church and touch the life of politics? What relation could there be between the Offertory procession and the young men and women pouring along the road to Aldermaston, between the Gélineau psalms and the world of "pop" singers? No doubt such questions almost ask themselves.

If we are inclined to suppose that a change in the modes of worship cannot have serious consequences for real life, this is because we have lost our hold upon the meaning of worship, that we no longer—outside the pages of the textbooks —see this as the central activity of the people of God from which everything else may be hoped for. The central activity of those who were brought into the Church by the first preaching of the Apostles was "the breaking of the bread, and the prayers".[4] It was from this centre, and through what this centre was, that the task of preaching the good news to every creature was in obedience undertaken. The entire effort of the Church, which has seen the rise and fall of civilizations

4. Acts ii. 42.

14

and has shown itself in every century capable of leavening the dough of unregenerate human nature, springs from and returns to "the breaking of the bread, and the prayers". It is true, the Eucharistic Sacrifice has an absolute value which is independent of the degree of fervour and understanding in those who offer it; but to contribute less fervour and understanding than can at a given time be had is (if the expression may be permitted) a degradation of the Liturgy, and is accompanied by a false separation between preaching and teaching and the Liturgy. When the priest says *Orate, fratres* with no thought that his brethren should heed or understand, when the Mass of the catechumens is recited at the altar while a sermon is preached to the congregation, when the Canon is ended and the people of God present at the sacrifice do not even know that it is their privilege to ratify it with the *Amen*, then the function of the Liturgy is obscured; and it is possible for an entire generation of Catholics to fail altogether to realize the nature of the sacrifice—*meum sacrificium ac vestrum*, the Church teaches us through the mouth of the priest—at which they are present throughout their lives.

The restoration of the Liturgy to the people is, then, not only a means of enabling both laity *and* clergy to participate intelligently—that is, as mature men, not as children—in public worship; it is also a renewal of the teaching mission of the Church and a renewal which presents us with a *norm*, the sacred tradition embodied in the Liturgy, which brings with it a sense of proportion in devotion and a realization of the relatively peripheral character of ephemeral fashions in devotion. The Liturgy thus becomes what in theory it has always been, the means by which we make our own the substance of the Faith. In this process of making our own the substance of the Faith many old things that appear to be new come to light. There is, for example, a fresh realization that we are the new Israel, "a chosen race, a royal priesthood, a consecrated nation";[5] and with this realization a new awareness of the orthodox doctrine of the priesthood of the laity.

Here is, perhaps, one of the chief fruits, so far as one can anticipate the later developments of a movement that is still in its earliest stages, of the Liturgical Movement: the growth in maturity of the laity in the body of the Church. In the modern period the laity has come to political maturity; but within the Church laymen have tended to remain childish. The anti-clericalism (and the clericalism) endemic in Catholic countries springs from this contradiction between political maturity and religious immaturity. With the Liturgical Movement and all that may come from it we are presented with the possibility of overcoming the contradiction and with it the tension and the sterility which have so often character- ized the politics of Catholic societies. The appearance of a maturity which is that of the complete man, a social and political animal who takes his membership of the super- natural society seriously and intelligently, is a solvent of mythical thinking. It is not accidental that the centres of resistance to liturgical reform and to that whole renewal of the life of the Church that goes with it are precisely those groups most deeply enslaved by the political myths of our time; nor is it accidental that the punishment for religious immaturity in Catholic societies should be the popularity of mass Communist parties, themselves strongholds of another kind of mythical thinking. The opposed myths are, as it were, parasitic one upon the other.

This renewal of the life of the Church through the Liturgy and the Bible is still in the main something to be prayed for, hoped for, worked for. That it is a matter of extreme urgency (not that we should be consumed with anxiety), as urgent for the missionary work of the Church as for the salvaging of the Catholic masses in the old centres of Catholicism, scarcely needs to be argued. I am tempted to think that the greatest

5. 1 Peter ii. 9.

possibilities are to be found in the United States. In such societies as those of England and France the egalitarian present is profoundly modified by the hierarchical past. American society has never known, in quite the European way, the pressures of the social and ecclesiastical hierarchies, and this gives its atmosphere a charm and an intoxication— if, as well, a certain crudity—that one cannot find in Europe. There is, of course, an enormous flaw in American egalitarianism : the failure completely to integrate the Negro community within the common society. But one guesses that the thousands of Negroes who come in a great torrent from Mississippi and Alabama and the rest of the Deep South to the industries and towns north of the Mason-Dixon Line are in part moved by the hope that the United States may be for them what it has been for the immigrants from Europe. And in relation to *this* problem American Catholics have a good record, better, perhaps, than that of the other religious bodies. It would be ironical, and splendid, if the most potent of the Catholic myths were to receive a mortal wound in the land of the late Senator McCarthy.

1960

# 2

## T. S. Eliot as a Political Writer

MR. ELIOT has never been deficient in candour and the courage to criticize himself. Ten years ago he remarked somewhat acidly on "the tendency . . . for those who have acquired some reputation, to write books outside the subject on which they have made their reputation",[1] and did not hesitate to instance his own work. Here he is unjust to himself. Even if he had never written a word about politics, it would still be evident that the author of *Coriolan* and *Murder in the Cathedral* had reflected much upon the life of our society and upon the relations of Church and State. Apart from this, Mr. Edwin Muir's comment on the politics of Shakespeare applies very well to Mr. Eliot. Mr. Muir writes:

> It has been maintained that Shakespeare had no politics. Now this may be true in a sense, if it means that he cannot be put down as a Conservative, or a Liberal, or a Socialist, or whatever the counterparts of these modern classifications were in his time. . . . But a man may have political sense, and political sense of a high kind, without falling into any of these categories; for his mind, while working politically, may not think in terms of any of them. To say that Shakespeare had no politics—if one takes the statement seriously—can only mean that he had no conception of what is good in society; and to assert that would bring an immediate denial from everybody. It has been said that he was above the conflict; it would be more true to say that he was above the classification.[2]

The nerve of all Mr. Eliot's work has been his feeling and his concern for the human good. From *Prufrock*, through *The*

1. *Notes Towards the Definition of Culture*, 1948, p. 86.
2. Edwin Muir, *Essays on Literature and Society*, 1949, p. 32.

*Waste Land*, to the *Four Quartets*, this feeling and this concern give strength and passion to the most remarkable English verse of our time. To recognize this is not to fall into the error, often noticed by Mr. Eliot, of appraising poetry by moral or religious criteria, but simply to note that high achievement in poetry comes to an integrated man who, as it were, has digested and absorbed the life of his time.[3]

We encounter Shakespeare as a political mind only in *King Lear*, say, or *Coriolanus* or the historical plays. But Mr. Eliot has written a great many essays which contain political remarks and has written directly upon political themes in, for example, the Commentaries in the *Criterion* and in such works as *The Idea of a Christian Society* and *Notes Towards the Definition of Culture*. Here he is perhaps more in the tradition of French and American than of English letters; and one is inclined to think that, despite the generous tributes he so often pays to Tawney, Demant, Christopher Dawson and other English writers, the deeper influences have been such writers as Irving Babbitt, Paul Elmer More and Charles Maurras. No one wholly English in culture could have brought himself in the nineteen-twenties to confess to "Royalism" as a political creed;[4] and though the Anglo-Catholicism with which Mr. Eliot linked his Royalism is by definition English, as worn by him it has a less insular cut than is common. This slight eccentricity to English styles of thinking has sometimes, though not always, been of immense advantage to Mr. Eliot in his political writings. In the heady days of the Popular Front he managed to keep his balance when many writers lost theirs,[5] and this without yielding to

3. "While the practice of poetry need not in itself confer wisdom or accumulate knowledge, it ought at least to train the mind in one habit of universal value: that of analysing the meanings of words." *The Idea of a Christian Society*, 1939, p. 8. This is true; but such a capacity could bring the poet to no more than pedantry if it stood by itself.

4. In *For Lancelot Andrewes*, 1928, Preface.

5. Cf.: "The delusion of the 'Popular Front', which is so seductive to the intelligentsia of every country." *Criterion*, Vol. XVI, No. lxiv, April 1937, p. 474.

the complacency which marked the Conservatism of Mr. Chamberlain and Lord Halifax.[6]

Mr. Eliot has in his political writings two main themes: Culture, and Church and State. He has written from time to time on political philosophy, and has frequently deplored the absence from contemporary English politics of any political philosophy; but by political philosophy he means not so much the analytical study of political concepts—our greatest practitioner in this field is certainly Thomas Hobbes, and he does not find Hobbes a sympathetic thinker [7]—as political *Weltanschauung;*[8] and political philosophy in this sense is an ingredient of culture as Mr. Eliot understands it rather than a critical study of the second-order questions (that is, meta-political questions) that arise out of reflection upon the terminology and concepts employed in political discourse. As a Christian thinker he is more interested in getting the right answers to political questions than in the appraisal of the logical relations between concepts. It is true, these two

6. Cf.: "I believe that there must be many persons who, like myself, were deeply shaken by the events of September 1938, in a way from which one does not recover; persons to whom that month brought a profounder realization of the general plight. It was not a disturbance of the understanding: the events themselves were not surprising. Nor, as became increasingly evident, was our distress due merely to disagreement with the policy and behaviour of the moment. The feeling which was new and unexpected was a feeling of humiliation, which seemed to demand an act of personal contrition, of humility, repentance and amendment; what had happened was something in which one was deeply implicated and responsible. . . . Was our society, which had always been so assured of its superiority and rectitude, so confident of its unexamined premisses, assembled round anything more permanent than a congeries of banks, insurance companies and industries, and had it any beliefs more essential than a belief in compound interest and the maintenance of dividends?" *The Idea of a Christian Society*, p. 64.

7. See the essay on Bramhall, in *Essays Ancient and Modern*, 1936. Hobbes is described as "an extraordinary little upstart", and as "undoubtedly an atheist". The former point is a matter of opinion, but the latter is by no means undoubted. My own view is that Hobbes is certainly a believer, having affinities with both Socinianism and Calvinism, and deriving much from the Nominalism of the later Middle Ages. He was a "mortalist", but certainly not an atheist.

8. Cf.: "What I mean by a political philosophy is not merely even the conscious formulation of the ideal aims of a people, but the substratum of collective temperament, ways of behaviour and unconscious values which provides the material for the formulation." *The Idea of a Christian Society*, p. 18.

enterprises have historically—and rightly—been run together; but the latter is the strictly philosophical enterprise.
At any rate, Mr. Eliot is concerned about what is wrong
with our society : the decay of religious belief, the vulgarization of culture, the bankruptcy of Protestant theology—he
has never seemed much impressed by the DialecticalTheology
of continental neo-Calvinism—the decline in natural piety
as this decline shows itself in the commercial exploitation of
natural resources and contempt for the past, the growing
flatness and imprecision of language. It is impossible to go
through the files of the *Criterion* without coming to know
both the breadth and the particularity of Mr. Eliot's interest
in the signs of barbarism and cultural decay. Nothing is too
small or too trivial for his attention : the protection of wild
birds,[9] the preservation of the squares and enclosures of
London,[1] the fate of the City churches.[2] Equally, he has something to say, though his pessimism grows darker throughout
the thirties, on the great problems of which the smaller bar-
barisms are no more than symptoms.[3]

Mr. Eliot is convinced—no doubt he owes in part this conviction to the work of Mr. Christopher Dawson—that religion is the vital element in culture; and he is equally convinced that the matter to be attended to in the consideration
of religion is the question of truth and not the question of
utility or aesthetic quality.[4] There is, all the same, a problem
to be solved, an ambiguity to be teased out, in what Mr. Eliot
has from time to time written about religion and culture;
and it has a direct bearing on what is for him the central

9. *Monthly Criterion*, Vol. VI, No. iii, September 1927.
1. Ibid.
2. *New Criterion*, Vol. V, No. i, January 1927.
3. E.g. he censures "urbanization of mind" and the indifference of the
major parties to the problem of rural depopulation, adding : "One sees
no hope either in the Labour Party or in the equally unimaginative
dominant section of the Conservative Party. There seems no hope in contemporary politics at all." *Criterion*, Vol. XVIII, No. lxx, October 1938.
4. "What is worst of all is to advocate Christianity, not because it is
true, but because it might be beneficial." *The Idea of a Christian Society*,
p. 58.

political problem, the relations of Church and State, as I shall try to show.

One aspect of his thought on these matters is well represented by the notorious avowal of his belief in Royalism, Classicism and Anglo-Catholicism in the Preface to the volume *For Lancelot Andrewes*, and by the essay "Lancelot Andrewes" in the same volume. Of course, he was to remark later that this running together of political views, critical prejudices and religious belief was liable to mislead the reader, adding that "I now see the danger of suggesting to outsiders [only?] that the Faith is a political principle or a literary fashion, and the sum of all a dramatic posture".[5] But the notorious sentence in the Preface is not the only, nor the most important, passage which suggests a view of the function of Christianity in culture which has certain affinities with the views of Maurras.[6] In "Lancelot Andrewes" he tells us that "the Church of England is the creation of the reign of Elizabeth. The *via media* which is the spirit of Anglicanism was the spirit of Elizabeth in all things." He speaks of the Church of England as "a masterpiece of ecclesiastical statesmanship". It is true, he adds the proviso that "we must not confuse the history of a Church with its spiritual meaning"; nevertheless, "a Church is to be judged by its intellectual fruits, by its influence on the sensibility of the most sensitive and on the intellect of the most intelligent, and it must be made real to the eye by monuments of artistic merit". And: "No religion can survive the judgment of history unless the best minds of its time have collaborated in its construction. . . ." No matter what provisos may be added, the terms employed are such as to imply what may be called the connoisseur's conception of religion. The criteria of judgment invoked are intellectual and aesthetic; the capacity of

5. *After Strange Gods: A Primer of Modern Heresy*, 1934, p. 28.
6. In reply to a suggestion that the intention of Maurras had been "to pervert his disciples and students away from Christianity", Mr. Eliot wrote: "I have been a reader of the work of Maurras for eighteen years; upon me he has had exactly the opposite effect." *Monthly Criterion*, Vol. VII, No. iii, March 1928, p. 202.

a Church to survive "the judgment of history" (is this to be understood as human or as Divine judgment?) rests upon human achievement—the willingness of "the best minds" to collaborate. Just as Maurras, the unbeliever, commended Catholicism on account of its organic connection with Roman and French history (and regretted the supreme claim made by the Catholic Church to the obedience of men, for the essence of this claim is that the Church is the New Israel, and thus to be a Christian is to be spiritually a Semite); so Mr. Eliot appears to be suggesting that the primary claim of the Church of England upon our attention is derived from its cultural achievements. All this has an air of paradox; for the grounds upon which Mr. Eliot here seems to be commending the Church of England are precisely those which have been stressed by unfriendly critics as witnessing to the merely human character of that institution. What is there in what Mr. Eliot here says that differs radically from the massive indictment brought by Newman against his old communion? Newman countered the arguments of those who urged that the Church of England must in some sense be a part of the Catholic Church, pointing as evidence of this to its vitality, by alleging that they confused the energy of a great secular and national institution with the life of the spirit. Anglicanism (he writes) is "the religion of gentlemen, of scholars, of men of substance, and men of no religion at all. If this be life, [then it is life] to impart a tone to the court and houses of parliament, to ministers of state, to law and literature, to universities and schools, and to society." [7]
Of course, even in "Lancelot Andrewes" Mr. Eliot is aware that the "spiritual meaning"—an unhappy phrase, for no institution is quite without spiritual meaning—of the Church of England is not to be exhausted by an account of Anglican history and culture from the reign of Elizabeth down to our own day; but to give to intellectual and aesthetic fruits such

7. John Henry Newman, *Lectures on Anglican Difficulties*, second edition, 1850, p. 40.

23

a degree of importance as he wishes to give them is theologically extremely odd—as though one were to commend Catholicism to the French of our own day by pointing to the excellence of Bossuet's prose.[8]

One conjectures that Mr. Eliot very soon perceived that the meaning most naturally put upon his theological and political views as they were expressed in For Lancelot Andrewes was not one he wished to defend. He made handsome amends five years later in After Strange Gods.[9] Yet it is this work, magnificently contemptuous in its reflections upon a society "worm-eaten with Liberalism",[1] which contains a passage perhaps closer in spirit to the writings of Maurras —and one which sounded extremely offensive in the acoustics of the year of publication (1934)—than anything else to be found in his writings.

> You are hardly likely to develop tradition except where the bulk of the population is relatively so well off where it is that it has no incentive or pressure to move about. The population should be homogeneous; where two or more cultures exist in the same place they are likely either to be fiercely self-conscious or both to become adulterate. What is still more important is unity of religious background; and reasons of race and religion combine to make any large number of free-thinking Jews undesirable. . . . And a spirit of excessive tolerance is to be deprecated.[2]

It can scarcely be doubted that in his reference to the "free-thinking Jews" Mr. Eliot is echoing the Maurrassien

8. It ought to be made clear that the present writer is a Catholic; but he thinks he would be inclined to say very much the same thing, though he might put it somewhat differently, were he an Anglican.

9. See especially pp. 27, 28.

1. Ibid., p. 13. He later observed acutely, in connection with the vogue of Communism among the intellectuals of the thirties, that "Communism flourished because it grew so easily on the Liberal root". Criterion, Vol. XVIII, No. lxx, October 1938, p. 272. This, of course, is Communism as an intellectual fashion, the Communism of the salon. Communism as a political movement—at least, as one with indigenous sources of strength—has flourished only in such countries as Russia and China. The Communist voters of such countries as Italy and France are delusive phenomena; the revolution they seem to portend is a mirage.

2. After Strange Gods, pp. 19, 20.

teaching on the role of the *métèque* in a society "worm-eaten with Liberalism".[3]

One would not wish to criticize Mr. Eliot simply on the ground that he has taken over from Maurras a doctrine which, from the days of the *Affaire*, has been used to give an appearance of respectability to violence, injustice and blasphemy. Such a doctrine may exaggerate a true doctrine, be a heresy; and since people are often deaf, it may in some circumstances be necessary to shout. But two considerations strike me as being apposite. First, such a doctrine is so closely connected with the vicissitudes of the Third French Republic that it is hard to see—certainly, Mr. Eliot does not enlighten us—its relevance to English or American conditions. The social evils of both countries are manifold; but it would be hard to show that these evils flowed from the role of the *métèques* in educational, artistic or political life. This view would run into particular difficulties as an analysis of American society; and it is American society that Mr. Eliot has primarily in mind in the first of the lectures in *After Strange Gods*. "*Métèque*" is, after all, a relative term, and too generous a use of the term would transform the vast majority of the inhabitants of the United States into *métèques*, and would raise the interesting question whether the Puritans of New England are entitled to call the Anglicans of Virginia *métèques*, or the Anglicans the Puritans. If we are to have as fine a nose as Maurras for the foreign infection, we shall in looking at American society be compelled to treat such names as Roosevelt, Eisenhower and McCarthy as being pre-eminently signs of the presence of the *métèques* in political life. Secondly, such a remark about the Jews as Mr. Eliot permits himself in these lectures (delivered at the University of Virginia in 1933 and published in 1934) has a peculiar resonance when we recall that the year 1933 was the year in which Hitler and his party made themselves the masters of

3. Another echo: Mr. Eliot can say of Virginia that it has been "less industrialized and *less invaded by foreign races*"! Ibid., p. 16. My italics.

Germany and called upon "reasons of race", if not of religion, to justify the most cruel and bloody persecution known to history.[4]

Altogether, one is inclined to suggest that Mr. Eliot's appearance as a softened and domesticated Maurras, the Maurras of Anglo-Saxon liberal society, sprang from a failure—a failure fully shared by those liberal and communist intellectuals who were the first to censure Mr. Eliot—to perceive that the advent of totalitarianism had raised moral and political questions of an entirely new kind. Modern industrial societies are such that counter-revolution in the name of tradition, hierarchy, the defence of religion, the preservation of the national community and so on produces exactly the same consequences as revolution in the name of progress, equality, emancipation from religion, internationalism and so on. Hitler and Stalin are faces on opposite sides of the same coin. What is surprising is that Mr. Eliot fails to see that his real affinities are not with Maurras (so radical in his positivism) but with those who are the prophets and apologists of the liberal societies of England and the United States: with Jefferson and Burke, with Acton and Maitland.[5]

4. Hindsight is, of course, easy. But the general intentions of the Nazis were known before 1933; the furnaces of Auschwitz were already on the drawing-board.

5. Mr. Eliot tends to underestimate the toughness of the English political tradition. After arguing that in Italy a pagan theory of the State is modified by the tradition of society in "a country which is still mainly agricultural and Catholic", he goes on to say: "The more highly industrialized the country, the more easily a materialistic philosophy will flourish in it, and the more deadly that philosophy will be. Britain has been highly industrialized longer than any other country. And the tendency of unlimited industrialism is to create bodies of men and women—of all classes —detached from tradition, alienated from religion and susceptible to mass suggestion: in other words, a mob." *The Idea of a Christian Society*, p. 21. Even if one is inclined to agree with Mr. Eliot's generalization, at a level high enough and over a time long enough, its application to the English people is doubtful. It must be harder to raise a mob in England than in any other country of western Europe, and the thing which strikes observers from Europe is the English capacity for co-operation and self-discipline. Mr. Eliot, for all his interest in the seventeenth century, has never read the paradoxical lesson of that period: that the victory of the Puritans over the Monarchy was the condition for the survival in England, alone of the European countries, of a medieval and Catholic tradition in

All this is no more than an episode in the development of Mr. Eliot's political thought. In *The Idea of a Christian Society* the *Maurrassien* note is scarcely struck; and in the *Definition of Culture*—the best and wisest of the books in this vein—it is quite vanished. But the episode is, all the same, significant; for the episode was only possible on account of an ambiguity in Mr. Eliot's conception of the Church. To care so desperately about culture, and about a particular historic culture, that the Church ceases to be even in principle detachable from the culture, and may even, as with Maurras, be valued solely by reason of its links with and its social and political role within the culture, this is to neglect what may be called the transcendence of the Church and to overemphasize the immanence of the Church; as did the late Hilaire Belloc in *Europe and the Faith*. How far Mr. Eliot has clarified his view of the Church (even in Anglican terms), and thus placed himself in a position to deal satisfactorily with the problem of Church and State, we must now inquire.

The central contention of *The Idea of a Christian Society* is, I take it, that "a liberalized or negative condition of society must either proceed into a gradual decline of which we can see no end, or . . . reform itself into a positive shape which is likely to be effectively secular"; and the only alternative to decline or secular reform is "a positive Christian society".[6] The present writer would not wish to quarrel with this. Now, granted the possibility and the desirability of a positive Christian society, the inquirer, whether Christian or not, is likely to ask for a sketch, if not for a blueprint; and one feature of the sketch will have to be a few lines which suggest the place of the Church, both as the community of Christians and as an hierarchical institution, in the Christian State. Mr. Eliot rejects the idea that such a relation is best founded

the State and in Law. This is the grain of truth in the Whig interpretation of history. It seems unlikely that the victory of the Anglican Counter-Reformation under Andrewes and Laud would have produced results of which Mr. Eliot would have approved.

6. *The Idea of a Christian Society*, p. 25.

upon a Concordat; [7] and seems to favour the idea of a religious establishment—in this country, the Church of England.[8]

Mr. Eliot's argument is intricate and I am not sure that I have altogether grasped it, perhaps because some of the steps in the argument have been suppressed. He begins by suggesting that the problem of Church and State "will take a different form according to the traditions [of the Christian country concerned]—Roman, Orthodox or Lutheran"; and still another form in those countries which have no one predominant religious tradition.[9] This is, of course, true as a matter of sociology. Does it carry with it the implication that the task of the Christian sociologist or political philosopher is to accept the religious tradition of the country in which he happens to be domiciled as a *datum*? Perhaps so; for Mr. Eliot restricts himself to the Church of England; seems to suggest—though in its context the sentence is slightly ambiguous—that the Church of England "can claim to represent the traditional form of Christian belief and worship of the great mass of the people" of this country; [1] and asserts without ambiguity that "if the idea of a Christian society be grasped and accepted, then it can only be realized, in England, through the Church of England".[2] Even on the level of history and sociology one might wish to quarrel with this. Many historians would wish to qualify the judgment that Anglicanism does represent the religious tradition of "the great mass of the people". There is much to be said for the view that all the English religious traditions are minority traditions, and that the great mass of the people have lived their lives outside these traditions. Hooker's view that Englishman and Anglican are interchangeable terms was no more than a legal fiction when he put it forward and has certainly not acquired any more reality since the end of the sixteenth century. The view that only through the Church of England can a Christian

7. Ibid., p. 26.   8. Ibid., p. 46.   9. Ibid., p. 45.
1. Ibid., p. 46.   2. Ibid., p. 47.

society be established in England is a matter of opinion; and no evidence is offered in support of this—to many Roman Catholic and Protestant dissenters—surprising assertion.

One might wish respectfully to suggest that Mr. Eliot is mixing his categories. A Christian society, in the sense in which Mr. Eliot wishes to use the term, is a theological and not a sociological category. This is made plain by what he has to say later about the "increasing recognition of the supranational Christian society" (by oecumenical conferences); and his argument that "no one today can defend the idea of a National Church, without balancing it with the idea of the Universal Church, and without keeping in mind that truth is one and that theology has no frontiers".[3] Precisely. And in some fine pages on the need in our society for "a *respect* for the religious life, for the life of prayer and contemplation" he tells us that "I should not like the 'Community of Christians' of which I have spoken, to be thought of as merely the nicest, most intelligent and public-spirited of the upper middle class—it is not to be conceived on that analogy".[4]

Now, if the idea of a Christian society is a theological and not a sociological category, it is quite beside the point to consider in any particular country which of the Christian bodies is by reason of history and national prejudice in the best strategic situation. This would be a Latitudinarian position, not unlike that of Dr. Arnold. Mr. Eliot is certainly not a Latitudinarian. The life of the Christian society is nourished by Grace; and while it would be blasphemous to set limits to the freedom of the Spirit, poured out far beyond the frontiers of Christendom, only on a Latitudinarian theory is it a matter of comparative indifference which institution of all those which claim to be in some sense orthodox churches is to be taken as the *datum*. Of course, in a passage to which I have already referred, Mr. Eliot refers to the Universal Church and to "the supranational Christian society"; but these are

3. Ibid., p. 53.    4. Ibid., pp. 60, 61.

(in the sense which they must be given by an Anglican writer) speculative ideas, hopes for an unspecified future, or, at best, spiritual realities without, as yet, any institutional embodiment. It is true, he writes that "the allegiance of the individual to his own Church is secondary to his allegiance to the Universal Church. Unless the National Church is a part of the whole, it has no claim upon me. . . ." [5] Here it is very hard to know in what sense a National Church, an actual institution, is a part of a Universal Church which, on any Anglican theory, has no institutional embodiment, and in what way the allegiance of an individual member of a National Church could show itself.

It is very much a question whether, on any theory of the Church, there is available today any solution better than that of the neutral society on the American model. Mr. Eliot is quite right when he says of the solution of the problem of Church and State by means of a Concordat that it is "a kind of compromise, of doubtful durability, resting on a dubious division of authority, and often a popular division of loyalty; a compromise which implies perhaps a hope on the part of the State that their rule will outlast Christianity, and a faith on the part of the Church that it will survive any particular form of secular organization".[6] Nevertheless, it is also true that a concordatory régime does at least preserve the indispensable distinction between Church and State, the things of God and the things of Caesar; that it does witness, in Mr. Eliot's own phrase, to "a faith on the part of the Church that it will survive any particular form of secular organization"; whereas the defect of an Establishment is that Church and State are so mingled that the necessary distinctions are lost. As Mr. Eliot himself puts it in a striking phrase, "bishops are a part of English culture, and horses and dogs a part of English religion".[7]

Mr. Eliot is so important and so stimulating a writer that a

---

5. Ibid., p. 54.  6. Ibid., p. 26.
7. *Notes Towards the Definition of Culture*, p. 32.

mainly critical treatment of his writings on the range of topics here considered needs no apology. Whatever the defects of that eccentricity to English styles of thinking which I remarked upon earlier, it has the great advantage that it has done much to mitigate the crudity and provincialism of so much English writing on questions of religion, culture and politics. The gaps and ambiguities in his presentation of his themes are from one standpoint virtues rather than vices. Nothing is so unsatisfactory and nothing wears so badly as that logical rigour which springs from a mania for systematization. In dealing with those "mixed" questions where the problems of religion, culture and politics run together, the *method* employed by Mr. Eliot—the examination of particular questions in the light of general principles not too narrowly defined and not too inflexibly stated—is certainly the right one; and it is in my view clear that Mr. Eliot's expertness in the use of this method has grown with time. *The Idea of a Christian Society* is a notable advance upon *After Strange Gods*; and *Notes Towards the Definition of Culture* is so much the finest of the works in this vein that the comparison with *Culture and Anarchy* is irresistible; and the comparison is perhaps in Mr. Eliot's favour. What, for example, could be finer than this interpretation of totalitarianism?

The identity of religion and culture remains on the unconscious level, upon which we have superimposed a conscious structure wherein religion and culture are contrasted and can be opposed. The *meaning* of the terms "religion" and "culture" is of course altered between these two levels. To the unconscious level we constantly tend to revert, as we find consciousness an excessive burden; and the tendency towards reversion may explain the powerful attraction which totalitarian philosophy and practice can exert upon humanity. Totalitarianism appeals to the desire to return to the womb. The contrast between religion and culture imposes a strain : we escape from this strain by attempting to revert to an identity of religion and culture which prevailed at a more primitive stage; as when we indulge in alcohol as an anodyne, we consciously seek unconsciousness. It is only by unremitting effort that we can persist in being individuals in a society instead of merely members of a disciplined crowd. Yet we remain members of the crowd, even when we succeed in being individuals.[8]

And the following characterization of the English religious situation makes his earlier writing on the same topic seem by contrast doctrinaire.

> In England, as in other Protestant countries, atheism has been mostly of a passive kind. . . . Many people live on an unmarked frontier enveloped in dense fog; and those who dwell beyond it are more numerous in the dark waste of ignorance and indifference than in the well-lighted desert of atheism. The English unbeliever, of some social status however humble, is likely to conform to the practices of Christianity on the occasions of birth, death and the first venture in matrimony. Atheists in this country are not yet culturally united: their types of atheism will vary according to the culture of the religious communion in which they, or their parents, or their grandparents were reared. The chief cultural differences in England have, in the past, been those between Anglicanism and the more important Protestant sects; and even these differences are far from clearly defined: first, because the Church of England itself has comprehended wider variations of belief and cult than a foreign observer would believe it possible for one institution to contain without bursting; and second, because of the number and variety of the sects separated from it.[9]

If—putting aside questions of philosophical and aesthetic criticism—one were asked to say what it is in Mr. Eliot's work that speaks to our time of what our time needs, quite apart from any guesses we may have as to whether or not our time will heed him, one might say this: he has kept steadily before us man's dependence upon and hunger for the Absolute; and his capacity for the Eternal. In a shabby and murderous age he has spoken to many who would never be found

8. Ibid., p. 68.    9. Ibid., pp. 72, 73.

beneath the pulpits; and to those—all of us—who find ourselves

> where is no secure foothold,
> And menaced by monsters, fancy lights,
> Risking enchantment.

All will salute the achievement of the poet and the critic. It
is desirable also to consider the body of thought from which
the work of the poet and critic draws its strength. Many will
no doubt find it acrid. They should consider whether the
fault is in the medicine or in their own palates.

1958

33

# 3

# Problems of Communist Language

ANY form of words which appears to say something of importance about human life and about the world seems in one way very simple and in another way very complicated. This is plain enough if we consider poetic expressions or scientific statements. Understanding these isn't simply a matter of grasping the syntax of sentences or the dictionary meanings of words. We can understand the words and have no difficulties about the syntax, and still be baffled. To grasp the full meaning we have to place the sentence or expression in its proper context, to assign it to the right family of sentences and expressions, to become aware of the complex of images, concepts, theories, historical usages and the rest that stands behind the words used in this way. Such a complex gives the words their vast range of reference and makes them a starting-point for speculation.

Political expressions stand within a complex, just as do poetic or scientific expressions. And just as we can fail to receive the full impact of a poem or fail to see that certain problems are raised by the use of a piece of scientific terminology, so we can fail to grasp the meaning and intention of a political expression through not seeing, or not being familiar with, the complex to which it belongs.

We may well recognize the words—such words, say, as "democracy", "progress", "compromise", "independence" —and we may have no difficulties about the syntax of the expression; but we may altogether misunderstand the expression through putting it into the wrong complex, through assigning it to the wrong family of statements. This often happens when west Europeans are trying to understand—or think they *are* understanding—Communist statements. And it often happens when Communists think they are understanding political statements made by west Europeans. But as I am neither a Soviet citizen nor a Communist, I am not concerned with this side of the misunderstanding. It is true, a great many Communist statements strike us as patently absurd or disingenuous. Perhaps they are. But if, when we characterize Communist statements in this way, we are simply drawing attention to the fact that these statements are odd or contradictory by the rules of western political grammar, we fail to grasp the problem.

To understand what the Communists are saying we have to familiarize ourselves with the complex that stands behind most important Communist statements. This complex is partly determined by the general philosophy of Marx and Engels. But Communism today is Bolshevism, with the special twist given to Bolshevism by the Stalin régime. Bolshevism is the interpretation and extension of Marxist theory during the first twenty years of this century; and it is largely the work of one man, Lenin; and the development of the theory is to be traced in a great mass of books and pamphlets and newspaper articles published during these years.

There are two—at first sight extremely puzzling—classes of Communist statement that one can show, by referring to some elements in the complex to which they belong, to be not so puzzling as they seem on the surface to be. And there is the more general question about the relation between the theoretical complex of Bolshevism and the real world to which, so Communists believe, it refers.

In a way, to pass from western political language to Communist language is like passing from one world to another. All the same, both we and the Communists live in *one* world. Such a theory as Bolshevism appeals to the facts and

35

it must in the end be judged by the facts; and perhaps perish by the facts.

The two classes of statement are these. In the first place, there are statements, some of them as early as the 1917 Revolution, some of them quite recent, which speak of the Soviet Union as "a lever for the . . . disintegration of imperialism", of the Soviet Union coming out "even with armed force against the exploiting classes and their states", of the Soviet workers as "the vanguard" of the world proletariat. And so on. These we may call the *revolutionary* statements. Then there are those statements which argue that the supposed connection between the Soviet Union and the world revolution is a grotesque misunderstanding on the part of non-Communist observers and that the Soviet Government would like nothing better than to settle down to "normal business relations" with the capitalist world.

For example, in 1936, Mr. Roy Howard asked Stalin if the Soviet Union had "to any degree abandoned their plans and intentions for bringing about a world revolution". Stalin replied: "We never had any such plans or intentions." And added that the widespread impression to the contrary was "the product of a misunderstanding". Again on 24th August 1939, *Izvestia*, fresh from denouncing the Nazis as reptiles and cannibals, commented on the recently concluded German-Soviet Pact in these terms: "Ideological differences, as well as differences in the political systems of both nations, cannot and must not stand in the way of the establishment and maintenance of good neighbourly relations." Such statements as these we may call *conciliatory*.

When revolutionary and conciliatory statements are put side by side they seem to be contradictory; and the commentators resort to various explanations: that the conciliatory statements are designed to deceive; that the revolutionary statements are a ritual survival from the heroic age of the revolution; that talk about world revolution is for internal purposes and that the conciliatory statements represent the Soviet Government's genuine desire to meet the West half way; and so on, up to the limit of the commentator's ingenuity. There may well be something in all these explanations; but our first task is to consider the complex ideas standing behind both classes of statement.

Two pieces of writing by Lenin strike me as relevant here. The first is "Compromises", an article published on 6th September (old style) 1917.[1] Lenin wrote this immediately after the provisional Government had suppressed the Kornilov Revolt.

In the Soviets, the majority, composed of Mensheviks and Social Revolutionaries, had swung to the left; and Lenin proposed in his article that the Bolsheviks should sponsor the slogan "All Power to the Soviets" and drop their demand for the dictatorship of the workers and the poor peasants. He argued that under a Soviet régime the Bolsheviks would be in a minority, but that in the present temper of the majority they would enjoy freedom to agitate and set out their views, and that this might provide the conditions under which the Bolsheviks could win a majority and establish a proletarian dictatorship. Lenin knows that some of the Bolsheviks will regard this change as an inadmissible compromise; and in defending the admissibility of this particular compromise he makes some observations on the place of compromise in the tactics of a revolutionary party. He points out that for a compromise to be acceptable *both* sides must gain something. (The compromise is acceptable to the Bolsheviks because "the tide of events is on our side". And only because he believes this is so does Lenin propose the compromise.) Lenin's point is that this compromise does not represent the sacrifice of a part of the revolutionary policy; neither is it simply a piece of Machiavellian deception—though Lenin certainly did not object to ruses in politics; compromise is, in a peculiar situation, another method of *carrying out* the revolutionary

1. In V. I. Lenin, *Selected Works*, Vol. VI, 1936.

policy; and it can always be abandoned and denounced should the situation change.

The other and more important piece of writing is Lenin's pamphlet *Left-Wing Communism an Infantile Disorder*—together with *Imperialism* and *What is to be Done?* perhaps the most important of his writings.

Lenin is addressing, in the summer of 1920, some of the ultra-left sections of the Communist parties in Europe. These had argued that it was wrong for Communists to take part in the work of bourgeois parliaments and to work within non-revolutionary trade unions. Lenin didn't agree with this view and tried to argue them out of it. He shows that "the whole history of Bolshevism, both before and after the October Revolution, is *full* of instances of manoeuvring, temporizing, and compromising with other parties, bourgeois parties included". He gives examples of such compromises.

The most interesting and, for my purpose, the most instructive, of these is the adoption by the Bolsheviks, at the beginning of the October Revolution, of the agrarian policy of the Social Revolutionaries. This policy—the division of the big estates among the peasants—was quite contrary to the old land nationalization policy of the Bolsheviks. But it split the Social Revolutionaries; and it won over, at a crucial moment, the great mass of peasant opinion, especially the opinion of the peasants in the army, who, as Lenin said, "voted with their feet". All this was gained by compromise. And later the peasant expropriators of the big estates were themselves expropriated by the Bolsheviks; the original programme of the Bolsheviks was in the end realized.

Compromise, then, in the tactics of the Bolsheviks does not mean Machiavellian deception. There is an element of this, or so at least a Russian peasant labelled "Kulak" would have thought in the thirties. But something really is given to the other party. Lenin was prepared to tolerate at the beginning of September 1917 a non-Bolshevik majority in the Soviets. The peasants really were given the land.

Equally, compromise does not mean sacrificing a part of the revolutionary objective. An admissible—from the Bolshevik standpoint—compromise is the best way possible of advancing, in a given situation, towards the revolutionary objective.

I think all this helps when we are trying to place both revolutionary and conciliatory statements. Most of the leading Communists are so familiar with the kind of literature I have been quoting that it has become, almost organically, a part of themselves. Probably they don't—they don't need to —pull down Lenin on "Compromises" or brush up their knowledge of *Left-Wing Communism*, just as a scientist talking to us about nuclear physics and the atomic theory may not give a thought to Democritus or Dalton. But, in the terms I used earlier, the writings of Lenin and the development of Lenin's ideas in the years since then stand behind every important statement they make—with a few interesting exceptions I shall refer to later. And what stands behind these statements is what gives them their peculiar intention and meaning.

It is therefore a mistake to say of this or that conciliatory statement made by the Communist leaders: Either they mean it—in which case we're delighted and we ought to meet them half way; or they are deceiving us—this is just conjuror's patter designed to divert our attention from what is really going on. The truth is usually more complicated. They *do* mean it: but not in *our* language—in their own. Of course, they may be—they often have been—wrong in thinking a particular compromise *will* lead them towards their revolutionary objective. This depends in part on how the other parties to the compromise employ their time.

All this is a plea for a better understanding of the Communist position. But the word "understanding" has its own ambiguities. I am not suggesting our failures to understand the Communists spring from a lack of sympathy with their position and aims. It is, of course, useful to be able to enter imaginatively into the position of an opponent, but such identification of oneself with an opponent does not entail having an attitude of approval towards his aims. The novelist who gives us a well-realized portrait of a villain or a fool does not thereby become an accomplice in villainy or folly. There has in one sense been too much sympathy with the Communists on the part of liberal thinkers in the West— too much good will of a rather vague and guilty sort; and too little study and hard thinking. One has the impression that some of us are so weighed down with feelings of guilt inspired by defects in the social order of the West that we are incapable of looking dispassionately at the Communist theories and policies. It doesn't follow from the obvious fact that much in Communism draws its power from the revulsion of good men from social evils that Communist theory and Communist policy have, so to speak, a hard core of righteousness. This might be so; but it would have to be shown to be so by means of a cool analysis; and those who plead for a better understanding of Communism in this sense start from the conviction that the hard core of righteousness is there and dispense themselves from showing it as a conclusion.

So far I have assumed that the *meaning* of Communist pronouncements can only be ascertained if one gets into the habit of placing them within the complex of Bolshevik theory and history. This seems on the whole true. But a new question then arises. Granted that the Communist leaders do interpret the world through the categories of Bolshevism, is it true that they are *practically* committed to Bolshevism? Let me give a parallel which I hope no one will think offensive. The Judgment and the Second Coming are fundamental Christian dogmas. But how many Christians, and I mean *believing* Christians, can be said to live in *expectation* of the Second Coming? Surely very few. Is it perhaps like this with the Communist leaders? Certainly they *believe* in the world revolution. But does the world revolution belong to politics or to eschatology?

## 2

In so far as the Communist parties attempt to justify their policies to themselves, they do so by drawing upon the theory of Bolshevism. Policy will be shaped in response to changes in the world situation—or rather, to the Communist interpretation of what these changes are and of what results they will tend to bring about. But the grammar of policy statements will be governed by rules derived from the theory; and we can only understand the statements by deriving the rules from the theory.

Of course, one has to hedge all this about with qualifications. Bolshevism as a theoretical system is pretty well complete by 1921. After that there are changes which seem in one way to be developments of the original theory and in another dilutions or vulgarizations of the theory. If one is well disposed towards the régime, associated with the name of Stalin, that followed the heroic age of Bolshevism one will be disposed to call them developments. If one is an admirer of the Bolshevism of Lenin one will be disposed to call these changes a dilution or a vulgarization or even a perversion of Bolshevism. And if one isn't committed in either of these ways one will be content to note their character without wanting to talk about them in the deep and thrilling tones of moral passion.

For example, Bolshevism down to the death of Lenin had no use for a living human authority which would be omniscient and infallible. Marx and Engels were thought to be as near omniscience and infallibility as makes no matter; but neither the Bolshevik party nor its central committee nor Lenin himself was thought of, in Lenin's lifetime, in this way. But in the later stages of the Stalin régime omniscience and infallibility were attributed to Stalin himself in a way that would have been repugnant to the first generation of Bolsheviks and that conflicted with the critical and iconoclastic side of Bolshevism. This led to a special kind of logical discourse—one which it is hard to fit into the general theory of Bolshevism—which consisted of taking certain oracular statements of the master and drawing out from these statements, by what purported to be deduction, conclusions agreeable to the Soviet Government. Again, the campaign against "cosmopolitanism"—a campaign seasoned with a dash of anti-Semitism—shows how far removed in some respects the Stalin régime was from the truly cosmopolitan and sceptical spirit of the years of revolution.

These and similar qualifications have to be made. But it remains true that even the most recent statements made by the Soviet leaders in their capacities as Communist pedagogues presuppose a comparatively undiluted primitive Bolshevism. A fierce contempt for all varieties of pacifism and for all schemes for an international order not founded upon the victory of the proletarian revolution in at least the main advanced countries is a characteristic sentiment in early Bolshevism. Lenin wrote in 1914: "The war . . . is a form of *capitalist* life as natural as peace. . . . The idea of refusing to serve in the army, of strikes against the war, etc., is mere foolishness; it is the miserable cowardly dream of an unarmed struggle against an armed bourgeoisie, it is a weak yearning for the abolition of capitalism without a desperate civil war, or a series of wars." We find the same spirit, though the expression of it is colder, less passionate, in Stalin's pamphlet *Economic Problems of Socialism in the U.S.S.R.* published in 1953, and in Malenkov's report to the Nineteenth Congress of the Soviet Communist Party in October 1952. Stalin, writing of the "peace" movement, emphasizes that this movement may "result in preventing a *particular war* . . . in the temporary preservation of a *particular peace* . . .". And he goes on to say that this "will not be enough to eliminate the inevitability of wars between capitalist countries generally. . . . To eliminate the inevitability of war, it is necessary to abolish imperialism." The emphasis in Malenkov's report is somewhat different; and by the use of hindsight we may even discover traces in it of the changes in tone that have come over Soviet propaganda since the death of Stalin; but his entire analysis takes for granted the validity of Lenin's theory of imperialism, notably when he interprets American foreign policy and states that "the antagonisms between the United States and Britain and between the United States and France become more acute, and will become still more acute in future".

Now, if we were to conclude that Communist policy is always and inevitably determined by considerations drawn from the theory of Bolshevism—if, in the words of Stalin, "to eliminate the inevitability of war, it is necessary to abolish imperialism"—then the prospects of a reasonable settlement between the Soviet Union and the West are poor. Certainly, to understand the *meaning* of many Soviet pronouncements we must place them within the complex of theory to which they belong. To suppose, as many people did suppose between 1941 and 1945, that the Soviet Communists are at bottom Fabian Socialists of a rather crude and uncultivated sort is to make it hard or impossible to understand Soviet pronouncements. But are there any signs that Bolshevism is ceasing to count *practically* with the rulers of the U.S.S.R.? Are there, in Soviet language, any indications that revolutionary talk is a smoke-screen behind which there is coming into existence a régime with interests and purposes very different from those of the Soviet Union in its earlier years?

If one looks back upon earlier revolutions it is easy to see during which years the new régime begins to move away from a genuine belief in the revolutionary mythology to which it still defers in its official pronouncements. The fortunes of the French Revolution after Thermidor illustrate the point. We can see that the Directory, the Consulate, the Empire, represent successively greater divergences from the myth of liberty, equality and fraternity. But this was not so plain at the time. Even so intelligent and generous a man as Hazlitt continued to believe, against what appear to us the most obvious of facts, that the Napoleonic régime was the incarnation of the revolution, the Napoleonic armies instruments of liberation; and this was precisely the impression that Napoleon strove to impose upon his contemporaries. If there were old Jacobins who could not be shaken even by the coronation of Bonaparte in Notre Dame, only a decade after the solemn inauguration of the cult of Reason in the same edifice, it is not surprising that happenings just as strange should fail to disturb the faith and loyalty of Communists in our own day. But historical parallels can be pressed too hard. Is it true that the inner life of Bolshevism is growing feebler and that under the surface appearances something different is growing up?

Now and then a pronouncement is made that doesn't seem to belong at all to the complex of Bolshevism. Such pronouncements are extremely rare; but it is significant that they can occur at all. There is, for example, Stalin's reply to Hitler's greetings to him on his sixtieth birthday, in 1939. "The friendship of the peoples of Germany and the Soviet Union, cemented by blood, has every reason to be lasting and firm." Perhaps one ought not to attach too much weight to words uttered on ceremonial occasions such as this. But even ceremonial pronouncements are, in the Soviet Union, always phrased with the greatest care and carry with them implications for policy. (When, before the war, Stalin said that life was becoming more joyful in the Soviet Union, this was treated not as a casual remark but as an utterance big with implications of immense gravity.) The key phrase is, of course, "cemented by blood". The reference seems to be to the partition of Poland which had just been accomplished. It was unnecessary for Stalin to have used these words. He cannot have thought they would be likely to make the

slightest difference to the German attitude. From the Bolshevik standpoint the joint attack on Poland could no doubt
have been justified as a necessity in the existing situation; but
for an old Marxist, aware of all that the cause of Polish independence had meant for European revolutionaries from 1848
down to 1917, it could only have been a bitter and shameful
necessity. But here is Stalin, without the slightest excuse,
using one of the typical cant phrases—"cemented by blood"
—of the despised imperialists.

Again, there is Stalin's comment on the Japanese surrender in 1945. "The defeat of the Russian troops in 1904
left bitter memories in the mind of the people. It lay like
a black spot on our country. Our people believed and
hoped that a day would come when Japan would be
smashed and that blot effaced. Forty years have we, the
people of the older generation, waited for this day." [2]
Now, it isn't at all extraordinary that in some respects the
Soviet leaders should wish to identify themselves with the
Russian past. What *is* extraordinary is that Stalin should
have treated the victory of 1945 as wiping out the humiliation of the Tsarist régime by the Japanese forty years before.
For the entire opposition to Tsarism, the Bolsheviks more
vehemently than others, had *rejoiced* over the Russian defeat.
Lenin's comment on the Russian defeat at Port Arthur had
been : "The European bourgeoisie has its reason to be fright-
ened. The proletariat has its reasons to rejoice." Stalin himself, then an agitator in the Caucasus, had greeted the news
in similar terms of exultation. Consequently, when Stalin
speaks in 1945 of the victory over Japan as a long-awaited
day of triumph and revenge, he speaks as though Bolshevism
had never existed and forgets—or conceals—his own past.

Such pronouncements as these seem to resemble the mo-
mentary twitching aside of a curtain. For a few seconds we
glimpse a room furnished and peopled in a way quite different
from what we had anticipated. Statements, then, which seem

2. In I. Deutscher, *Stalin. A Political Biography*, 1961, p. 528.

to belong to a family of statements different from that of Bolshevism are occasionally made by Soviet statesmen.

If this fact stood by itself we might be quite unable to calculate its importance. Men are inconsistent. Not everyone is an accomplished theoretician. Statements can be made to deceive and to win the support of groups that don't share or don't understand the theory of the ruling group. We have to relate what is said, not only to a theoretical background but also to acts of policy.

If one works one's way through the literature of Bolshevism, especially the literature of the crucial ten years between 1914 and 1924, one thing is quite certain: the immense importance which is attached to a proletarian revolution in Germany. Great importance is also attached to revolts against imperialism in Asia, for according to Lenin's theory such revolts seriously weaken the social structure of the metropolitan countries. But it is the German revolution which will provide the struggling Soviet régime with the resources of technical ability and material equipment it needs. By 1939 the situation had changed a good deal. The Soviet Union had become a great industrial power. But although the deferred German revolution could no longer be thought an absolute necessity it still remained, as a means of strengthening the Soviet state and extending the world revolution, desirable.

Now, the evidence seems to suggest that Stalin's purpose in the last stages of the war was to build up a defensive zone in eastern Europe, not to encourage a proletarian revolution in the advanced countries. Part of the evidence is to be found in the tactics imposed upon the French and Italian Communist parties. But the decisive evidence is to be found in Stalin's German policy. Apart from his sponsoring of a punitive peace *with* annexations and indemnities—an incomprehensible policy if the stake for which he was playing was a Soviet Germany—and his acquiescence in the division of Germany into zones of occupation, his boldest attempt to split the home front in Germany was the organizing of the Free German Committee under Seydlitz and Von Paulus; an effort to exploit, not revolutionary and internationalist sentiment but Conservative and Nationalist sentiment. The Old Bolsheviks had staked almost everything on a German revolution. Stalin showed not the least trace of confidence in such a possibility.

I am far from wishing to suggest that in this Stalin was mistaken. It doesn't show, even, that Stalin had "lost faith" in Bolshevism. What it does show is that the original expectation that proletarian revolution was a possibility, even a probability, in advanced industrial societies had been abandoned, perhaps for ever. The palace revolutions carried through in eastern Europe through Communist control over the police and the army have not the slightest resemblance to anything approaching proletarian revolution in the classical sense. But if it is true that the Soviet leaders have ceased to count on proletarian revolution in Britain, France, Germany, then the central doctrines of Bolshevism have simply evaporated. And they have evaporated, not so much through any "degeneration" of the régime, through the growth of a new ruling class which knows not the original prophets, but rather because Marxism and Bolshevism are simply wrong about the social tendencies of industrial societies.

It is just false that these societies lurch from one desperate crisis to another yet more desperate, and that the workers in these societies grow more revolutionary in their temper and more disposed to entrust their fortunes to the leadership of the Communist parties. On the contrary, these parties are strong in countries where industrial development is backward and an impoverished peasantry presses hard upon the means of subsistence. This is the great fact against which Bolshevism as a theory has broken itself. The language of Bolshevism is still employed; and certain parts of the theory—especially the theory of imperialism as it relates to Asia and Africa—may still be thought valid; in trying to make sense of the international situation the members of the Soviet Government may feel that a purely empirical approach is dangerous and deceiving and may therefore use the old theoretical scheme as a working hypothesis; but we may look forward with some confidence to further and more dramatic changes in Communist language. Sooner or later the new generation in the Army and the Party will break the links—other than those of historical sentiment—that bind them to the heroic age; though language that is no longer taken seriously as a guide to action may for a long time keep its importance as ritual speech and, because both the other powers and the Soviet rulers themselves will for long find it hard to distinguish between what they have to take seriously and what may be dismissed as a matter of form, the survival of such ritual speech may continue to bedevil the foreign relations of the Soviet Union.

There is no guarantee that this development will be to the advantage of the rest of the world. Napoleon was in many respects a more formidable threat to Europe than the armies of 1793; and his inheritance of some of the ideas and social policies of the revolution he had stabilized enabled him to disintegrate, socially and politically, the old régime in much of Europe. But Napoleon—here the parallel is a little closer to the Third Reich than to the Soviet Union—believed himself to be the instrument of destiny. Consciously Machiavellian politicians—and that the Soviet leaders should be such is the best we can immediately hope for—are perhaps easier to get on with. In some ways a Robespierre or a Napoleon is a grander figure than Talleyrand; but a Talleyrand is better at picking up the pieces and has a greater sense of his human limitations.

To offer a free translation of what Péguy used to say ("Tout commence en mystique et finit en politique"): "Everything in politics starts out as a *mystique*; and everything ends up as a political job." This is discouraging if we look for absolutes in politics, especially if it takes the form of seeing a particular régime as the chosen instrument of some dialectic of history, Marxist or other. Such a belief about a particular régime seems to me a delusion and a dangerous one; and not only dangerous when it weighs upon a Communist statesman.

1953

# 4

## The New Left in Britain

ON 18th March 1921 the Red Army, under the command of Tukhachevsky, crossed the ice of the Gulf of Finland and captured the fortress of Kronstadt, then held by the insurgent sailors of the Baltic Fleet, the pride of the Revolution. A dreadful blood-letting followed. This was the first in a series of episodes in the history of Bolshevism each one of which was, for some, the occasion of a moral revulsion from the Soviet régime and the international political movement associated with it. All are linked with death: the débâcle of Stalin's Chinese policy sealed by the massacre in 1927 of the Shanghai Communists at the hands of Chiang Kai-Chek's troops; the great famine which was a direct consequence of the policy of collectivizing the peasant farms; the theatrical trials of the thirties in which a whole generation of Bolshevik leaders and Red Army commanders perished for a variety of fictitious crimes ranging from plots to poison Stalin to lighting bonfires under Maxim Gorky's bedroom window to exacerbate his bronchitis; the pact between Ribbentrop and Molotov which was the signal for the partition of Poland, the enslavement of the Baltic states and the opening of the second world war; most recent of all, the suppression of the Hungarian revolution by the Red Army. The list is by no means complete. Each episode brought about a falling away from the Communist parties. Each time a central core stayed firm and survived through a period of difficulty to welcome yet another influx of new members. Are we to expect a continuation of this process, more Shanghais, more Kronstadts, more Hungaries, to be endured and overcome by the Communist parties? My answer is that, so far as Europe and more particularly this country are concerned, we have come to an end of the process. The crushing of the Hungarian revolution was the last time of all. We shall never again witness honest revolutionaries (or would-be revolutionaries) uttering cries of anger, surprise and shame as they leave the Communist parties. A piece of tempered steel may be bent a thousand times and return to the straight; but all the time within the steel there are molecular changes; and in the end the metal grows weary—and breaks.

But why should the case of Hungary be so different? If Communists can be brought to believe, as they have been, that Trotsky was a spy in the service of Britain, Germany and Japan and that his only contribution to the October Revolution was the negative one of vainly attempting to frustrate the infallible and predestined leadership of Lenin and Stalin, why should they not be brought to believe that the Hungarian revolution was a counter-revolution of Fascists crushed by an alliance of the Red Army and the Hungarian workers and peasants? And why, as the rattle of the Soviet tanks in the streets of Budapest grows fainter with the passage of time, should we think them incapable of recruiting a fresh generation of dupes?

This will not and cannot happen because Hungary followed Khrushchev's speech at the twentieth party congress; and in consequence no one—not even the Communists themselves—believes the official Soviet account of what happened in Hungary; nor will such absurdities ever be believed again.[1] It is unnecessary to give an extended account of Khrushchev's speech (never published in the Soviet Union, though its contents are pretty well known there). In it he described how lying, torture and false witness had been the systematic policy of the Soviet State; that history had been falsified at the orders of the State; that the Government was guilty of genocide; and so on. The speech was, it is true, confused,

1. Perhaps one ought to qualify this by adding: not in Europe.

ambiguous and contradictory, and necessarily so, in view of Khrushchev's personal implication, together with all his colleagues, in the crimes he denounced. The explanation offered —an extraordinary one in the mouth of a Marxist—was that everything was a consequence of the personal whims of Stalin in his later years. The earlier period of Stalin's rule was left a discreet blank. But enough was said to make it quite plain that much of what was alleged against the Soviet régime by the non-Communist press in the last twenty years, and denounced by all Communists as the lies of an unscrupulous propaganda, was true. This would seem to leave the Communists with very little credit; but they might have escaped had it not been for Hungary. In this case what were transparently lies of exactly the kind that had marked the Stalinist period were served up once again. But this time no one was deceived.

These matters are worth going into in some detail because one element in the "New Left" is that group of former Communists, most of whom left the party over Hungary, responsible for editing and writing *The New Reasoner*. *The New Reasoner* described itself as "a quarterly journal of socialist humanism". During its brief life (ten issues in all were published) it was perhaps the most brilliant representative of what is known in Communist party circles as *revisionism*. While it touched on a great many issues—economics, the arts, education—and published poems, short stories and some remarkable drawings, notably by Mr. Paul Hogarth, its central concern was an attempt to understand the transformation of the Marxist revolutionary movement into Stalinism, an attempt which included a determination to discover the authentic features of Marxism which, so it was believed, would be revealed once the Stalinist mask had been torn away for good. Those who edited the magazine and those who wrote in it from this point of view were quite unlike the earlier emigrations from the Communist movement. Apart from those who in the twenties and thirties formed the small dissident Communist groups, Trotskyists and others—ineffectual and short-lived organizations—ex-Communists had on the whole either entered or re-entered the social democratic parties and been reconciled to parliamentary democracy, or they had faded out of politics altogether. But here was a group of youngish men, many of them university teachers, who repudiated both Stalinism and later Soviet policies *and* social democracy. They were rebels with a cause and without a party. This time there was no serious attempt to set up a new Communist party purged of the errors of Stalinism. The admired models—admired with some reservations—were the Polish Workers' Party under Gomulka and the Yugoslav Communist Party. But they evidently judged that in Britain the time for an organized revolutionary movement was not yet.

Fundamentally their criticism of the Communist party was a moral one. The elements of this criticism are to be found in an article published in the first issue of *The New Reasoner* by Mr. E. P. Thompson. It is entitled "Socialist Humanism: An Epistle to the Philistines".[2] The ironical reference to St. Paul is not altogether misplaced, for in essence Thompson is, like St. Paul, correcting and chastising the errors of those to whom he writes and setting out the true and saving doctrine; and he has the same sense of urgency—the secular equivalent of the day of the Lord is thought to be not far off. The argument is suffused with generous and romantic feeling. He brings out in their full horror the morally repulsive features of Stalinism and tries to show at the same time that Stalinism is to be understood by means of a Marxist analysis, that it is "the ideology of a revolutionary *élite* which, within a particular historical context, degenerated into a bureaucracy". Stalinism involved, according to Thompson, a distortion of what is central in Marxism. In particular he repudiates the notion that Marxism gives any serious support to

2. It ought to be said that Mr. Thompson would not now write in such terms. But this does not deprive the article of its historic importance.

the view that the sole test for a Communist of the morality of an action is whether or not in given circumstances it advances or retards the fortunes of the revolutionary party. He writes that violence may be inescapable under the conditions of war and revolution; but it must never be glorified; "the Christian precept, 'Forgive them, for they know not what they do', must reassert itself whenever and to the degree that contingencies allow".

A later article by Mr. A. H. Hanson subjected Thompson's article to what is in my view a definitive criticism; and two articles by Mr. Alasdair MacIntyre, "Notes from the Moral Wilderness", discussed in a much deeper and more sophisticated way the moral implications of Marxism. But I am not concerned with the coherence or rightness of Thompson's views. I am concerned with them as representative of a type of reaction to Stalinism and to Soviet Communism generally. Now, Thompson wishes to maintain that Stalinism is in large part to be explained by the special circumstances in which Bolshevism came to power in a backward and isolated country and succeeded in establishing control over the world revolutionary movement and imposing its own image upon it. At the same time, he wishes to maintain that the *truth* of revolutionary Marxism is untouched by this historical development. We have everything to hope, he argues, from the success of a revolutionary Marxist movement purged of the errors of Stalinism—the dream of Nagy in those intoxicating few days before the Red Army intervened in Hungary, the dream of all those "national" Communists in eastern Europe who romanticized Soviet reality during the brief period of the "thaw", and saw in Khrushchev's revelations at the twentieth congress a sign of repentance and self-criticism.

It would not be unfair to put Thompson's case in these terms. Mankind is, as Marx prophesied, engaged in a revolutionary transition from one form of society to another. One of the signs of this transition is the emergence of the Soviet Union, the Chinese People's Republic and their client states.

These states have laid the foundation of the new society within which mankind will pass from the kingdom of necessity into the kingdom of freedom, even though they still wear the distorting mask of Stalinism—the mask has slipped, not fallen. Nevertheless, there is within the international Communist movement a strong movement of revolt against Stalinism; and there is at least the potential of a revolutionary movement in the capitalist societies, for injustice and want persist within the affluent society; and the strategy imposed by the nuclear stalemate subjects these societies to moral and political tensions that may in the end destroy them. If the Communist opposition to Stalinism, and those in the capitalist societies prepared to see political struggle in the perspectives of revolution, were to come together, then there would be a reasonable hope both of a revolutionary transition to socialism, and of the establishment of socialist societies, neither of which would be marked by the lying, cruelty and injustice that have disfigured Stalinism. For the revolutionaries, so Thompson implies, have learned the lesson of Stalinism.

Setting aside for the moment the question of the general validity of the analysis of capitalist society by Marx, Lenin and later thinkers in this tradition, we may ask what reasons Thompson and those who think like him have for believing in the possibility of a revolutionary régime that will nevertheless be tolerant and humane. Until only yesterday they maintained against what they held to be the slanders of the bourgeois press that the Soviet State *was* such a régime. In the issue of *The New Reasoner* in which Thompson's "epistle" appeared, Professor Levy, another distinguished ex-Communist, writes that "horror was undoubtedly the first natural reaction of every balanced person on the Left, at the publicly disclosed Khrushchev revelations". *Revelations!* What are we to think of the sense of reality of men for whom the limited disclosures of Khrushchev were *revelations?* The writings of Trotsky and Souvarine, countless memoirs by fugitives from Soviet concentration camps, eyewitness accounts of the deportation of hundreds of thousands of Poles in cattle-trucks to the Arctic and central Asia, reports by George Orwell and others of the role of the Soviet political police in the Spanish Civil War, all these have been readily available over the last twenty years. More. At the very beginning of the Russian Revolution, one of the most gifted and sensitive Marxist theoreticians, Rosa Luxembourg, predicted with the utmost exactness that once the Bolshevik party had established its dictatorship and destroyed multi-party democracy, the dictatorship of the party would degenerate into the dictatorship of a group within the party, and that the dictatorship of a group would degenerate into the dictatorship of an individual—and this at a time when the very name of Stalin was unknown outside Bolshevik circles. It is strange that those who left the Communist party at the time of Hungary and still wish to maintain that Stalinism is an unfortunate distortion of a revolutionary norm to which they remain faithful should think that it is the liberals and the social democrats who need to justify themselves vis-à-vis Communism.

Whether or not the successor state of a proletarian revolution can provide the framework of a relatively free and humane society, this looks like an empirical question, even though, as in all cases where we are asking questions about a future state of society, there cannot in the nature of things be anything resembling a controlled experiment to determine the answer to the question. We cannot even be certain that anything answering to the description of a proletarian revolution *can* take place—it is by no means clear that the October Revolution in Russia provides an instance of such a revolution. Nevertheless, such questions are not idle. The anatomy of revolution has been studied in great detail by a vast number of brilliant writers from Thucydides to Trotsky. We really know a great deal about revolutions and their successor states. And when, therefore, we put this question, some answers will be more sensible, more worthy of belief, than others. Once we see that an answer to this question must necessarily depend upon historical considerations, then it seems perfectly clear that to expect of the successor state of a revolution, proletarian or other, a high degree of humanity or liberty is to expect the improbable. Bonapartism or Stalinism are in a high degree typical of what we should expect. At the very least, it is up to Thompson and his colleagues to show under what conditions we are entitled to expect something very different.

In repudiating Stalinism, Thompson and those who think like him have, I submit, repudiated too much or too little. They have repudiated too much if they still see the politics of socialism in the free societies of the west in the perspectives of revolution; for history gives us absolutely no reason to suppose that the consequences of a revolutionary seizure of power can be other than a brutal and authoritarian régime. They have repudiated too little if they really want our society to be transformed into one with a higher degree of freedom and humanity and the possibility of a richer life for ordinary people. A political strategy seriously concerned with such an end must set aside as irrelevant even the most "revisionist" version of the concept of the seizure of power through a violent revolution.

But I think it may be a mistake to discuss revolutionary Marxism—Stalinist, Trotskyist or "revisionist"—as though it were a possible but mistaken policy. It has no application to the countries of developed capitalism. The trend of social and economic development in these countries is quite different from what Marx expected, and quite different from what we should have expected had Lenin's theory of imperialism been true. The Labour movement altogether lacks the will to revolution, even in such countries as France and Italy where there are mass Communist parties. Dreams of revolution are the opiates of groups of intellectuals and have political significance only as distractions from the serious business of political analysis.

Further, I want to suggest that these ex-Communists have missed the central phenomenon in the politics of our day: the appearance of the totalitarian state. The difference between *any*—even the most corrupt—free society and a totalitarian society is far sharper than the distinction between a capitalist and a socialist society. With varying degrees of sophistication the ex-Communist revolutionaries still want to maintain that basically, whatever the distortions of the present epoch, the Soviet and Chinese societies represent a higher stage of development than the capitalist societies of America and western Europe. To maintain this, one has also to maintain that the political liberties, with their legal safeguards, that still characterize these societies are of relatively slight importance compared with the economic and class relations within them. Such a conclusion is both tragic and absurd. Tragic, because there *are* in these societies powerful forces making for totalitarianism, and revolutionary Marxism, precisely because it siphons off scarce political talent that is badly needed to deal with the genuine problems of our society, helps rather than hinders these forces. Absurd, because only in a free society can the debate over Stalinism and "revisionism" be pursued in security and without commitment.

2

The repentant Stalinists have contributed much to the spirit of the New Left: toughness, a feeling for the drama of political conflict, a conviction of the importance of theory at the level of world history; above all, perhaps, they have for those who never endured the Stalinist servitude the charm that clings to veterans of famous wars. They are, or have been, the nearest thing to professional revolutionaries the British political scene affords. Numerically, though, they are greatly outnumbered by young men who were never

Communists, or were Communists only for a short period, who are interested in Marxism as a theory without regarding it as in any sense a master science; for this is a generation that takes Freud and Keynes for granted, moves easily in the world of academic sociology, in philosophy may be influenced by Wittgenstein or Sartre, and has personal commitments that vary from a cheerful secularism to Quakerism or Catholicism. What the former Stalinists see in the social and political scene of our day is fundamentally determined by an analysis which is carried over without radical change from their Stalinist period; whereas the other members of the New Left look at the contemporary scene with a gaze less disciplined by theory, or perhaps with a gaze affected by a variety of influences—George Orwell, R. H. Tawney, even Cobbett, the Chartists, Mill and Matthew Arnold. They are as likely to have been given a push to the Left by the 'personalism' of Mounier or the sociological conclusions of Professor Wright Mills as by an encounter with *Socialism Utopian and Scientific* or *State and Revolution*.

All this means that if we look at the New Left more broadly than I have done so far—if, in terms of the organs of the Left, we move from *The New Reasoner* to *Universities and Left Review*—the pattern of thinking is not so plain. What I now have to say is in the first place a very crude attempt to state what seem to me the general characteristics of the thought of the New Left, excluding those characteristics that are the peculiar contributions of the former Stalinists. Of course, many of these characteristics are to be found in the thought of the former Stalinists. But this is in a sense coincidental. Beliefs held in common may be derived from very different sources and be given quite different justifications.

It is widely held that the social and economic changes in our society since 1945 can properly be described as "a social revolution". Indeed, both the major parties compete for the credit that is thought to attach to this revolution. Certainly, there

have been many remarkable changes: a vast increase in the
public services concerned with social welfare, a public health
service which is, in spite of many gross defects, probably in
advance of anything to be found elsewhere, the elimination
of the greater part of that primary poverty (that is, poverty
which is a consequence of an absolute lack of resources, as
distinct from poverty which is a consequence of the bad use
made of resources) which was an evident feature of our great
cities before the war, the visible bodily health of so many of
our children, above all the persistence of a degree of full
employment such as no pre-war economist would have dared
to hope for. No one who lived through the thirties will be
disposed to minimize the scale and importance of these
changes, and it is natural to fall into the hyperbole of describing these changes as in sum "a social revolution". The
New Left, with varying degrees of emphasis, argues that
the hyperbole disguises the extent to which the *structure* of
our society remains unchanged under the welfare state; more,
it is argued that the class structure is in fact more rigid and
that social power is more effectively in the hands of those
who control corporate business than it was in the capitalism
of the thirties; and finally, that the general belief that a
social revolution has taken place disguises the extent to
which gross poverty and harsh conditions of life persist,
especially among the old, the mentally and physically sick,
and that section of the working-class—the railwaymen, for
example—with incomes well below the average.

What has been said so far could amount to no more than
the assertion that the changes that have taken place, welcome
enough, are less dramatic than they are often claimed to be.
Much more than this is involved. The assumption made by
what we may roughly call the Fabians—by this I understand
what is essentially the *centre* in British politics, a centre
stretching from Mr. Gaitskell and Mr. Crosland (the most
gifted apologist the centre has) to the Bow Group—is that
the social changes of the last fifteen years are a first instal-

ment of changes still to come, changes in the direction of a society to be characterized by an ever higher degree of welfare, education, justice and social equality. It is *this* assumption that is challenged by the New Left. Their argument is that the fundamental social evils that are left untouched under welfare capitalism as we know it today are firmly linked with the structure of capitalism and can only be modified in a serious way, or abolished, by a far more radical transformation of the social structure than the present Labour party envisages. It is this position that gives point to what is serious, as distinct from what is comic, in the long debate in the Labour party over Clause 4 of the Constitution.

I have no competence to assess this argument in detail. But it is a serious argument, advanced by responsible and expert academic people and backed by detailed study of our economic and social structure. It is very much more impressive than superficially analogous arguments employed by the left-wing intellectuals of the thirties, partly because very much more is known about the working of our society now than was known—or could have been known—then. That it carries with it all the political implications that are customarily attached to it is another matter, and one where common sense rather than the specialized knowledge of the expert is relevant.

The argument that those gross social evils that can be given some kind of statistical assessment are structural to capitalism and are to be remedied only by structural changes of a fundamental kind does not stand alone. It is linked with a diagnosis of our cultural situation, a diagnosis that might well stand even if the social and economic critique of welfare capitalism should turn out to be less well founded than the New Left believes.

This diagnosis functions at two levels. First, there is a critical account of the ideology of our society as it is expressed through the various mass media and notably through the use of advertisement. This is often brightly and amusingly done but is only a part of a vast literature obsessively concerned with questions of status—"top people", U and non-U, and so on—and is, allowing for differences of tone and intention, as characteristic of the *New Yorker* as of the organs of the New Left. And then there is the concern with problems of culture at a deeper level, a concern most typically represented by the work of Mr. Richard Hoggart and Mr. Raymond Williams. Indeed, it would not be extravagant to say that without *The Uses of Literacy* and *Culture and Society 1780–1950* the New Left would be a very different kind of movement from what it now is.

Both these works are well known and there is no point in summarizing them here. Hoggart examines the use of the printed mass media to condition ordinary people to accept the values of what he calls "the candy-floss world", and does this against the background of a study of the older working-class world he remembers from his childhood in Hunslet. Williams gives us what is in effect a history of social criticism from the end of the eighteenth century to our own day. It is history seen from the angle of one whose training is in the discipline of literary criticism, and it is organized to elucidate that family of concepts grouped under the word "culture", from culture understood as the activities and products of the arts and the intellectual pursuits to culture understood as the whole way of life of a society. The effect of both these works has been to render the New Left more critically aware of the quality and texture of the individual lives and concrete relationships of people within our society than was the old Left and more distrustful of easy solutions to problems. The influence of Hoggart and Williams has thus worked against the tendency to simplify social problems, a tendency natural in men predisposed to a revolutionary estimate of the gravity of our situation. At the same time, Raymond Williams, relating himself to the radical tradition in British politics and social criticism—D. H. Lawrence, R. H. Tawney and Leavis count for more than Marx—nevertheless finds himself at the conclusion of his argument gripped by the central problems of politics simply because any thorough analysis—and his analysis is both thorough and penetrating —of culture considered as the way of life of our society raises problems that can be solved only—if not completely— at the level of politics. His conclusion is that we cannot find our way out of the frustrations of our culture under the leadership of an *élite* that will use the mass media to educate the common people (an unspoken assumption that rules the approach of many educated people to this set of problems); "we need [he writes] a common culture, not for the sake of an abstraction, but because we shall not survive without it"; [3] and he goes on to argue that what seems the most obvious difficulty in the way of a common culture, even given the will to bring it about, the difficulty that increased specialization is, technically, the very life of our civilization, can be overcome only "in the context of material community and by the full democratic process" [4]—that is, through common ownership together with democracy.

As to what is involved if we are to lend a new life to this worn-out term "democracy", here Williams strikes me as better than any other writer associated with the New Left. The Conclusion to *Culture and Society* should be read as a whole; but the following passage gives some idea of the quality of the argument. Williams has been showing our disposition to overcome physical and social difficulties through the domination and manipulation of physical objects and men. He continues:

> . . . we come to realize . . . that where the dominative mood extends to man himself, where human beings also are isolated and exploited, with whatever temporary success, the issue in the long run is a cancelling in spirit of the full opportunities offered by the material gains. A knot is tied, that has come near to strangling our whole common life, in this century.

3. Raymond Williams, *Culture and Society 1780–1950*, 1958, p. 317.
4. Ibid., p. 333.

. . . We react to the danger by attempting to take control, yet still we have to unlearn, as the price of survival, the inherent dominative mode. The struggle for democracy is the pattern of this revaluation, yet much that passes as democratic is allied, in spirit, with the practice of its open enemies. It is as if, in fear or vision, we are now all determined to lay our hands on life and force it into our own image, and it is then no good to dispute on the merits of rival images. This is a real barrier in the mind, which at times it seems almost impossible to break down: a refusal to accept the creative capacities of life; a determination to limit and restrict the channels of growth; a habit of thinking, indeed, that the future has now to be determined by some ordinance in our own minds. We project our old images into the future, and take hold of ourselves and others to force energy towards that substantiation. We do this as conservatives, trying to prolong old forms; we do this as socialists, trying to prescribe the new man.[5]

These are wise words, to be reflected upon and returned to at leisure.

To do even the sketchiest justice to the New Left something must be said about the Campaign for Nuclear Disarmament and the·policy of unilateral nuclear disarmament. The New Left is united upon the policy, backs the campaign and even has a slightly proprietorial attitude towards it.

Unilateralism has many roots, from the bogus unilateralism of those Communists who support it because they conceive it to be to the advantage of the Soviet Union—they earlier opposed it—to pacifists who oppose armaments of any kind and the use of force in any circumstances. Setting aside these two wings of the movement, it would, I think, be just to say that unilateralism is founded upon a moral judgment rather than upon political calculation. As the case for unilateralism is presented by the New Left, it is often tied to a set of predictions of what the consequences of Britain's ridding itself of the deterrent would be: a policy of "active

5. Ibid., p. 336.

neutralism" that would exercise an attractive influence upon the uncommitted sections of the world, especially in Africa and Asia, that would strengthen the libertarian tendencies in the satellite states of the Soviet Union, especially in Poland, that would hinder the spread of nuclear weapons to those countries that do not as yet possess them, that would release social and economic resources now immobilized by the psychology of the cold war and by the influence upon the economy of the arms programme. These predictions may or may not be reasonable. Commonly those who make these predictions seem to me to underrate the possibility that a totally disarmed (so far as nuclear weapons are concerned) western Europe, with the United States no longer interested in the security of the region, would offer in some circumstances an exceedingly strong temptation to the Red Army. But this does not touch the heart of unilateralism. The heart of the campaign lies in the simple judgment of a multitude of ordinary people who regard the use of nuclear bombs against the populations of other states, even in response to aggression, as altogether immoral; and I believe that the bulk of the supporters of the campaign would still be unilateralists even if there were no substance in the hopeful predictions of the New Left, even if unilateralism were likely to bring about Soviet aggression. If I am right, the identification of the New Left with unilateralism is in a sense accidental. The refusal to contemplate the use of nuclear weapons in any conceivable circumstances is a judgment of conscience [6] that altogether transcends the political categories with which it is connected in the mind of the New Left. But it is important to add that the serious and persistent concern of the New Left with questions of social morality gives it every right—granted its major premises—to include in its general indictment of our society the fact that it is, like the

6. A valuable and perhaps epoch-making discussion of this judgment of conscience, from the Catholic standpoint, is Walter Stein (Editor), *Nuclear Weapons and Christian Conscience*, 1961.

Soviet Union and the United States, committed to the policy of the great deterrent.

A critical analysis of our social and economic system; a diagnosis of our society considered as a total way of life; a repudiation of the morality of the great deterrent; all these add up to a policy and an outlook, distinctive and with an obvious appeal. Such a policy, such an outlook, just because they aspire to a complete vision of our social condition, are not strictly comparable with the policy and outlook of the supporters of our traditional parties. Presuppositions and theoretical considerations are always present, unspoken and unanalysed, in the background of politics; but it is a peculiar characteristic of the recent British political tradition that they are left unspoken and unanalysed; and it is felt to be better so. Here the New Left is our most important dissenting group. Their dissent is on the ground that the issues of politics are today of such crucial importance to the entire human race that we can no longer be content with empiricism and pragmatism in politics. The question of politics has become what it was for the Greeks or for the medieval thinkers or for the men of our own Civil War: the question of what it is for man to live well, both as an individual moral agent and as a social and political animal.

In so far as the New Left has anything like a formulated position on this question, it is indicated by the concept of "humanism". Much has been written on this topic by members of the New Left; and it has to be said quite bluntly that, Raymond Williams and Alasdair MacIntyre apart, this is the weakest part of the New Left's contribution. What is man? We ought to know the answer to this question, for we are surely better acquainted with ourselves than with, say, the brutes or the stars. But the question persists and is a perpetual source of puzzlement. Even if the New Left should be wrong in its analysis and deceived in its expectations, it has the great merit of having forced us back upon this question and shown us its relevance to a mature consideration of politics.

## 3

The coming together of the two elements that compose the New Left, the ex-Communists and the others, is symbolized by the merging of *The New Reasoner* and *Universities and Left Review*. And the union has now been celebrated by the appearance of *Out of Apathy*, a collection of essays which is the first of a series of New Left Books.[7] The essays are of very unequal value. The one essay which is quite certainly of more than transient interest is Mr. Alasdair MacIntyre's "Breaking the Chains of Reason". In it he asks the question : What is man ?

It may be that MacIntyre is not strictly to be counted as a member of the New Left. He is a professional philosopher with an uncommon store of learning, especially in psychology and theology, and although he is in his methods very much a part of the contemporary philosophical movement, the catholicity of his sympathies and interests is evident in most of what he writes, in that his manifest debts are not only to Frege and Wittgenstein, but also to Plato and Aquinas, Hegel and Marx. Politically he stands a little apart from the other contributors to *Out of Apathy* and may be presumed to have more crisply conceived notions of revolutionary policy and organization.

MacIntyre begins with a judgment on the condition of the intellectuals. He sees them as having lost the role of the rebellious critics of society able to speak to men in terms that are politically effective, a role they enjoyed between the collapse of medieval society and the arrival of the bureaucratic, intellectually fragmented society in which we now live. Prisoners of their specialisms, they are as much the impotent spectators of life as are the workers (as seen by the intellectuals), stupefied with football, gambling, television and the gutter press. They are conformists, worshippers of things as they are, expressing and receiving the gospel of

7. E. P. Thompson and others, *Out of Apathy*, 1960.

conformism at the level of sophistication represented by the respectable newspapers and the intellectual weeklies.

What has gone wrong? MacIntyre's view is that the contemporary intellectual is confused by a mistaken analysis of certain central concepts having to do with life in society: reason, purpose, intention, freedom. These concepts are central, and interrelated, because they are all of them necessary to an understanding of what it is to live as a human being, one who reflects, chooses and acts. It is distinctively human to choose freely in the light of rational considerations. In this sense freedom is the essence of man. In so far as the area of rational choice is more limited than it need be, man falls below the human level and, like the brutes and the physical world, comes under the rule of necessity. In so far as the area of rational choice is enlarged, man becomes more fully what he has it in him to be. It is important not to lose sight of the connection between freedom and reason. "Without freedom reason operates only within limits, and so its constructions, however intricate, remain beyond those limits uncriticized, and, in so far as uncriticized, irrational. Without reason freedom becomes merely a lack of constraint which leaves the individual the plaything of all the forces which impinge upon and influence him, but of which he remains unconscious." [8]

The contemporary intellectual has lost the connection between reason and freedom, or fails to see its importance. This is a consequence, MacIntyre argues, of the inner weakness of the academic world. Whereas at one time the academic world preserved the concept of human nature, for the separate disciplines of history and philosophy and literature met in the study of a single civilization, that of classical antiquity, now the concept, and with it a sense of the interrelatedness of these disciplines and of their relevance to the life of the present, has been lost. The university-trained intellectual is thus no longer a critic of his society but an apologist for it; for he has lost sight of the rational ground

8. Ibid., p. 201.

of all criticism, the concept of human nature, which can be understood only if the connections between the separate disciplines are made in and through the study of the human sciences.

At this point MacIntyre moves from the level of sociological explanation to that of a purely intellectual analysis of theory. The central theoretical error of the human sciences is that they have missed the peculiar character of their subject matter through a mistaken reliance upon mechanical explanation. The psychologist in the case of the individual and the social scientist in that of the group have attempted "to discover laws as simple as Newton's laws of motion, from which observed regularities in human conduct might be deduced. . . . To explain, to predict, to control; to be able to see human behaviour as the outcome of physiological or environmental determinants; and to unify this understanding in a scheme as simple as Newton's: these have been the goals." [9]

It is not necessary to follow out MacIntyre's detailed demonstration that explanation in terms of the mechanical model breaks down through a series of conceptual confusions that are inescapable, for the subject matter of the human sciences is such that the mechanical model is theoretically too poor to illuminate the fundamental problems. Its only successes are in limited contexts where what is specific to human nature can be disregarded—those contexts, for example, where the differences between the behaviour of rats in mazes and the conditioned behaviour of human beings are not substantial. Of course, the breakdown of the mechanical model can issue, not in the reaffirmation and application of reason to human problems, but in the view—parasitic upon the mechanistic view—that human life is inexplicable, beyond the power of reason to grasp.

How is this analysis relevant to Marxism, to socialism? MacIntyre lacks the space to make all the connections, but

9. Ibid., p. 210.

roughly the relevance seems to be this. Marx, in the spirit of the younger Hegel, sees the essence of human nature as freedom. But freedom always has a concrete form, an historical expression. We enlarge our freedom, or fail to do so, under the conditions of a particular historical epoch. In our own epoch human freedom can be extended only through the struggle for a society founded upon common ownership and the participation of all men in the running of this society. Such a state of affairs is both technically and socially feasible; only through the establishment of such a state of affairs can we hope to remedy the evils that are a consequence of a class-divided society. To be a committed revolutionary socialist is, therefore, to point the way to one's fellows to the realization of what, as human beings, they cannot but desire. Revolution is in our day the authentic mode of human existence: social democracy, liberalism, conservatism, are forms of bad faith.

It is significant that the fundamentals of MacIntyre's argument do not necessitate any reference to the writings of Marx or Hegel. He could perfectly well have stated it without any reference to, say, Marx's third thesis on Feuerbach, for the concept of human activity there employed can only seem peculiarly Marxist in an intellectual climate dominated by the notion of mechanical explanation. And MacIntyre's Marxism is idiosyncratic and highly selective. The Marxism which has counted for so much in the history of the modern world, of which Leninism is an authentic expression and Stalinism a revealing caricature, is very different from the Marxism of MacIntyre. Its attractive power—and its irrationalism—spring from its amalgamation of the notion of mechanistic explanation with the notion of human freedom. Its obvious historical analogue is that of Calvinism. The Calvinist doctrine of Predestination could have issued in passivity or antinomianism. Notoriously, however, it issued in moral earnestness and a furious activity; for a virtuous life was the sign, though not the cause, of election; and anxiety over whether or not one was chosen for eternal salvation by the inscrutable Divine decree could be overcome through the active living of that kind of life which was a sign of election. When Dimitrov cried out from the dock at Leipzig: "The wheel of history moves slowly on to the ultimate, inevitable, irrepressible goal of Communism!" he expressed the essence of the faith of generations of Marxists, the belief that history was on the side of the proletarian revolution, more, that the dialectic of history is an instance of that dialectical law which is written in the history of the Cosmos itself. But the belief that the stars in their courses fight for the victory of Communism does not—here the analogy with Calvinism is relevant—issue in passivity, but in the life of revolutionary activity; and in so far as this life brings about the results desired it vindicates the belief.

MacIntyre can make out a case for his version of Marxism, just as thirty years ago Professor Sidney Hook had a case for portraying Marx as in the fundamentals of his method an anticipator of the pragmatism and instrumentalism of Dewey. But in both cases, the reading of Marx has to be selective and, more importantly, Marx has to be distinguished very sharply from Engels and from Lenin, indeed, from almost all Marxists. Marx himself, it is true, made the remark that he was not himself a Marxist; but MacIntyre's redefinition of Marxism is so drastic that it leads to paradoxical consequences. When Engels at the grave of Marx said that Marx had done for history what Darwin had done for biology, when Engels, in the most popular of all his works, a work treated by Marxists from that day to this as *the* compendium of Marxism, *Socialism Utopian and Scientific*, treats Marxism as a *science*, he certainly wishes to claim for Marxism considered as a theory of society and of history not less but *more* than the natural scientist claims; for in Marxism is to be found the logic of the sciences themselves. It is no less than the master science, that supreme science of human nature that poor David Hume searched for and didn't find, that was to serve as "the only solid foundation for the other sciences". This claim is made so generally by the followers of Marx, there is such a constant tradition in its favour, that we have to take MacIntyre as a kind of protestant Marxist who dates the corruption of the faith from the apostolic age itself. But what has made Marxism a shaping force in the history of the modern world is the Marxism of Engels, of Lenin, even of Stalin; and its charm and power spring from its combination of the notion of history as determined by law, and thus a proper subject for scientific investigation, and the notion of revolutionary activity—the responsibility of the individual to shorten the birth-pangs of the new society.

Marxism as a method of explanation is tied to the inappropriate mechanical model. It is one more version of the old dream that methods so successful in the natural sciences will surely pay dividends in the human sciences. For the reasons MacIntyre gives this simply won't do. Any analysis of our situation which is to be politically useful has to discard Marxism along with much other lumber. Of course, this doesn't mean that there is nothing to learn from Marx. There is, after all, much to learn from Freud who, with his followers, fell into very similar logical confusions.

Nevertheless, Marxism continues to fascinate the New Left, as it has for so long fascinated the European labour movement. Its pretensions to be the science of human affairs may be groundless, but there is something about it which seems to speak to our condition. It does so because it is true that we are, as the Marxists presuppose, both agents and victims, though not victims of the historical process, conceived as the Marxists conceive it, and agents of the proletarian revolution. The power of the Marxist myth lies in its being a myth of sin, suffering and redemption. The Fall in Marxism is the transition from primitive communism to class society. (Anyone who doubts this, thinks it forced, should read what Engels has to say in *The Origin of the Family*,

*Private Property and the State* about the vestigial morality of that early state surviving among modern primitives.) The redemption, in the fullness of time, is the work of the most suffering class of modern society, the proletariat; and through the passion of the proletariat mankind passes into communism, a return to man's primitive integrity but at a higher level. Death is swallowed up in victory or, if with the Marxists you prefer the categories of Hegelian logic, the negation is negated. It is the power of this myth that has made of Marxism for so many what Marx himself said of religion: "the heart of a heartless world".

What is man? MacIntyre thinks the question is relevant to a consideration of politics in a revolutionary epoch such as our own. He is surely right. But if we are to take this question seriously we have to move beyond the extraordinary parochialism, in its thinking about this subject, of the New Left. So far as religion and ethics are concerned there is little sign—MacIntyre apart—that they have eaten very much more than the thin positivist gruel of nineteenth-century rationalism. Hegel and Marx, Freud and Wittgenstein, are indispensable witnesses to be examined and cross-examined. But there is at least a *prima facie* case for thinking that if man's predicament is that of one who is at once agent and victim, then other witnesses may need to be heard: St. Augustine and Pascal, for example, and the greater men who stand behind them.

The New Left is a young and not altogether coherent movement, and what its impact upon British politics will be is hard to foretell. It is obviously "going places". The cultural wing, so to speak, represented by Hoggart and Williams, already has a vast influence. Even the political and economic thinkers influence a considerable public through their writings in the weeklies and in one of the respectable newspapers. (There may be a certain irony here.) Perhaps the surest sign that their influence is to be reckoned with is that there begin to be signs that intellectuals in the Labour party are disposed to borrow clothes, gestures and tricks of speech from them. It is not out of the question that they may achieve in our day the kind of success the Left Book Club had in the thirties. All this would be a reason for taking the New Left seriously, even if there were not very much better reasons for doing so.

What ought, in my view, to be giving the New Left some concern is what I may call "vestigial Bolshevism". In an age when the very existence of man on the planet Earth is in question, images of violence and catastrophe have a certain appeal. If our situation is so desperate, then perhaps the remedy must be a desperate one too. If we live in a bureaucratic society where passivity and "I'm all right, Jack" represent—if they do—the temporary mood of the people, then perhaps nothing short of an explosion will shatter the calm. But serious political analysis cannot be tied to temporary moods, nor does the possible folly of nuclear warfare—a folly which is impartially threatened by states quite differently organized socially and politically (threats of nuclear warfare are not a peculiarity of capitalist societies)—provide a good reason for a radical breach with the political tradition of our own country. The New Left may be roughly right in thinking that welfare capitalism has only scratched the surface of social evils and that common ownership would be a predominant feature of a more satisfactory society. This can be argued and will continue to be argued so long as we preserve the legal framework of our society and a sufficient diversity of institutions to prevent the concentration of power over the means of communication in the hands of a single corporate group. What has been achieved in terms of social advance over the past century is immense and ought not to be undervalued. The habit of social peace has been compatible with a high rate of social change. There seems no reason to suppose that our institutions have suddenly become so rigid that they cannot contain further social changes without breaking.

I have already said that dreams of revolution are the opiates of intellectuals. They are more than this. They nourish a spirit of contempt for the profoundly unrevolutionary mass of the people who are by no means so befuddled by the mass media as intellectuals sometimes think, both in this country and the United States. And this spirit of contempt is simply irreconcilable with the creation of that common culture desired by the New Left. I have already quoted Raymond Williams's warning that we have a strong impulse to *force* ourselves and others to realize our images of the good life. "We do this as Conservatives, trying to prolong old forms; we do this as Socialists, trying to prescribe the new man."

1960

# 5

## The Justification of Political Attitudes

IN contemporary writing "attitude" has a variety of meanings and employments and in recent work in ethics it has become a vogue word. Professor Stevenson's use of it I sometimes find hard to understand; but in one respect I shall follow his example and offer no definition of "attitude". It has a range of familiar meanings in ordinary speech and writing. In some of its instances the term makes a strong "propositional" or "cognitive" claim, in others this claim is made tentatively or not at all. Some attitudes belong to the family of theatrical gestures and poses, and we may if we wish make it a question whether or not such are *really* attitudes. In most of its uses it is a faded metaphor drawn originally from "a technical term of the Arts of Design".[1] Faded metaphors are not dead, but deeply sleeping, and we shall not be surprised if from time to time there are stirrings.

One difficulty I ought perhaps to deal with at once. There is a sense of attitude which (some might hold) would make talk about justification otiose. Mr. Hare, for example, asserts (in connection with Stevenson's use of the term) that " 'attitude', if it means anything, means a principle of action".[2] Now, some might think that the only case in which one could speak of justifying an attitude of this kind would be where one simply drew attention to the principle exhibited. The principle might not be such that it could be justified by reference to other principles or to any facts about the world. Here the attitude—"a principle of action"—would itself be ready

---

1. *Shorter Oxford English Dictionary.*
2. R. M. Hare, *The Language of Morals*, 1952, p. 70.

to provide a justification of a particular piece of *conduct*. I do not think this difficulty is serious, even if one allows that it does not make sense to ask for the justification of some or any moral principles. It would not be plausible to say of all principles of action in politics that they were of this order; and where they are of this order it will still be possible to justify them in the sense allowed by Mr. Hare: "if pressed to justify a decision [of principle] completely, we have to give a complete specification of the way of life of which it is a part".[3]

In speaking of "justification" it will not always be necessary to speak of "the justification of attitudes". Traditions, laws, customs, decisions, may all in one sense or another be justified. A justification of any one of these will entail the justification of a related attitude. It would be clumsy and unnecessary to reduce all statements about justification to statements about the justification of attitudes entailed by them. In political discourse, as distinct from talk about such discourse, we may wish on occasion to speak of attitudes rather than the states of affairs towards which they are directed; for to emphasize the attitude is to emphasize the practical character of political discourse, to make it plain that here deliberation is for the sake of action.

I

Questions about justification in politics are or may be put in a context made in part by the political philosophers of the last three or four hundred years. There is a good deal of doubt as to what precisely such philosophers were trying to do and some interesting suggestions have recently been made.[4] I want to point out what I think to be a neglected

3. Ibid., p. 69.
4. I have in mind such discussions as those in Mr. Mabbott's *The State and the Citizen* and Mr. Weldon's *Vocabulary of Politics*.

aspect of their work, and one which has a bearing on questions of justification.

Medieval philosophers conceived of political attitudes as a relatively tractable sub-species of moral attitudes. Princes could certainly be wise or foolish; but the wisdom requisite in a ruler was rather the moral virtue of Prudence than the command of a technique. His acts and edicts were judged by their agreement with or their divergence from the *jus naturale*. St. Louis, dispensing justice from under the oak in the wood of Vincennes, is a type of the wise ruler of the Middle Ages. Here questions of justification are connected immediately with questions of moral principle; and though there may be puzzles and difficulties—whether or not particular wars are justifiable, whether tyrannicide may be a duty, what circumstances justify the revolt of subjects from their prince—they can in principle be settled by the expert casuist.

When the cake of custom is broken political thinking is given a new style. Questions about justification are in the end no doubt reduced to questions about moral principles; but a great many questions are questions about art; and many of the traditional questions are dismissed as irrelevant or even dangerous.[5] We may examine an instance of the new style in the work of Hobbes.

Hobbes's work is an attempt to show man what his political situation is and what, given this situation, he must do to make himself secure and enjoy the fruits of civilization. Security is the one necessity and attitudes must be appraised according to whether or not they tend to increase security. Although his work has the appearance of a deductive system, this appearance is one of the many rhetorical devices he employs to convince the reader that one thing alone is needful. Within this quasi-systematic framework he draws our attention to a variety of models which illuminate the

5. Cf.: "Cardinal Bellarmine and Calvin both look asquint this way," Sir Robert Filmer, *Patriarcha*.

State considered as a work of art and encourage us to think it possible and desirable to bring into existence a State after the pattern of the models.

The rhetorical devices and models are exhibited in the "Introduction" to *Leviathan*. The world, man and the State are all of them products of art. We are familiar with the principles of this art, both as subjects of it—"that most rational and excellent work of nature, *man*"—and as practitioners of it—makers of "engines that move themselves by springs and wheels as doth a watch"; and thus potential makers of Leviathan. Hobbes wishes to persuade us into an ambivalent attitude towards the tasks of politics. The spectacle of an art practised supremely well—an intricate piece of juggling, a bridge suspended over a gorge—at once intimidates and reassures us. Given the hardness of the task, the smoothness of the performance seems miraculous, beyond human power; and yet, we reflect, this *is* a human performance, contrived by human wit and within the power of all those with the appropriate abilities. The construction of the State is supremely difficult—Hobbes does not hesitate to compare the making of "the body politic" to "that *fiat*, or the *let us make man*, pronounced by God in the creation"; and so swiftly would the seventeenth-century public have added the words—"in the image of God"—omitted by Hobbes, that we may take them as invisibly present on the page. Again, to drive home the belief, induced by the rhetorical structure of the whole passage, that the task of politics is supremely difficult, Hobbes qualifies the inference that if the State is "an artificial man", then the principles of political art can be derived from self-scrutiny, by suggesting that "he that is to govern a whole nation, must read in himself, not this or that particular man; but mankind"; and this is "hard to do, harder than to learn any language or science". All the same, the task is within human capacity—this is the point of the assertion that the art of constructing and governing the State is a sub-species of the art of clockwork;

and we must meet it with skill and courage or decline into the sickness of sedition and die in the agony of civil war.

My suggestion is that although Hobbes himself may well have supposed he had given an elaborate theoretical justification of the political attitudes so deftly induced by the rhetoric of *Leviathan*, the real point is different. He impresses upon us a vision of the situation of European man in his period; and the vision itself is both cause and justification of the attitudes induced by it, somewhat in the way the warning crack of the pit-prop is both the cause and the justification of the precautionary action of the miner. It is significant that the vision is, at least in part, shared by one whose theology and philosophy are at some distance from those of Hobbes—I mean Pascal.[6] And the same vision, though here it is mingled with a different and opposed vision, is expressed poetically in *King Lear*.[7] Indeed, *Leviathan* is closer in spirit to *King Lear* than it is to Euclid's *Elements*.

The vision of Pascal and Hobbes is powerfully conveyed; and the rhetoric in which it is clothed speaks almost as eloquently to our condition as it did to men in the seventeenth

6. Cf.: "Les choses du monde les plus déraisonnables deviennent les plus raisonnables à cause du dérèglement des hommes. Qu'y a-t-il de moins raisonnable que de choisir, pour gouverner un État, le premier fils d'une reine? l'on ne choisit pas pour gouverner un bateau celui des voyageurs qui est de meilleure maison. Cette loi serait ridicule et injuste. Mais parce qu'ils le sont et le seront toujours, elle devient raisonnable et juste, car qui choisira-t-on, le plus vertueux et le plus habile? Nous voilà incontinent aux mains, chacun prétend être ce plus vertueux et ce plus habile. Attachons donc cette qualité à quelque chose d'incontestable. C'est le fils aîné du roi; cela est net, il n'y a point de dispute. La raison ne peut mieux faire, car la guerre civile est le plus grand des maux." *Oeuvres de Blaise Pascal*, edited Léon Brunschvicg, Paris 1925, Vol. XIII, pp. 239–40. "*Injustice.*—Il est dangereux de dire au peuple que les lois ne sont pas justes, car il n'y obéit qu'à cause qu'il les croit justes. C'est pourquoi il lui faut dire en même temps qu'il y faut obéir parce qu'elles sont lois, comme il faut obéir aux supérieurs, non parce qu'ils sont justes, mais parce qu'ils sont supérieurs. Par là, voilà toute sédition prévenue si on peut faire entendre cela, et [ce] que [c'est] proprement que la définition de la justice." Ibid., p. 245. See also Erich Auerbach, "The Triumph of Evil in Pascal", *The Hudson Review*, Vol. IV, No. 1; and Jacques Maritain, "The Political Ideas of Pascal", in *Redeeming the Time*, 1943.

7. "There is a real sense in which *King Lear* incorporates the living parts of both *Ecclesiastical Polity* and *Leviathan*." John F. Danby, *Shakespeare's Doctrine of Nature*, 1949, p. 18.

century. But can we be satisfied with it as a justification of the kind of political order commended by them? Pascal is perhaps more acute than Hobbes in seeing that if "la guerre civile est le plus grand des maux", then everything is justified which can be shown to make for the avoidance of civil war, and that apart from this questions of justification ought not to be raised at all.[8] There is an infinite distance between the moral and the political order. Questions about justification —questions, that is, belonging to the moral order—are in the world as it is constituted not so much illegitimate as pointless. In the world of politics we are to submit ourselves without question to the evils which God permits. Perhaps this way of thinking about politics can best be understood as mythological—taking myth in a sense a little resembling that given to it by Sorel.[9] We may say that Hobbes and Pascal show us, by means of a rhetoric, the world within which the particular justifications and attitudes they commend have their meaning. But the connections of the justifications with each other and with the world within which they, as it were, make sense are connections of aesthetic appropriateness rather than of logical implication.[1] It is possible to accept the

8. Hobbes gets himself into a tangle when, for example, he attempts to justify the enforcement of the sovereign's orthodoxy without committing himself to the uncongenial doctrine that the sovereign can command belief. ". . . a Christian king, as a pastor and teacher of his subjects, makes not thereby his doctrines laws. He cannot oblige men to believe; though as a civil sovereign he may make laws suitable to his doctrine, which may oblige men to certain actions, and sometimes to such as they would not otherwise do, and which he ought not to command; and yet when they are commanded, they are laws; and the external actions done in obedience to them, without the inward approbation, are the actions of the sovereign, and not of the subject, which is in that case but as an instrument, without any motion of his own at all; because God hath commanded to obey them." *Leviathan*, Chapter 42. Pascal's cutting of all knots is more satisfactory than this.

9. ". . . it is necessary to appeal to *ensembles* of images capable of evoking *en bloc and by intuition alone*, in advance of all reflective analysis, the mass of feelings that correspond to the various manifestations of the war carried on by socialism against modern society." Cited in Richard Humphrey, *Georges Sorel Prophet without Honor*, Cambridge, Mass., 1951, p. 188.

1. I cannot see, for example, that there is or can be any logical connection between the mechanistic psychology of the early chapters of *Leviathan* and what is later said about Pride and Vanity.

Hobbesian picture of the world and at the same time to reject the political attitudes commended by Hobbes without committing a *logical* error; just as we may enter imaginatively into the world shown to us by Shakespeare in the plays concerned with kingship and without ever leaving this world find fault with Prince Hal's attitude to Falstaff. But in either case this would be an odd thing to do: Hobbes's and Shakespeare's worlds exercise their own kind of compulsion; but in neither case is the compulsion that of a logical nexus.[2]

Attitudes, expressed and evoked, may have deeply felt connections with each other of such a kind that they constitute a unified attitude—a kind of political *Weltanschauung* —which may be immensely effective in winning support despite—even, in some cases, on account of—the logical incoherence of the constituent parts. The blend of Marxism and liberalism in the outlook of the late Harold Laski (at least, after he had abandoned his early pluralism) is logically incoherent. Its logical incoherence was plain enough for all to see; but this did not make it the less influential.[3] Indeed, very often in politics there is an obstinate belief in the validity—a kind of extra- or supra-logical validity—of a nexus of feeling between logically incompatible propositions. On particular questions Hobbes and Pascal were right or wrong, what they said was true or false. But the enduring charm of what they said about political man is more to be grasped through the analogy of the poetic whole than through the analogy of Newton's *Principia*. This may go some way to explain what at first sight seems puzzling, and puzzling not only in connection with the thinkers I have

2. Some nineteenth-century critics were much troubled by Hal's dismissal of Falstaff after he becomes king. But this was surely a failure to take seriously the conception of kingship presented in these plays by Shakespeare. There is no logical objection to our censuring Hal; but to censure him is inappropriate within the only world in which the issue has meaning and importance.

3. A curious example of how men dwelling, as they think, within a system may hit upon correlative ideas of a very surprising character is provided by Engels's adherence to the doctrine of the eternal cycle. See *Dialectics of Nature*, Translated and Edited by Clemens Dutt, 1941, pp. 24, 25.

named: the co-presence of logical incoherence and a felt power to illuminate political relations.[4] The systems of the political philosophers achieve their effects in so far as they displace our customary centre of vision and substitute for it a centre from which everything looks new and strange. Who can view tradition in the same way after reading Burke? or the justification of a régime after reading Marx? or imagery in political speech after reading Sorel? Isn't it rather to miss the point to assert that there is no such partnership or contract "between those who are living, those who are dead, and those who are to be born" as Burke stated? that the theory of Surplus Value is of no empirical economic interest? that it just isn't true that you can manufacture heroic virtue and the tragic sense of life by propagating the myth of the General Strike? Certainly, there are contexts in which one may be obliged to say this kind of thing; but they are not the only possible comments nor are they in the end the most useful.

Justification within systems of this kind is not a process of inference such that we can say of it that it is valid or invalid. Here the political philosopher "brings it off"—or doesn't—in the way the painter or the poet succeeds or fails. To succeed is to shift the centre of vision so that what is really there is seen in a new perspective and as disclosing unsuspected relations. I do not deny that there is embedded in the work of those who have philosophized about politics in "the new style" a good deal of plain moral philosophy and genuine sociology; and it is often worth while to isolate such pieces of work and to evaluate them by the use of the appropriate criteria; but posterity has placed these philosophers in their niches, and they have an enduring influence, by reason of their power as framers of new visions of man's political relations. I do not wish to suggest that the right way to deal with these philosophers is to invoke only

4. *Du Contrat Social* is perhaps the most striking example of this paradox.

aesthetic criteria in judging their work—this is how some would come to terms with Dante's theology and how we should all come to terms with Hesiod's theogony. In the end we have to say of the world seen from the centre which they propose that it is more or less like the world as we know it. But there is much in the world as we know it which we should not have noticed, much in its texture we should have let pass with too casual a glance, had our vision not been schooled by the philosophers, even by those we may wish to classify as sentimentalizers or caricaturists or pernicious moralists.[5]

## 2

We believe that Heaven, and we know that men, by a natural law, always rule where they are stronger. We did not make that law nor were we the first to act on it; we found it existing, and it will exist for ever, after we are gone; and we know that you and anyone else as strong as we are would do as we do.

(Thucydides, *History of the Peloponnesian War*, V. 105.)

This would be a simple way of justifying political attitudes. It would be necessary only to describe how men behave and to explain to anyone who wondered whether they might not behave otherwise than they do that his wondering was unreasonable, in the sense that it would be unreasonable to wonder whether pigs might not fly or dogs preach sermons. The law to which the Athenian envoys appeal is not a rule but a generalization about how all men (and gods) behave at all times. It is not clear what, if any-

5. I am aware that this view of "the new style" is one-sided; but it emphasizes a neglected aspect. "Writers on the history of philosophy are inclined to attend too exclusively to one aspect only—to the ideas explicitly stated, canvassing their fabric, but disregarding the tone of thought which gives them their impetus." Friedrich Waismann, "Verifiability", in *Essays in Logic and Language* (First Series), 1952, p. 150. To analyse the works of these philosophers as rhetorical structures rather than as logical systems—though the rhetoric may be a function of the logical structure, the logical figures may have a rhetorical point—is one way of bringing out what Dr. Waismann calls "the tone of thought".

thing, would count against such a generalization, though it is easy to produce examples of the behaviour which gives the generalization its apparent force; but such a generalization, loose and indefeasible though it may be, conveys very well the notion that all talk of justification which is not descriptive of behaviour but asserts, with or without explanations and justifications, that certain modes of behaviour are to be preferred to others, is just idle chatter, idle (as the Marxist would argue) in the way talk about softening the bourgeois heart is idle or (as we should all argue) in the way talk about how nice it would be if cats did not stalk thrushes is idle. Such talk is indeed not nonsense: but it is directed, or appears to be directed, to ends that are unattainable. It may be symptomatic of what is undisclosed by—even hidden from—those who speak the words: it may, that is, be "ideological". Justification in the ideological mode would then be complex behaviour symptomatic of undisclosed fears, ambitions and so on. To criticize such justification would not be to refute it but to expose its hidden roots. It was in this sense that Marx held that the criticism of religion is the beginning of all criticism. The *philosophes* had tried to show that particular religious doctrines were false. Marx and Engels thought this beside the point. What one had to do was to explain religion as a social institution and to change society so that the roots which nourished religion would be cut.[6]

If we may transform the Athenian envoys into Marxists, their standpoint could crudely be rendered thus: All talk about justification, in Athens or in Melos or in any other city, is symptomatic of hidden purposes and dispositions. Talk about justification is not to be met as argument—true, false, valid, invalid, right, wrong, do not apply—but to be interpreted as complex and, initially, obscurely motivated behaviour.

6. Cf.: Karl Marx and Friedrich Engels, *The German Ideology*, Edited with an Introduction by R. Pascal, 1938, pp. 13 ff.

This is a case for handing over the study of the justification of political attitudes to history and sociology. Arguments advanced to justify attitudes would be considered as
symptoms and as causes modifying the behaviour of those to
whom the arguments are directed. No doubt all or most argument in political and moral matters is designed to influence
behaviour; and if we are convinced by an argument, and
change our behaviour as a result of this conviction, then
there is a proper sense in which it may be said that the argument has caused us to change our behaviour. But the point
of the Marxian critique of ideology appears to be that the
moral discourse of the feudal nobility or the bourgeoisie,
the political theory of Aquinas or Locke, have the appearance of argument over matters about which men can be
right and wrong; but they belong not to the family of rational discourse—a family with only two important members, natural science and dialectical materialism—but to
the family of groans, smiles and other betraying gestures;
and as such they can of course function as causes. Justifications would then indeed be attitudes (related to the theatrical
attitudes), or expressions of them; but they would be related
to justification as we commonly use the term in much the
same way as rationalization is related to reasoning.

It has often been urged that the Marxian view of these
matters is self-refuting. Marxism, too, must be ideological
or—to use Mannheim's convenient term—utopian. But
Marxism inconsistently claims that it is an argument to be
met, not a social phenomenon to be investigated. It seeks
to justify political attitudes while asserting that no justification of a political attitude is what it appears to be. The
Marxian arguments as they are commonly presented certainly generate paradoxes of this kind; but they are re-
movable by the usual devices, though I do not know that a
Marxian logician has yet appeared to do this job.

There is a particular set of Marxian arguments which deal
with a question of justification: the arguments designed to

show that some wars are "just", others "unjust", and that different and opposed attitudes are therefore appropriate.

There are "progressive" and "reactionary" wars. In such wars it is one's duty to side with one or other of the belligerents. It may even be one's duty to do what one can to *begin* a war. (Marx and Engels tried to encourage a Prussian attack upon Russia in 1848.) And there are "imperialist" wars; in these it is one's duty to use the situation created by the war to transform the war between coalitions of states into a civil war between social classes. The principles which enable one to determine the right attitude to any given war are expressed by Lenin as follows:

> The Socialist, the revolutionary proletarian . . . says: "The character of the war (whether reactionary or revolutionary) is not determined by who the aggressor was or whose territory the 'enemy' has occupied; it is determined by the *class* that is waging the war and the politics of which this war is a continuation." [7]

Behind this passage stands the Marxian scheme of historical development. The industrial proletariat, under the philosophical leadership of the "bourgeois intelligentsia",[8] is the class predestined by history to create a socialist society. Whatever is thought to further its approach to power is to be supported, whatever delays its advent is to be opposed.

This seems a simple maxim, though it is not always easy to apply, as the late Harry Pollitt discovered in 1939. But this is a characteristic shared by many maxims we should find it hard to do without. As a justification of attitudes it seems to display the following features.

1. The victory of the proletariat and the creation of a

---

7. *The Proletarian Revolution and Kautsky the Renegade*, in V. I. Lenin, *Selected Works*, Vol. VIII, p. 177.

8. "The vehicles of science [i.e. social science] are not the proletariat, but the *bourgeois intelligentsia* . . ." This statement (by Kautsky) is quoted with approval by Lenin in *What is to be done?* See *Selected Works*, Vol. II, p. 61.

socialist society is a good such that I ought to prefer it to any other good.

2. There are good grounds for supposing that the creation of such a society is likely or inevitable in the future.

3. My action now will make a difference to the date of this desirable consummation.

4. I am obliged to prefer to immediate satisfactions action which will tend to accelerate the process of development towards socialism, even though it may be likely or certain [9] that I shall not participate in the socialist society.

Here the moral principle is that in situations where I am confronted with a variety of goods I ought always to choose the greatest (for most men in the future). I arrive at what I ought to do by connecting with this moral principle the judgment that socialism is the greatest available good. My attitude is in practice fortified by the conviction that whatever I may do or refrain from doing the arrival of socialism is inevitable; though this conviction might conceivably be a ground for choosing immediate satisfactions and leaving socialism to the historical process.[1]

Beliefs about the future and about the probable consequences of my actions are everywhere admitted to be facts relevant to the making of a moral judgment. We shall differ, if we do, from the Marxists in thinking that what we may believe about the future with some degree of assurance is confined to the near future. The more distant the future, the more speculative our beliefs will be; and we may well feel that speculative beliefs ought not to be taken into account in making decisions. Of course, the Marxists would claim that their predictions are as certain as those of the natural scientist and are similarly grounded. Unfortunately—or perhaps fortunately—these predictions turn out to resemble prophecies of the kind put out by palmists and crystal-gazers:

9. As in the case of the Communist martyr.
1. But very few Calvinists were antinomians

they are confirmed because, given the form in which they are cast, they could not not be confirmed.[2]

### 3

To see the world of politics from the centre of vision proposed by Hobbes or Pascal or Rousseau is to be disposed to adopt the complex of attitudes induced by a sympathetic reading of their works. To examine, with the Marxists, justifications which are facts for the historian and the sociologist but in connection with which questions of truth or falsity, validity or invalidity, cannot be raised, is either to dismiss all talk of justification as idle chatter or to admit only that kind of justification which involves an appeal to a speculative theory of historical development. We are not obliged to keep to the centre of vision proposed by a philosopher in the way we are, in a sense, obliged to keep to the centre of vision of a poetic work. The poem is its own cosmos; and we either accept its peculiar perspectives in order to dwell within it, or we ignore the poem altogether. But the political cosmos of the philosopher is a comment on the actual scene—part chaos, part cosmos—and it is a piece of advice for us to accept or reject or separate into sound and unsound parts. We may therefore ask if there are independent reasons for adopting the attitudes that belong to a particular political cosmos. In the case of the analysis of attitudes proposed by the Marxists, we may admit that some attitudes are "ideological" and that there may be an element of "ideology" in

2. It would be interesting to compare the Marxian treatment of the question of the "just war" with the discussions of the same topic by moral theologians, from Aquinas (e.g. *Summa Theologica*, IIa IIae Q.40 Art.i. : "Utrum bellare sit semper peccatum") down to the present day. Such a comparison would, I think, show that the moral theologians are concerned with questions of responsibility—e.g. who is the aggressor?—dismissed by the Marxists as irrelevant technicalities, with questions of intention, and with consequences which are predictable in the ordinary sense in which we might say, for example, what the probable consequences would be for the civilian population of the bombing of certain targets. There is no suggestion in these discussions that war may be justified by an appeal to long-term historical consequences.

all or most attitudes; but we may still ask, after sociological analysis has done all it can do, what we ought to do, what attitudes in politics we are justified in adopting. The contemplation of the dreary succession of political mythologies may induce in us a weariness or inertia which will push us towards "the theory . . . that, so far as good and bad customs or rights and wrongs or matters of religion are concerned, whatever any state makes up its mind to enact as lawful for itself, really is lawful for it, and in this field no individual or state is wiser than another".[3] We could then, like Gallio, refrain from judgment.[4] This is a soothing theory but it is not very plausible. It suggests that those situations in which the agent finds himself faced with acute questions of political obligation [5] have a certain illusory character. I shall assume that in so far as in politics we deliberate about action and the ends of action—not only in connection with questions of art—political philosophy is the study of "the moral foundations and the casuistry of political obligations".[6]

The agent faced with acute questions of political obligation—the priest in South Africa requested to officiate at a marriage between persons forbidden by the law of the State to marry but whose marriage neither Divine Law nor Canon Law forbids, the biologist in eastern Europe required publicly to disavow neo-Mendelian theories of genetics: I forbear to multiply examples—must be prepared to stake his life upon his belief in the rightness of his moral attitude. His moral attitude must be an expression of "a truth which is true *for me . . . the idea for which I can live and die*".[7] He cannot be satisfied with what Newman calls a *notional* assent to

3. *Theaetetus* 172 A (Cornford's translation).
4. Acts xviii. 14, 15.
5. "The questions about obligation become acute only in revolutionary situations. . . ." P. Nowell Smith, Symposium "Science and Politics", Aristotelian Society. Supp. Vol. XXIII, 1949, p. 161. Perhaps so. But we are today living through a revolutionary situation that seems to have gone on for a long time and shows no signs of ending.
6. E. F. Carritt, *Ethical and Political Thinking*, 1947, p. 142.
7. *The Journals of Soren Kierkegaard*. A Selection edited and translated by Alexander Dru, 1938, p. 15 (entry for 1st August 1835).

the attitudes sanctioned by his cultural milieu. At the same time, although his attitude and the decision that follows from it are those of a single individual in a particular situation, he does in a sense decide for all men, he commits mankind. This is involved in the concept of "right action": in an unfashionable but useful idiom, "lex naturalis nihil aliud est quam participatio legis aeternae in rationali creatura".[8]

Fully to explore the situation of such an agent would be to venture a long way into the metaphysic of morals. This is certainly a part of moral philosophy: I see no reason to suppose that moral philosophy is rightly restricted to "the logical study of the language of morals",[9] greatly though I admire the work of those who have in recent years so notably advanced this part of the subject. But what I have to say belongs wholly to the phenomenology of morals, and this (I assume) includes the examination of the language of morals, though the focus of interest is not the logical structure therein exhibited.

To say "x is wrong" = "x violates rule R" can only be to assert a moral judgment if we expand it to include "and you ought not to violate R". If, to one who doubts that x is wrong, the only reply is the reassertion of R, we are sometimes inclined to say that in the last analysis each chooses his own moral principle. If one who doubts that x is wrong is ignorant of none of the facts judged to be relevant by one who believes x is wrong, and if there is no way, other than by drawing attention to the facts and asserting their relevance, of showing that x is wrong, then it may seem that we are driven to accept what Professor Gallie has called the "polyarchic" view of morality: the view which maintains "that, far from there being one single set of valid moral standards, there are an indefinite number of these, embodied in different moralities whose cardinal principles are not

8. Thomas Aquinas, *Summa Theologica*, Ia IIae Q.91 Art. ii.
9. Hare, op. cit., p.v. I do not suggest that Mr. Hare thinks it should be so restricted.

mutually corrigible".[1] A polyarchic view *might*, though this seems to me doubtful—Gallie admits that it is difficult "really to believe it" [2]—give us "the truth which is true for me"; but a decision founded upon a moral principle belonging to one out of a number of moralities with "mutually incorrigible" cardinal principles could not be said to commit mankind. I do not think that if the polyarchic view were correct the agent faced with an acute question of political obligation would have a sufficient ground for taking a decision upon which to stake his life. Morality A might require him to take a certain decision; but it would logically be open to him to choose morality B, which did not require this decision, without loss of moral face. Indeed, there is logically nothing against his adhering to A on Mondays, Wednesdays and Fridays, to B on Tuesdays, Thursdays and Saturdays, and to C on Sundays, however uncomfortable in practice these transitions might prove to be.

I must confess to being dissatisfied with this position, for two main reasons. In the first place, while it makes sense to say we choose to accept or to act upon a principle, it does not seem to make sense to say that we choose the principle itself. Moral principles are accepted or rejected, not chosen. The supporter of the polyarchic view might want to say that this is just psychological: everyone is brought up within a moral tradition and the principles of this tradition present themselves as external to the agent. But even where we come to formulate our moral attitudes after a consideration of moral systems which conflict with the tradition in which we were nurtured, a moral principle presents itself to us as that which has authority to bind our decisions. It is surely sometimes the case that we accept a moral principle as

1. W. B. Gallie, "Liberal Morality and Socialist Morality", *Philosophy*, XXIV, 91, October 1949, p. 319. I do not suggest that acceptance of a position such as that sketched above *logically* commits one to a "polyarchic" view; but that the "polyarchic" view may at first sight offer itself as a plausible device for overcoming the difficulties of this position. Quite other reasons may, of course, be given as justifications of the "polyarchic" view. 2. Ibid., p. 320.

authoritative only with extreme reluctance. If the authority of a moral principle were constituted by our choosing it, then we should choose differently. But "choosing" just will not do this job. I am not saying that "choosing a moral principle" is an impermissible locution, though I myself find it a strange one. What I do say is that if we examine all that we see to be involved in coming to know what we ought to do, including our expressing the awareness of obligation in terms of a principle, we see that it is an empty locution, for nothing answering to it does or can take place.

My second reason for being dissatisfied with the polyarchic view is that it seems to me plain that "our moral attitudes to things are always reactions to their features",[3] that our attitudes of moral approval and disapproval are so connected with our beliefs about actual and prospective states of affairs that our attitudes can be said to be appropriate or inappropriate, correct or mistaken.[4] For example, whatever may be said or thought by some people in Alabama or the Union of South Africa, it is a truth in the natural order that "God hath made of one blood all nations of the earth"; and it follows from this being true that some attitudes are appropriate and correct, others inappropriate and mistaken. When I say that such and such *follows* from x's being true I must not be understood as asserting any kind of logical doctrine. If it should be urged that I appear to be asserting a synthetic necessary proposition, then I do not object to this being said;

3. Jonathan Harrison, Symposium "When is a principle a moral principle?" Aristotelian Society Supp. Vol. XXVIII, 1954, p. 121.
4. Cf.: "Can we then suppose that appetite may receive its last and decisive specification from the perceived merit of the object? That, in the last resort, the desire becomes such because the object is perceived to be such? At least no other account can be accepted of moral approval and disapproval. Our moral prejudices and principles already fixed may partially specify our judgments. But what they still leave open, what we recognize as a new case and painfully reflect upon, we believe ourselves to judge by an informing of our appetite (or aversion) by the object itself. And though we do not suppose our judgment infallible, we believe that in principle it can be done, or else we must abandon every belief in ethical judgments." Austin Farrer, *Finite and Infinite*, 1943, p. 147. "Honesta vero dicuntur, quae in seipsis habent, unde desiderentur." Aquinas, op cit., Ia Q.5 Art. vi.

though I do not think that any philosophical difficulties as to how there can be such propositions in ethics are good reasons for doubting that such and such (a judgment that attitudes are appropriate or inappropriate, correct or mistaken) follows from x's being true about the world. To the objection that I appear to be deriving statements in the optative mood from statements in the indicative mood, I would reply that I admit the charge but fail to see its relevance—I am not arguing that here "it follows" is an instance of deductive inference. These and other difficulties that might be raised are certainly difficulties for the moral philosopher and I do not profess to be able to see my way through or round all of them. But they are difficulties about where to place moral discourse on the logician's chart. If we are in doubt as to where we ought to place moral discourse in relation to those kinds of discourse which have been well charted by the logicians, we do not have to settle this doubt before we can come to know what we ought to do and to know that our knowing what we ought to do is connected with our knowing what is the case about the world, and connected in a peculiar way that we can only characterize by pointing to instances.

Where we place moral discourse on the logician's chart, or whether we give it a place on the chart at all, these questions no doubt depend upon how we choose to limit the paradigm of rationality; and difficulties arise in connection with the justification of any such paradigm, difficulties of a kind similar to those which arise in connection with the justification of moral attitudes. The reasons which have compelled some to assimilate moral discourse to such modes as groans, cheers or imperatives are well known and carry immense conviction, for the paradigm of rationality which they presuppose is—largely for historical reasons—taken as the obvious one. A moral judgment is not an empirical statement, not even a very queer one: we cannot, then, establish the correctness of any moral judgment by an empirical procedure. This surely implies that the ground of any moral judgment is—in terms of the paradigm presupposed—non-rational: feeling, or a choosing for which no logically sufficient reason can be given. We seem then to be driven back upon the polyarchic view. Moral judgments, injunctions and prohibitions, and the principles and attitudes to which these are formally reducible, all are such that they can be exhibited as logically interconnected *within* moral system A, B or C; but each system is—or may be: I am not concerned with how far different moral systems do in fact overlap—an isolated universe of discourse; and while each system is, as a functioning system, a part of the world of fact, there is nothing in the nature or structure of the world of fact to provide a sufficient reason for thinking any one moral system to be rationally more respectable than any other. This allows us to say that the moral system of the Nazis is irrational in so far as it is connected with a racial theory which is empirically false, but merely different in so far as the judgment that it is good to propagate a false racial theory is made a postulate of the system. That we find ourselves with such a conclusion as this on our hands seems to me a sufficient ground for drawing the limits of the paradigm of rationality more broadly. It should be pointed out that the above judgment was not in fact a part of the Nazi moral system; there is a sense in which it *could not* have been a part of the system—the theory (though false) had to be asserted as true, because it was thought, quite rightly, that it is a minimum requirement of any moral system that its primary moral judgments should seem to follow from the structure of the world of fact.

I should like to make it quite plain that I am not arguing that a particular moral judgment is ever *entailed* by a formal rule. We should certainly be inclined to say that a value judgment which could not be "explicated" in terms of a formal rule was not a moral judgment; but no particular moral judgment is ever entailed by the formal rule which it exemplifies. Again, no particular moral judgment can be confirmed or disconfirmed by induction. It is very clear that ethics is not like logic or natural science. The moral life is neither calculation nor applied science. In the end we have to decide; and the landscape is illuminated, the structure of the world of fact is or may be seen as congruent with our moral judgments, once the decision has been taken. But the structure is not constituted thus and thus by our coming to this or that decision; and when we discover we are mistaken about the structure of the facts we know we are committed to a revision of our moral judgments.

To stake one's life upon a principle need be neither a leap in the dark nor a surrender to a local or epochal prejudice; it may be as well-grounded a decision as any other. If in our approach to such a decision we hear a faint rustle of scepticism (are not other attitudes consecrated in Polynesia and Tibet?) we may nevertheless be confident, not in our infallibility, for the queerest doctrines have their martyrs, but in the rationality of our procedure.

## 4

Not all questions about political attitudes seem reducible to questions about moral attitudes. I have argued that while it is sensible to say that we choose to accept or to act in accordance with a moral principle, it does not make sense to say that we choose the principle itself. Now, if we were prepared to say that men have a duty to be Liberals or Tories, Democrats or Republicans, to agitate for proportional representation or the reform of the House of Lords, we should be compelled to say that political principles can no more be chosen than can moral principles. Very few people think we have duties of this kind, though under the influence of political passion we sometimes write or speak as though men have a duty to subscribe to certain political principles and as though men who dissent from our own principles convict themselves of moral error in so doing. Of course, there are disputes in politics in which the choice between one side and the other is a matter of moral obligation. I should think myself morally obliged to vote against a party which proposed the establishment of a colour bar in industry or social life; and in so thinking I commit myself to the belief that everyone able to vote is morally obliged to vote in this way. I may be wrong in thinking a particular dispute imposes a moral obligation upon those able to do something about it; but that there are *some* disputes of this kind seems plain enough. This seems to entail that there may be political principles I am obliged to reject on the ground that decisions in accordance with them are morally wrong and tend to bring about bad states of affairs, though there may in a given situation be no principles I am obliged to accept.

On the whole, I am inclined to think this is true. It would be very strange to say that anyone who is acquainted with those social facts which are accessible to most members of the electorate is obliged to be a Conservative—or a Liberal or a Socialist. There are good reasons for adopting any one of these political attitudes; but none of these reasons is as good as the reasons we commonly have for deciding what our domestic and parochial duties are. If we consider political attitudes in the wider sense in which it might be held that Conservatives, Liberals and Socialists share a common attitude to be contrasted with attitudes of, say, Communists or Falangists or South African Nationalists, then the matter is not so clear. There seem to be political attitudes which are morally objectionable, not on account of the human frailty and error of those who entertain them, but by reason of what they are as dispositions. This is not to say that parliamentary democracy has an absolute moral value, that we are obliged to implant it, so far as this is in our power, in all those societies which do not as yet enjoy it. It is merely to say that, given what we know about the world and given the accumulated insight of our moral traditions, certain choices between attitudes may confront us with acute questions of morals. The casuistry of such situations is often more complex than that of the situations commonly treated by the moralist; but it is not unreasonable to ask the moralist to reflect upon the world he lives in.

1955

# 6
# Words and Things

MR. GELLNER'S book [1] achieved a *succès de scandale* before it had been out very long. Professor Ryle's refusal to have it reviewed in *Mind* on the ground that it was abusive and levelled accusations of disingenuousness against identifiable teachers of philosophy provoked in the columns of *The Times* an impassioned exchange of letters in the course of which a great many issues were firmly knotted together beyond all reasonable possibilities of disentanglement. The Thunderer summed up in favour of Mr. Gellner and Lord Russell (who writes an Introduction to *Words and Things* and began and concluded *The Times* exchanges of letters) in what must be the first leader devoted to a philosophical topic within living memory. Such a hubbub could scarcely, in our culture, have been provoked by purely philosophical differences. It has in fact been a party fight in which much more than philosophical differences have been at stake. The position of Oxford in relation to the provincial universities and the University of London; the connection of philosophers with the cultural "establishment"; the obscure mechanisms by which reputations among professional philosophers are made and marred and advancement secured or frustrated; all these and other issues have been caught up into the controversy. All these issues are in fact raised by Mr. Gellner in his book, and legitimately enough from his point of view—he is a philosopher who is now professionally concerned with sociology —but the nature of his book, as a critical account of certain philosophical doctrines and simultaneously a treatment of

1. Ernest Gellner, *Words and Things. A Critical Account of Linguistic Philosophy and a Study in Ideology*, 1959.

these doctrines as "ideology", that is, as in some sense doctrines the rationale of which can only be understood in terms of obscure social motivations, presents the philosophical reviewer with some difficulties. Any such reviewer is bound to rise up from a reading of *Words and Things* with strong feelings of sympathy for Professor Ryle, even if he takes the view (as does the present writer) that the refusal to arrange for a review in *Mind* was, so to speak, strategically wrong and tactically absurd.

What Mr. Gellner begins by criticizing and ends by savaging had best be set out, in the first place, in the words of the author.

> Linguistic Philosophy is a certain cluster of views about the world, language and philosophy. This cluster has a considerable measure of unity and inner coherence. It merits treatment as "a philosophy", that is, a distinctive outlook, a way of looking at things, with its associated style of reasoning and of setting about solving problems, of recognizing problems and solutions. This philosophy underlies the views and practices of what has become the dominant school of philosophy in British Universities, and particularly in Oxford, since the war. Before the war it was upheld by an influential *avant-garde*. Its main origin is to be found in the later views of Ludwig Wittgenstein.[2]

Mr. Gellner, then, is making the following claims, which it will be convenient to tabulate: (1) Linguistic Philosophy (I shall follow Mr. Gellner's example and call it hereafter LP) is a *Weltanschauung* (Mr. Gellner argues later that it is a concealed or unacknowledged *Weltanschauung*); (2) this *Weltanschauung* has a high degree of inner consistency of doctrine; (3) corresponding to this consistency in *doctrine*, there is community of *appraisal* (that is, agreement upon what is to count as a philosophical problem) and of *method*; (4) LP is dominant in British universities; (5) the doctrines and methods (and the *Weltanschauung*? I am not clear

2. Gellner, p. 17.

whether Mr. Gellner wishes to maintain this, though it seems at times to be *insinuated* by him) of LP are derived in the main from *The Blue and Brown Books, Philosophical Investigations* and *Remarks on the Foundations of Mathematics.*

Plainly, there are various possibilities here. (1) could be true and (2) false, for the unity of a *Weltanschauung* is not necessarily—perhaps not commonly—constituted by the logical consistency of the doctrines of which it is composed. (1) could be true, (2) false and (3) true. If (1) is false, (2) is false; but (3) could be true, if we delete from (3) the backward-looking reference to consistency in doctrine. (3) could be true in part and false in part, or wholly true or not at all true. (4) we might allow to be true, provided this does not commit us to more than admitting that there is some sort of *compositum* properly labelled LP; but it need not have any of the characteristics ascribed to it by Mr. Gellner. (5) is admittedly true in some degree of *some* sense of LP, though not necessarily of Mr. Gellner's sense of LP and perhaps not at all in the case of some of those (I have in mind the late J. L. Austin) considered by Mr. Gellner to be typical practitioners of LP. There are of course other possibilities than those I have considered. It may be that there is a unity of doctrine and/or of method among those who may *properly* be designated as practitioners of LP but that the only sense which can be given to this statement makes it analytic, though not on this account useless. It may be that the philosophers Mr. Gellner names as practitioners of LP are one in doctrine, but that Mr. Gellner has misstated the doctrines which they hold or has misconceived how they hold together. Or it may be that Mr. Gellner's plunge into sociology has led him to the view that a loose social grouping of philosophers who share certain mannerisms, tricks of speech, conventions of discussion, aesthetic and moral prejudices (if, that is, and in so far as they do share these things) and what not, must really share a common outlook and have a common intellectual strategy even when the evidence for this is thin in terms of the doctrines they formally profess. This last, if it should turn out that Mr. Gellner is arguing from the existence of a discernible culture pattern to the existence of an underlying unity of outlook, could be an intelligent guess; this would depend upon what we took as counting for and against the plausibility of guesses in this field; but it could also be analogous to the disordered visions of those who conclude from the existence of shared culture patterns among Jews or Freemasons or Jesuits to the existence of hidden conspiracies.

I have dwelt on the manifold possibilities raised by Mr. Gellner's opening statement of his theme in order to bring out the magnitude of the task Mr. Gellner has set himself. To discharge it respectably he has not only to consider a great many possibilities; he has, in order to decide whether, and how far, the hypotheses he advances are confirmed, to examine and evaluate a great mass of writing from the point of view of its philosophical content and method. After he has done all this, he has then to show that as philosophy it won't do; and it will be difficult or impossible to do this without at least adumbrating more satisfactory ways of doing philosophy. Having done this, he faces a final task, that of considering all he has hitherto taken at the level of philosophy as the ideology of a social group and of showing that there are strong reasons for taking LP as an ideology. It would not be excessive to say that Mr. Gellner, if he is to do his job well, has to give to the work of a number of philosophers (if I have counted correctly Mr. Gellner mentions as practitioners of LP twenty-nine philosophers of whom twenty-eight were living at the time of writing) the patience and devotion Broad gave to the study of McTaggart; and follow this with a sociological study such as Max Weber might have undertaken in his prime.

Of course, Mr. Gellner has done neither of these things. He has written a far more modest book than his programme requires. What he writes is often acute and sometimes amusing and here and there grossly unfair; it is acute as criticism of some philosophical positions maintained by some practitioners of LP; it is amusing somewhat in the manner of Mr. Stephen Potter's work on Gamesmanship and Lifemanship; it is grossly unfair in that it lumps together philosophers of the most diverse views and treats their repudiation of specific doctrines attributed to them by Mr. Gellner as confirmation of his thesis that *really* they hold these doctrines. At times Mr. Gellner uncomfortably resembles the man who undertakes to show that the Jews run the world and treats the absence of Jews from particular positions of power not as counting against his contention but as evidence for the ability of the Jews to run the world without appearing to do so.

It is impossible to traverse the whole ground covered by Mr. Gellner. I propose to do three things: first, to examine an instance of his critical method where it seems to me perversely employed; then, to indicate one or two of the points where Mr. Gellner is very acute—points that, further developed, would have led him to write a valuable book very different in character from *Words and Things*; and lastly to discuss the fundamental question inescapably raised by the whole argument, a question that remains to be asked even if Mr. Gellner's *particular* arguments are rejected and even if *all* the LP positions are *much* stronger than he would allow, the question, namely, as to whether or not all philosophy is rightly characterized as the description and analysis of concepts (and therefore in one important sense rightly to be described as LP).

Mr. Gellner has much to say about the Argument from Paradigm Cases (APC); and regards it as one of the four pillars of LP. "The Argument from Paradigm Cases is absolutely essential to Linguistic Philosophy: it pervades it and it is presupposed without qualification, denials notwithstanding." [3] He states (without giving references or authorities) the APC in these terms:

> The argument is this: stress that, after all, words mean what they normally mean (unless and until redefined). Their meaning is their use. We often have occasion to use the word "table". It means whatever it is used to refer to and, as we often do use it, that to which it refers to (*sic*) *is* a "table". Therefore, tables exist.[4]

This is of course fantastic, and it is significant that the only cited example of the APC which is in any way like Mr. Gellner's account of it is Professor Flew's highly idiosyncratic argument to show how we learn to use such expressions as "of one's own free will". One would not gather from Mr. Gellner's account that the APC is primarily concerned with a thesis about how we learn the use of expressions. He does make this plain later but only after he has set the tone for his treatment by the comic account given above. The point of the APC in connection with epistemological problems connected with tables is not to "prove" that there are tables but to show that one who uses the word "table" in the standard way, pointing to a table, and then goes on to say that perhaps there aren't really tables wishes simultaneously to heed and to disregard the rules for the use of the word "table". What he says is without sense in the same way that one who asserts $p \sim p$ has said what is without sense. Mr. Gellner later wants to say that the APC involves a claim that a *correction* of the rules for the use of a word or expression is never in order; but what the APC suggests is that many corrections are rendered absurd because those who make the corrections want *at the same time* to use the word or expression according to the ordinary rules. This is how the late Sir Arthur Eddington was able to find it extraordinary that he could lean on his study table and be supported: he wished simultaneously to change and to abide by the rules for the use of the word

3. Gellner, pp. 30, 31.          4. Ibid., p. 31.

"solid".[5] In fact, Mr. Gellner himself seems to hold the APC in the absurd form in which he states it (namely, that if a word has a standard use this means that what it is used to refer to exists; with the corollary that if it can be shown that what it is used to refer to doesn't exist, then the word loses its point and ought to be abolished). He writes:

> Somebody who denies the existence of witches is making a perfectly legitimate move within the broader game of asserting or denying what kind of species of beings exist (sic): and at the same time also *he is recommending the abolition of a whole genre of speech, witch-language.* (My italics.)[6]

And so, too, one supposes, for all those who deny the existence of fairies, Prester John and men on Mars.

Reckless and slapdash, Mr. Gellner's treatment of the APC, only a part of which has been touched on here, is typical of his general treatment of the philosophical arguments he attributes to those philosophers he is attacking. Either he states the argument in loaded ways such as would certainly be repudiated by the philosophers under discussion; or he draws strange conclusions from fragments of quoted arguments. His capacity for misunderstanding a plain statement is immense. For example, he takes G. E. Moore's remark in his autobiography—"I do not think that the world or the sciences would ever have suggested to me any philosophical problems. What has suggested philosophical problems to me is things which other philosophers have said about the world or the sciences"—and infers from it that Moore *"explicitly states that he never found the world itself or science philosophically puzzling".* (My italics.)[7] Of course, what Moore is saying is that he would never have found the world or the

---

5. Later on Mr. Gellner discusses "solid" and asks rhetorically (p. 63) of such expressions as "tables are not really solid": who is misled? Eddington was misled. That such expressions do induce a state of muddle in undergraduate students is, I am confident, common knowledge among teachers of philosophy. Perhaps undergraduates at the London School of Economics are very clever.

6. Ibid., p. 35.    7. Ibid., p. 59.

sciences philosophically puzzling had it not been for the things philosophers said about them.

If one gives oneself a licence to roam over a vast body of work by many philosophers it will be hard luck if one doesn't find now and then some rich specimen of fallacy or idiocy. Mr. Gellner has acquired a fair collection of such fallacies and idiocies;[8] but they have strength only in so far as the general indictment brought against LP is strong. It would after all be possible to range over Professor Popper's *The Open Society and Its Enemies* and come back with an anthology of curious pieces. One could, that is, play with Popper the game Popper plays with Plato, Hegel and Marx, the game Mr. Gellner plays with those he designates as linguistic philosophers. But what has this to do with philosophy?

And yet Mr. Gellner is, as one knows from his published papers, an excellent philosopher. There are in *Words and Things* the elements of a formidable criticism, not so much of LP in Mr. Gellner's too wide and inclusive sense, as of the philosophical presuppositions and methods of some practitioners of LP, notably J. L. Austin and Mr. Warnock. The too general accusations of triviality, lexicography and the superstitious worship of ordinary usage which are directed against all twenty-nine linguistic philosophers have a certain plausibility here. At least, there is a case to be argued. Again, Mr. Gellner, in accusing linguistic philosophers of very frequently presupposing positivist doctrines while innocently disowning any connection with them, makes an important point, though it needs more documentation and discussion than he gives it. He writes: "Linguistic Philosophy absolutely requires and presupposes Positivism for without it as a tacit premiss, there is nothing to exclude any metaphysical interpretation of the usages that are to be found,

8. E.g. ". . . at least one linguistic moral philosopher claims to have cured a young man's nihilism by pointing out to him that the logic of the expression 'nothing matters' is different from that of 'nothing chatters'." Ibid., p. 217.

and allegedly 'taken as they are', in the world." [9] This is too sweepingly put, but the point is worth making. Above all, perhaps, one is inclined to sympathize with Mr. Gellner, in his self-chosen role of the angry young man of British philosophy, when he makes the accusation of triviality against some of the philosophical work that has made most noise in professional circles in recent years.[1] But he ought in decency to point to examples of serious work that is far from trivial and is neither lexicographical nor superstitious, but is on the contrary serious and illuminating, though written within the tradition of which Mr. Gellner disapproves.[2] And whatever one may think of *The Concept of Mind*, it is not a trivial work, but a tough and magnanimous piece of writing.

The fundamental question raised by Mr. Gellner is that of philosophical method. It is not at all clear what he thinks philosophers can do. He thinks they ought to take science seriously, and contemporary moral predicaments ("the social and intellectual transformation which humanity is undergoing"). Sometimes he falls into a naturalism grosser than that of which he accuses LP. He says of Absolute Idealism and Logical Positivism that "they are local-temporary versions of what are perhaps archetypal attitudes of the human spirit".[3] This is no more than a variation of Coleridge's remark (I think) that we are all of us born Aristotelians or Platonists. This is all very well, but if we are to take it seriously we are plunged into a naturalism and a consequent scepticism that would make of philosophy exactly what Mr. Gellner does not want it to be. Apart from such illuminating asides, Mr. Gellner seems to want to maintain that philosophy *must*, if it is to be an important and valuable activity, con-

9. Ibid., p. 86. This was long ago pointed out by a linguistic philosopher, Mr. John Holloway, in *Mind*, Vol. LXII, No. 245, pp. 99 ff.
 1. Gellner, p. 218.
 2. I have in mind Miss Anscombe's *Intention* (can't Mr. Gellner see here the affinity with Aristotle as well as with Wittgenstein?), recent papers on ethical topics by Mrs. Philippa Foot, Mr. Strawson's *Individuals*; and many other books and papers.
 3. Gellner, p. 214.

sist in more than the description and analysis of concepts, for if it is this then in one sense philosophy is necessarily LP. He especially dislikes Wittgenstein's aphorism that "philosophy only states what everyone admits". Admittedly, there are more ways than one of taking this aphorism; but taken in one sense this is surely a truism, and a way of pointing out something essential to philosophical method, namely, that it is dialectical in the Socratic sense. Particular linguistic philosophers may wish to tie this aphorism to their own metaphysical prejudices or to what Mr. Gellner happily calls "the mid-morning view of the world", when all that is terrible, mysterious and enigmatic seems to have vanished with the night and its dreams. But these are prejudices to be sifted dialectically like any others.

I want to maintain, as against Mr. Gellner, that Wittgenstein's aphorism is a philosophical truism; that philosophy does consist in the description and analysis of concepts, with the entailment that it is therefore in an important sense LP. It will not follow from this that this or that contemporary practitioner of LP is a sound philosopher; only that these are philosophers in the traditional sense—in the *only* sense we can give to philosophy. (Mr. Gellner makes too much of the fact that they proclaim themselves revolutionaries. Hasn't this always happened when the *style* of philosophy has changed?) I shall take as the distinctively philosophical fields of discourse those of metaphysics and epistemology.

Now, what are the marks of metaphysical and epistemological questions (I shan't attempt to draw a clear distinction between these two sets of questions)? I think they have two distinguishing marks: (1) a certain kind of generality; (2) a certain kind of obscurity, in that a great part of the attempt to answer one of these questions consists not in finding out what the right answer is but in getting clear about what the meaning of the question is, what it is that is being asked.

If we ask what the difference is between "knowing" and "believing", in one way this is of course to ask what the dif-

ference is between knowing and believing a particular proposition, say, "Statham is at the top of the bowling averages
for the season 1959"; but the particular proposition is taken
not in its particularity but as an instance of a type of proposition, and this is why in philosophical discussions we
often use the variable $p$ instead of a particular example. But
one can't dispense with the particular example, for one
doesn't in discussing this question have a licence to substitute
absolutely anything for $p$. For the question might arise
whether the necessary and sufficient conditions for saying
that X knows that $p$ are the same if we substitute for $p$ not
"Statham etcetera" but "God is love" or "Lying is always
wrong". But though particular examples are always necessary in philosophy in order to bring out the logical complexity of questions that at first sight look simple, the particular examples are always bearers of a certain kind of
generality, such that if we are satisfied with a certain analysis
of "John Smith knows that Statham etcetera" then we are
committed to an analysis of X knows that $p$ for whatever
range of propositions $p$ stands for when "Statham etcetera"
is a permissible substitution. (What the criteria are for
settling what is "permissible" is another question.) Another
way in which this question has generality is this. It is not a
question that could be answered by a psychological investigation of what went on in people when they were in a state
of knowing something and believing something. In the first
place, the division between states of knowing and believing
presupposes that we already know (in some sense) what is to
count as an instance of knowing or of believing, which is
precisely the point at issue; and nothing that went on,
psychologically speaking, in people—saying certain things,
acting in certain ways, having certain images in their minds
—could ever be a sufficient condition for saying that they
knew or believed something, since it would never be self-
contradictory to say that X said something or did something
or had certain images and knew that or believed that $p$ (or

did not know or did not believe that *p*). Thus to ask what the difference is between "knowing" and "believing" is not to ask a question that can be settled by observation and experiment, by an examination, that is, of a particular range of facts. If there were *not* a particular range of facts which could roughly be designated prior to all philosophizing, then of course the philosophical question couldn't arise. If no one had ever framed and used temporal propositions the philosophical problems connected with time couldn't have arisen. But the force of the philosophical question is quite different from the force of any factual question. We can imagine a society in which all the factual questions we now raise were raised and answered, but in which no philosophical questions were ever raised. I think such a society would be something a bit less than a human society; but it would certainly be a society of rational creatures, for it would be unconvincing to write into our definition of rationality a capacity for philosophical reflection.

There is a further point about generality. Philosophy has often been described as the study of "reality" or "being" or "existence as a whole" and so on. This seems to me unobjectionable, though it is unfashionable. It is an apt description of what almost all—though I don't know that I need to insert *any* qualification—those who are accounted philosophers have done. The objections to this way of putting the point are that it seems to suggest that a philosopher is a kind of super scientist, either a synthesizer or a man with superior faculties. I don't know if any considerable philosopher has ever set himself up to be one or the other. (Hegel looks a bit like a synthesizer. Plato seems to have thought "the philosopher" was a man with superior faculties who was acquainted with those Forms which the rest of us know only by hearsay; but in both these cases I dare say another interpretation is possible.) However this may be, the sense in which it seems to me unobjectionable to say that philosophy is the study of "reality" is this. Thinking involves the use of concepts that are categorial in the sense that they seem necessary to any general discourse about what there is. Such concepts as those of "Englishman", "hammer", "mammal", etcetera, are means of being articulate about local and particular subject matters. But if we take such concepts as "time", "space", "cause", "particular", "thought", "person", and so on, we seem to be confronted with concepts that are necessary not for thinking about particular subject matters but for thinking at all. The range of their possible application is such that an ability to use them seems to be presupposed in human discourse upon any topic. Analysis of such concepts as these (as in the *Metaphysics* of Aristotle) is the study of "reality" in that they have application and are used to make assertions that are true or false; and since statements have a logical structure the analysis of this structure and of the concepts employed in them is an analysis of what we are committed to, logically speaking, when we make statements, true or false. This I take it is the point of Aristotle's analysis of the concept of substance or Hume's analysis of the concept of cause. Sometimes people have talked as though Aristotle's analysis of substance is the analysis of *substances* into metaphysical constituents of a mysterious kind, as though substances were mixtures or puddings the ingredients of which were form and matter.

It may be objected at this point that what I have said about the study of "reality", that in its unobjectionable sense it is the analysis of concepts having a high degree of generality, is really a disguised form of the philosophy of Kant and is open to all the objections that have been urged against Kant, notably that it interposes an impenetrable structure of concepts between us and what there is so that our knowledge is knowledge only of phenomena which are organized out of an unknown given in accordance with *a priori* concepts. My short answer to this would be that the notion of the actual universe as being quite other than we describe it as being has no sense. To say that there is a universe, as distinct from the phenomenal universe, which cannot be talked about, seems to me to make no existential claim at all. The possibility of using concepts is presupposed in positing anything. Perhaps this is what Kant meant in his best moments. I cannot see then that there is any objection to saying that philosophy is primarily or even solely concerned with the description and analysis of concepts in the sense in which I have tried to explain this. It is the study of reality in general because it is the study of concepts at a high level of generality; and the point of these concepts is that they are presupposed in making true and false statements.

The analysis of concepts is not like the analysis of chemical substances. If the analogy were at all close, industry would be the chief virtue of the philosopher. Concepts are not particulars with a structure *there*, waiting to be analysed. Concepts have a role, or a set of related roles, in discourse; and the elucidation of one concept has to set out upon lines of inquiry to which no determinate limit whatever can be set. To take an analogy. We might be asked to explain to someone ignorant of English law and politics what a *citizen* was. This might involve, if the inquirer were very ignorant and had very little relevant experience of other political societies, an explanation of such terms as *law, residence, sovereignty,* and so on. And this would not be an explanation of terms one by one, but an explanation of a system of related terms such that *law* cannot be understood without an understanding of *sovereignty,* *sovereignty* without an understanding of *law.* The same problem arises if we have to explain the use of such terms as *mass, momentum, motion* in physics. Now, problems of explanation in such fields are relatively tractable. But if in philosophy we are concerned, as I have argued, with concepts that are categorial in the sense that their use is a pervasive feature of all our discourse, then the problem of explanation is not simply more difficult: it is quite other. If I set myself to explain a particular set of notions pertaining to law or to physics to one who has hitherto been ignorant of these notions, it is presupposed that both myself and the one to whom I am offering explanations have a language in common, and this language functions as an instrument with which I can explain the more specialized terms of the subject-matter I am concerned with. For example, if I want to explain *law* and *sovereignty* I may be able to do so because we both of us understand the terms *rule* and *command*. But if we are concerned with the most pervasive features of discourse, there are no concepts to be presupposed as being already understood.

This is, of course, ambiguous, and by design; for it is surely absurd to say that those concepts which are pervasive features of our discourse are not already understood. For what is it to understand a concept if it is not to use it? What can philosophy tell us that we don't already know? To quote something Mr. Geach has written:

> . . . if somebody knows how to use the English word "red", he has a concept of red; if he knows how to use the first-person pronoun, he has a concept of *self*; if he knows how to use the negative construction in some language, he has a concept of negation.[4]

The way out of this difficulty is by seeing that the concept of understanding is ambiguous. For example, understanding the grammar of a language can be taken in two ways. In one way, we should say that whoever speaks grammatically—in accordance with the rules—understands the grammar of the language. (This is akin to Geach's sense of "has a concept".) But the ability to speak a language in accordance with the rules of grammar does not imply an ability to state what these rules are. We can imagine someone who speaks faultless English as a consequence, simply, of reading good authors and conversing with those who use the language correctly. It is true that such a one, reflecting upon his practice, might excogitate the entire corpus of English

4. *Mental Acts*, pp. 12, 13.

grammar, might come to know what the rules were that he was continually heeding. This holds, I think, for that kind of reflection which is distinctively philosophical. The analysis of concepts in philosophy is not a journey into an unknown country. We are exploring ground with which we are already familiar—in one sense too familiar, since what stumps us is a request for an account of how we get from point A to point B when the journey from point A to point B is one we are continually making. *This* is the point of Wittgenstein's aphorism: "Philosophy only states what everyone admits." This is why the method of philosophy is always in an open or a hidden way dialectical. Philosophers who have maintained the existence of sense data have not been drawing our attention to the existence of hitherto unknown entities, like electrons or vitamins. Their question has always been: "Isn't this how it is? Don't you know quite well that round coins look elliptical from certain angles? Don't you admit that if there are hallucinations this isn't to say that nothing is perceived by the subject of the hallucination?" This is the method of philosophy from the *Theaetetus* to the *Critique of Pure Reason*, from the *Metaphysics* to *The Concept of Mind*. Differences between philosophers are not fundamentally differences about what the task is but about how to set about it; and from these differences flow some of the differences between the conclusions of philosophers.

But it doesn't at first seem at all a plausible interpretation of the history of philosophy to say that all philosophers have been concerned with the description and analysis of concepts and have differed only in the conclusions they have come to. It may be obvious that certain works, e.g. parts at least of Aristotle's *Metaphysics*, Aquinas's *De Veritate*, parts of Berkeley's *Principles*, are concerned with the description and analysis of concepts; but what of the great systematic philosophers, Spinoza or Leibniz or Hegel? Aren't they concerned with expressing a vision of the world, a vision such that a new battery of concepts, those of a peculiarly philosophical kind, is needed to express it? One can't deny that there is this difference between those philosophers who are primarily interested in piecemeal analysis and those who are ambitious to construct a system, that is, a coherent set of what we might call super-concepts in the light of which our ordinary concepts are revised or reinterpreted, so that our vision of the world, once we enter the system, is more or less at variance with how the world is commonly taken.

My answer to this would be that the differences here are differences over what the force of the description and analysis of our concepts is taken to be. What moves us to the activity of describing and analysing a concept is a certain kind of intellectual discomfort in the face of different ways of using a concept-designating expression. Familiar examples are those concepts which revolve round such seemingly central concepts as "truth", "freedom", "body", "mind", "pleasure" and so on. The starting-point is, I think, the same in all cases. But reflection can take two quite different courses. In the one case, the assumption is that our concepts are more or less all right as they stand, and that what is required is the removal through a more thorough exploration of the logical interrelationships of the concepts concerned of what initially appears to be incoherence or contradiction. (Think for example of *identifying* a man, an argument, a negative charge, a fallacy, a tune . . . or: "I changed my views, I changed my shirt, I changed the course of history, I changed my style of handwriting. . . .") In the other, the assumption is made that the appearance of incoherence and contradiction presented by what are taken to be the philosophically interesting examples is a sign that we need new concepts or purified concepts; and this in the end tends to issue in these paradoxical doctrines which are taken by the lay public to be peculiarly philosophical: "time is unreal . . . we can never be certain of the truth of any factual statement. . . ." Or in the strange questions which seem to be cries from the heart of the philosopher: "Can machines think? How can I know that others are in pain? How can I be certain that there are physical objects in space?"—questions that asked in one tone of voice are disguised statements that things are far from being what we commonly take them to be: that there is appearance and reality; or in the elaboration of such concepts, not a part of ordinary discourse, as "cognition", "apperception", "monad", etc. When I say here that reflection can take two different courses I am not saying that we can go through the list of philosophers and classify them as having taken one course or the other. In most cases they take now one and now the other, hesitate between one and the other. Think of the Plato of *The Republic* and the Plato of the *Theaetetus* or the Wittgenstein of the *Tractatus* and the Wittgenstein of the *Investigations*.

My conclusion here is that to say philosophy is concerned with the description and analysis of concepts is not to characterize philosophy in the way that it is often taken to be. It is a truism—though not for that reason without value—and by itself does not prescribe what force is to be given to description and analysis and what their limits are. To characterize philosophy in this way is not to characterize it as a study in which talk about monads or the Absolute or phenomena and things in themselves is out of place by reason of what philosophers are and can only be concerned with. We cannot outlaw or put under a philosophical ban certain philosophers on the ground that if philosophy is the description and analysis of concepts strange-sounding conclusions are *ipso facto* ruled out. If they are ruled out, this can only be on the ground that they are entailed by misdescriptions and incorrect analyses.

What I have been concerned to do is to try to show that there is a nucleus of strictly philosophical problems, that these are concerned with the description and analysis of concepts and above all, though not exclusively, with those concepts which have a high degree of generality and little history; that this is what almost all philosophers have been concerned with (when, that is, they have not been doing embryonic science), and that the shifts in the history of philosophy and the differences between philosophers have to do with different conceptions of how to set about this task and with differences of view as to what a given piece of description and analysis entails. If what I have said so far is right, then the history of philosophy will have a certain unity, a unity of topics if not of method. In so far as no one method has so far prevailed for more than a limited period, in so far as the sequence of philosophies in time is a sequence of very different styles of philosophizing, we cannot view the history of philosophy as cumulative in the way that the history of physics or of mathematics is cumulative; for, despite what Marx and Hegel have said, it seems quite plain that later philosophies are not in any obvious way higher syntheses of earlier philosophies. That they are historically related doesn't need to be demonstrated. For one thing, they are knit together by having a special relationship to logic, which *is* a developing and cumulative science, and this relationship is necessitated by what is central to philosophy, its task of description and analysis. It isn't accidental that it was a philosophical logician, Frege, who provided the tools with which philosophers cut their way through a number of tangles early in this century. If we ask in what consists the obvious superiority, as idealist metaphysicians, of Bradley and McTaggart to Bosanquet, the answer would lie in their power as logicians. Another way in which philosophies are historically related is this: the problems of philosophy are set to the philosophers of one generation by the philosophers of an earlier generation. Indeed, this is why the teaching of the history of philosophy is an indispensable part of philosophical education. To show Aristotle and Plato grappling with the problems of permanence and change as these had been elaborated by their predecessors and contemporaries, to show Kant in a situation created by the juncture of Hume's analysis of cause with what were taken to be the plain implications of Newton's physics, to show the role of Russell, Moore and Wittgenstein in setting the problems which now excite the schools, these are not simply exercises in the history of ideas, though they can be reduced to this: they are classic instances of the ways in which the task of conceptual description and analysis is mediated to the philosopher of a particular time and place. It is not accidental that the *Metaphysics* of Aristotle contains an historical account of Greek philosophy, that the Platonic dialogues having the highest philosophical interest are concerned with the doctrines of other philosophers in the sense that these doctrines give Plato's own reflections their purpose and direction.

Wittgenstein writes in the *Investigations*: "It is what human beings *say* that is true and false; and they agree in the *language* they use. That is not agreement in opinions but in form of life."[5] If Mr. Gellner had weighed the implications of this remark he would have written a more temperate and less misleading book. LP is very often old philosophy writ small.

1959

5. *Philosophical Investigations*, I, p. 88e, 241.

# 7

# Poetry and Dialectic

> Non enim omne quod fingimus, mendacium est; . . .
> cum autem fictio nostra refertur, in aliquam significa-
> tionem, non est mendacium, sed aliqua figura veritatis.
> Alioquin omnia quae a sapientibus et sanctis viris, vel
> etiam ab ipso Domino, figurate dicta sunt, mendacia
> deputabuntur.
>
> ST. AUGUSTINE [1]

> It haunts me like all shadows. All shades
> Of meaning whipping in and out are there.
> This torturer is a great lover of professors,
> Psychiatrists, chaplains, sits on their faces' skin
> But when I look at them it's on my own,
> Then flies to another place, leaves me in arrears.
>
> RICHARD EBERHART, "Of Truth" [2]

I

PHILOSOPHY is essentially, irredeemably, hopelessly dialectical. This is its glory and its shame: its glory, because it is
in and through the play of dialectic that the powers of the
mind are most fully known and manifested; its shame, for
it is precisely the enchantment of dialectic that seduces us,
so that we fall into sophistry in a moment. Everything can
be brought within the dialectical situation, nothing is exempt
from it. We can conceive of no thesis which could not be
put to the question, no response to a question which could
not generate further questions. The description and analysis
of concepts, the central task of philosophy since it first detached itself from mythopoeic thinking, presents us with a
limitless process, sinuous, fluid, surprising in its sudden starts
and turns, flashing and glittering, beginning from any point

---

1. St. Augustine, *Quaestiones Evangeliorum*, in Migne, *P.L.*, xxxv, 1362.
2. Richard Eberhart, *Burr Oaks* (Chatto & Windus), 1947.

we choose and having no assignable term. Now, because philosophy can put everything to the question, it tends from time to time to show a certain roughness and even savagery towards other types of discourse; and is by way of response roughly and savagely treated in its turn. Pride in the traditions of the community and devotion to the gods of the city, these have always feared what they took to be the corrosive effects of the dialectic, so that the indictment of Socrates, that "Socrates is guilty of not believing in the gods in whom the State believes, and of introducing other strange divinities; . . . and of corrupting the young men", represents a recurring moment in the history of philosophy. The rediscovery of dialectic in the twelfth century presents us with another paradigmatic man and situation in Abelard faced with his accusers; and if in the modern age, in liberal societies at least, the martyrdom of the philosopher is most likely to be that martyrdom feared by Kierkegaard, that of being trampled to death by geese, the philosopher, in so far as he is faithful to his vocation and does not pervert the instrument of dialectic to defend the idols of the tribe or paper over the cracks in fashionable arguments, is still a man on the margin, ambiguous, of doubtful loyalties, taken to be lukewarm by fervent believers and, by average sensual men, passionate about trivial issues and fine distinctions.

A matter on which philosophers have been inclined to be passionate is poetry. The relationship between these two modes of discourse, the dialectical and the poetic, resembles in Plato and perhaps in other philosophers that type of relationship between men which is characterized by the coexistence and interpenetration of love and hate. If the poet is driven out of the good society, it is only after he has been crowned; for in virtue of his gift he is sacred and wonderful; what he says may be destroyed by the dialectic, but his words are memorable. They are incantations of power drawn from a hidden source and having, therefore, that awful quality which belongs to all that comes up out of the darkness of the earth, the abode of demons and the shadows of men who were once alive; or if, since Apollo has two homes and two faces, the words of the poet fall from the heavens, in falling into the region of mutability their heavenly origin is obscured and can only be recovered if they perish in the fire of dialectic.

In our own period the tension between poetry and dialectic slackens. Poetry is the object of liking and despising, not love and hate. The poet is no longer feared or admired as a messenger of the infernal or heavenly powers. He is now a purveyor of elegant fictions, acceptable if you happen to like his fables and jingles—they may help to pass the time—but a man to be classed with tumblers and comedians rather than with philosophers, men of science and entrepreneurs. As late as Milton it was possible to speak of poetry to persons other than men of letters as a central human activity and one as indispensable to life as bread; but with the coming of the middle-class revolution philistinism becomes the philosophical orthodoxy. By this I do not mean that all philosophers have been insensitive to poetry, still less that there have not been attempts by poets and critics—one thinks of Blake, Wordsworth and Coleridge—to work out the rationale of poetry within our culture; but the theory of poetry current in the philosophical schools has been such as to make it appear that the implicit claim of poetry to be a central human activity had no ground.

To say that poetry moves in the sphere of delight and not of truth seems at first unexceptionable; and this is orthodoxy in Bacon and Hobbes; it lies behind the celebrated attack upon poetic discourse in Sprat's *History of the Royal Society*, an attack motivated by the fear that the energies of poetry impel it beyond the sphere of delight into that of truth, where it is a trespasser. What it may in the end come to is brought out by Locke who, as one would expect, produces a

mean-spirited gloss upon the tradition. He considers the case
of the child with "a poetick Vein":

> ... if he have a poetick Vein, 'tis to me the strangest thing in
> the World that the Father should desire or suffer it to be
> cherished or improved. Methinks the Parents should labour to
> have it stifled and suppressed as much as may be; and I know
> not what Reason a Father can have to wish his Son a Poet,
> who does not desire to have him bid Defiance to all other
> Callings and Business; which is not yet the worst of the Case;
> for if he proves a successful Rhymer, and gets once the Repu-
> tation of a Wit, I desire it may be considered what Company
> and Places he is like to spend his Time in, nay, and Estate too:
> For it is very seldom seen, that any one discovers Mines of
> Gold or Silver in *Parnassus*. 'Tis a pleasant Air, but a barren
> Soil. . . .[3]

Whatever is overthrown by dialectic can be set up again
only by dialectic. If, therefore, we find unwelcome the conclusion that poetry is something optional, decorative, well
enough when we have no serious business in hand but not to
be mentioned in the same breath as money, power and scientific discovery—unwelcome and, on purely intuitive grounds,
absurd—we must take up the argument again and see if a
patient analysis can give us grounds for thinking that truth
is applicable to poetic discourse and for putting that value
upon it which belongs to those types of discourse in which
we make plain to each other and to ourselves the character
of human life and of its predicaments.

2

I shall say that the making of poetry is the making of
fictions. To say this may strike us as too strong, or as not
strong enough. It will appear to be too strong if we reflect
that there is no reason why true narratives should not be
cast in poetic form; and not strong enough if we note that

3. John Locke, *Some Thoughts concerning Education*, para. 174.

the class of fictions is wider than the class of poems. The latter difficulty will, I hope, disappear when I explain what I take to be the peculiar character of poetic fictions; but the former difficulty is the harder to meet. Andrew Marvell, for example, wrote:

> He nothing common did or mean
> Upon that memorable Scene:
>> But with his keener Eye
>> The Axes edge did try:
> Nor call'd the Gods with vulgar spight
> To vindicate his helpless Right,
> But bow'd his comely Head,
> Down as upon a Bed.[4]

This is an account of the execution of Charles I. In what sense is it proper to class it as a piece of fiction? In the following sense. If we were to take it as a piece of historical narrative, then a number of questions would be appropriate that are not appropriate. The historian speaks in his own person and is responsible for what he says in general and in detail; and this is why the historian can tell lies and make mistakes. Now, if the speaker here were Marvell in his own person, it would be appropriate to test his account by asking, for example, what evidence there was that Charles looked at the axe, did not make a speech in defence of his constitutional right, and placed his head upon the block as he might have placed his head upon a pillow. I dare say that what Marvell here says is fair enough as an account of what an observer might have confirmed as not conflicting with anything that happened in Whitehall that day; but this, if true, is accidental to the poem and neither adds to nor subtracts from the poem considered as something made by Marvell. But how do we know that this isn't an attempt at historical narrative in verse or that, if it is, the question of its reliability as such a narrative is so irrelevant that it is proper

4. Andrew Marvell, "An Horatian Ode upon Cromwel's Return from Ireland," Miscellaneous Poems, 1681.

to class it as a fiction? First, the class of fictions is wider than
the class of false or imaginary accounts. A particular piece
of poetic narrative or a particular incident in a novel may
indeed be, as we say, founded on fact and may not conflict
with what is commonly taken to be the order and character
of past events. This is nothing to us unless there are unmistakable signs that the intention of the author is historical;
and that what we are confronted with is verse or a novel
warrants a presumption, though of course a rebuttable presumption, that the intention is not historical. Secondly, and
this is what may strengthen the presumption to the point
where it cannot be rebutted, the signs of poetic fiction are
those formal structures that can be shown by analysis to be
integral to the poetic effect but without function so far as
historical narrative is concerned. (Of course, the matter is
much more complicated than this. In particular, we might
well inquire why it is we might want to say of a particular
historian that he is "a great artist", thus appearing to classify
him with the poets and the novelists; and the answer would
be that he *is* a maker of fictions, though not on that account
a liar.) As to there being fictions we should not wish to call
poetic, these will be fictions having little formal interest,
where *how* the thing is said doesn't matter: the excuses of
schoolboys, the compliments of courtiers, the vows of lovers.
Each of these might by a person of talent be raised to the
level of poetic discourse; but the more successfully this was
done, the less would be our interest in it merely as excuse,
compliment, vow, conceived and expressed in a particular
situation; and the greater its formal interest, the more it
would tend to be loosened from the situation which was its
living context, thus passing into that world of poetic fictions where the remarks of Dr. Johnson and of the father of
Miss Elizabeth Bennet are equally at home.

It will be seen that my use of "poetic" is a wide one; that
it covers not only verse but verbal fictions of every kind,
novels, plays, fairy-stories, polished anecdotes, witticisms

and so on. This is, I think, an extension of the sense of "poetic" Aristotle has in mind in his *Poetics*; and it is worth noting that at the beginning of his book he looks for a moment at a problem closely resembling the problem I have just been dealing with. He finds that many people want to call "poetic" any metrical composition. "Even if a theory of medicine or physical philosophy be put forth in a metrical form, it is usual to describe the writer in this way; Homer and Empedocles, however, have really nothing in common apart from their metre; so that, if one is to be called a poet, the other should be termed a physicist rather than a poet." [5] That is, the sense of poetry in which Aristotle is interested is that which takes as the distinguishing characteristic of the poetic activity what he calls *mimesis*; and this in part at least overlaps with what I call the making of fictions. Further, it will be remembered that when Aristotle later makes his difficult remark that "poetry is something more philosophic and of graver import than history", [6] he prefaces it by saying that Herodotus put into verse would still be history and not poetry.

Before I come to the special problems of poetic discourse I wish to say something on a more general problem concerned with all verbal discourse: the problem of how words and expressions and sentences of various logical types get the sense they have. I do not wish to offer a solution of this problem, but rather to indicate the impossibility of what is often taken to be the solution; for what is often, and wrongly, taken to be the right solution is connected with certain gross errors in poetic theory.

There is a persistent tradition in our thinking about language, and it is one that has remained vigorous in the face of heavy attacks in recent years, that a thought is one thing and the way it is expressed another. Campbell is in the tradition when he writes in his *Philosophy of Rhetoric* (a

5. *Aristotle on the Art of Poetry*, translated by Ingram Bywater, with a Preface by Gilbert Murray, Oxford, 1920, pp. 24, 25.
6. *Aristotle*, p. 43.

work that went through many editions—it is the work that was lying on the table beside Hume when Boswell paid his famous call on the dying philosopher) that "there are two things in every discourse which principally claim our attention, the sense and the expression; or in other words, the thought, and the symbol by which it is communicated".[7]

Now, this view cannot be wholly absurd, for we are strongly inclined to agree with it as soon as it is propounded; it seems to chime in with our most natural prejudices in the matter. Faced with the fact that there are different ways of saying the same thing within a language, and between languages, it seems to us quite right to say that where $P^1$ and $P^2$ are roughly interchangeable sentences they have in common the thought they can both be used to express. Indeed, it could scarcely be wrong to say this. What is often taken to follow from this truism is something that seems all right when we are talking about or reflecting upon, as distinct from *using*, a sentence, namely, that to the distinction between the sentence and the thought it is used to express, and we must make this distinction if we admit that $P^1$ and $P^2$ express the same thought, there corresponds a distinction of objects standing in a certain relation one to the other: the thought; and the sentence which gets its meaning through "standing for" the thought.

It is to Locke that we must once more turn, this time for the supremely commonplace expression of the theory.

> Man . . . had by nature his organs so fashioned, as to be fit to frame articulate sounds, which we call words. But this was not enough to produce language; for parrots, and several other birds, will be taught to make articulate sounds distinct enough, which yet, by no means, are capable of language. Besides articulate sounds therefore, it was farther necessary, that he should be able to use these sounds as signs of internal conceptions; and to make them stand as marks for the ideas within his own mind, whereby they might be made known to others,

7. George Campbell, *The Philosophy of Rhetoric*, seventh edition, 1823, p. 47.

and the thoughts of men's minds be conveyed from one to another.[8]

That Locke is here talking about two sets of objects, words and sentences (which acquire meaning by having the relation of "standing for" to ideas), and thoughts, is made clearer in a later part of the *Essay concerning Human Understanding*.

> . . . we must observe two sorts of propositions that we are capable of making. First, mental, wherein the ideas in our understanding are without the use of words put together, or separated by the mind, perceiving or judging of their agreement or disagreement. Secondly, verbal propositions, which are words, the signs of our ideas, put together or separated in affirmative or negative sentences.[9]

Locke's view is variously wrong, but I must content myself with two arguments against it. First, no one when challenged is prepared to say that he is acquainted with anything at all corresponding to Locke's story. It *must* be like that, we sometimes hear; never, I think, Yes, that's how it is. The "must" is here significant. It suggests that we are not being given an introspective account, but an account of what is held to follow logically from our talking about propositions as expressing thoughts. A genuine introspective report would be something like: When I divided 762 by 3 it was as though there were red blobs dancing about inside. Now, another might say: When *I* divided 762 by 3 it was as though a sewing machine were going very fast inside me. And still another might say: I've tried very hard to introspect and I have absolutely nothing to report. But if they all rap out, when asked to do this piece of division, 254, we have the best possible evidence that they are expressing the same thought. Locke's argument gets its apparent force from its seeming to be a description of what goes on when we introspect; but it is a pseudo-description—not a *misdescrip-*

8. John Locke, *An Essay concerning Human Understanding*, III, 1.
9. Locke, *Essay*, IV, 5.

*tion* of what goes on, but rather what we take to be a description but isn't so. Again, if Locke's account of what it is for words and sentences to have meaning were correct, it would be impossible ever to teach anyone the meaning of a word or a sentence. But this is absurd, for we do teach people the meanings of words and sentences. If sounds get their significance from being the "signs of internal conceptions", then we could only teach their significance by showing another both the sound and the internal conception of which it is the sign. But Locke says that "the thoughts of men's minds" are "conveyed from one to another" *by words*. Thus, we could not *show* that relation which, according to Locke, transforms sounds into words; therefore, we could never make a sound that would for another count as a word. The argument is self-contradictory.

To talk about a sentence and the thought it expresses is clearly allowable, for we can translate at least some English sentences into sentences in other languages, and we can also have two different English sentences that express the same thought. For an example of the former I take the last paragraph of *Le Rouge et le Noir*:

> Madame de Rênal fut fidèle a sa promesse. Elle ne chercha en aucune manière à attenter à sa vie; mais trois jours après Julien, elle mourut en embrassant ses enfants.[1]

A recent translation into English runs as follows:

> Madame de Rênal was faithful to her promise. She did not attempt in any way to take her own life; but, three days after Julien's death, she gave her children a last embrace, and died.[2]

It would seem hard to say that here we do not have the same thoughts in the original and in the translation. Of

1. Stendhal, *Le Rouge et le Noir*, 1830.
2. Stendhal, *Scarlet and Black*, translated and with an introduction by Margaret R. B. Shaw (Penguin Books), 1953, p. 511.

course, the two passages are not *equivalents*. Resonances, flavours, atmospheres, that are attached to the French expressions are not so attached to the English. In an attempt to give the force of: "mais trois jours après Julien, elle mourut en embrassant ses enfants", the translator has departed from a literal rendering and gives us: "but, three days after Julien's death, she gave her children a last embrace, and died". This slight dislocation of the order of the French sentence indicates that the translator is using stylistic devices that belong to English and not to French in an effort, necessarily vain but all the same worth making, to give us an equivalent as well as a translation. But the same point could equally be made in cases where two English sentences may be said to express the same thought and where, at the same time, there is plainly no equivalence. This may easily be verified by comparing archaic and modern translations of the Scriptures.

To talk about the sentence and the thought it expresses is allowable; but we have no warrant for the inference that here there are two objects, as it were, the sentence and the thought. We cannot talk about a sentence as now expressing, now not expressing, a thought; for if it did not express a thought, have a sense, we should not know enough to characterize it as a sentence. What would a sentence without a sense be? We are tempted to answer: a succession of noises, or a series of marks in some material; but if this were all we knew we should have no ground for saying it was a sentence. We may distinguish between a cheek and the bloom upon it; but there is no inference from this distinction to the existence of two independent objects, so that the bloom upon the cheek could exist apart from the cheek. I do not wish to argue, for I do not think it is true, that words are the only bearers of sense, the only vehicles of thought, though they are certainly the most common; but the notion that there can be thought quite apart from a vehicle of thought is a superstition, so far, at least, as human thinking is concerned; and while we may suppose that there is thinking other than human thinking, we could not say in what this thinking consists.

Locke's view of the relation between thinking and using language lies behind, provides a justification for, the theory of poetic discourse I now wish to criticize. This theory has taken a beating at the hands of literary critics in recent years and has even been given a special name: the heresy of paraphrase. Nevertheless, it is highly influential at all but the most sophisticated levels; and some discussion of it is necessary before we can consider what it means to speak of truth in poetry. It is the theory that *what* is said in a poem is one thing, *how* it is said another.

The theory has seemed most obviously correct in the case of didactic poetry and in the case of those poems which give us an exposition of some quasi-systematic view of nature or of human affairs. Pope prefaces his *Essay on Man* with some remarks in this tradition. He writes of the *Essay* as "forming a *temperate* yet not *inconsistent*, and a *short* yet not *imperfect* system of Ethics. This I might have done in prose; but I chose verse, and even rhyme, for two reasons. The one will appear obvious; that principles, maxims, or precepts so written, both strike the reader more strongly at first, and are more easily retained by him afterwards . . .".[3] Pope's idea is that thoughts are like naked bodies. They may be seen for what they are through the diaphanous medium of prose; or they may have their features emphasized and made more attractive by the pretty and revealing clothes of verse. Pope is less than just to his own achievement in the *Essay*. He expresses the same idea, though this time more subtly and with some awareness of other possibilities, in the *Essay on Criticism*.

> True Wit is Nature to advantage dress'd;
> What oft was thought, but ne'er so well express'd;

3. Alexander Pope, *An Essay on Man*, 1734, "The Design".

Something, whose truth convinc'd at sight we find,
That gives us back the image of our mind.[4]

Here, as well as the image of a body dressed to advantage, we have the image of the expression of thought as bringing out sharply the lines of the thought so that it "gives us back the image of our mind", displays in all its brightness the thought we have been peering at, and not seeing properly, in the depths of the mind. (This latter image has its value; for it suggests, what I shall later argue is a fundamental characteristic of much poetry, that it is a means of self-knowledge.)

The shadow of this theory remains long after the practice of criticism seems to have shown that a serious defence of it is impossible. The greatest of the romantic critics, Coleridge, held it to be true of poetry "that whatever lines can be translated into other words of the same language, without diminution of their significance, either in sense or association, or in any worthy feeling, are so far vicious in their diction".[5] The contrary view seems to underlie Arnold's characterization of poetry as "a criticism of life"; and the common nineteenth-century view of Shakespeare as a great didactic writer, a sage, the wisest and best of men, rests not only upon the belief that straightforward inferences of a moral and religious kind may be founded upon his work but also, or so I think, upon the belief that the meaning of the plays can in some way be stated, in a non-poetic mode of discourse, outside the plays.

We may allow that the practice by critics of the method of close textual analysis has made the old theory highly implausible, since this practice has shown that to elucidate the sense of a poem involves showing how the sense is determined by the particular order of words, succession of images, covert references and allusions, even, in some instances, typo-

4. *An Essay on Criticism*, 1711, lines 297–300.
5. Samuel Taylor Coleridge, *Biographia Literaria*, 1817, ch. i.

graphical devices, in the poem under analysis. It is these words in this order that constitute the poem; and the sense of the poem, a sense that can be elucidated but not stated, is so entirely a function of a particular verbal structure that it seems impossible to maintain, what Pope certainly appears to maintain in the passage I have already quoted, that a poem consists of a core of meaning that could be stated in a series of propositions and, surrounding the core, a set of embellishments delightful in themselves and having, in relation to the propositional meaning, the function of high-lighting and emphasizing what the poet wishes to single out as being of peculiar interest. All this has been shown by a number of brilliant critics from whom Mr. Cleanth Brooks (the originator of "the heresy of paraphrase") in the United States and Mr. William Empson in this country may be picked out, not necessarily as the most distinguished practitioners, but as sufficiently exemplary.

But, we may ask, does it *have* to be like this? If we allow that it is a characteristic of at least some expressions in ordinary discourse that they can be translated without loss of meaning either into other expressions in the same language or into expressions in another language, how can we be sure that poetry is *essentially* such that this can never properly be done in the case of poetic discourse? After all, the kinds of poetry most in fashion in the last thirty years, the work of Donne and Marvell, of Hopkins, Eliot and Yeats, lend themselves easily to the method of close analysis; but it does not follow from its being impossible to offer adequate paraphrases of these specific kinds that the thing is impossible in relation to other specific kinds. What holds of a species does not necessarily hold of the genus. From the marine habitat of whales or the manner of movement of bats we cannot legitimately infer anything about the habits of all mammals. Some further argument is necessary if one wishes to hold (as I do) that belief in the possibility of paraphrasing poetic discourse is always a heresy, no matter what the poem in question may be.

My argument is that it follows from the nature of poetic fictions as such that belief in the possibility of paraphrase is always heretical. I have already suggested that it is characteristic of a fiction that certain questions cannot appropriately be asked about it. We cannot ask how many children Lady Macbeth had; or what courses Hamlet pursued at the University of Wittenberg; or what kind of caterpillar caused the sickness of the rose in Blake's poem; or whether Mr. Jingle's talking, in the year 1827, about the 1830 Revolution is or is not a case of extrasensory perception. We are tempted to suppose we can ask such questions because poetic discourse moves in the mode of possibility; so that nothing can be said poetically that would not be appropriate in discourse of another kind. If we say

> The king sits in Dunfermling toune,
> Drinking the blude-reid wine [6]

this has the sense it has because the state of affairs it feigns to describe is a possible one; and we could use the same expression, or an expression of the same type, to refer to an actual state of affairs. If one says

> I wish I were where Helen lies!
> Night and day on me she cries:
> And I am weary of the skies, [7]

then this could be said truly and sincerely by a man in such a situation. Similarly, poetic discourse can have the form of an exhortation, a command, a scientific generalization, a moral judgment, a thesis in theology, a philosophical theory. Whatever can be said in forms of discourse which have straightforward applications can be said poetically in the mode of possibility. A distinction between the poetic and other kinds

6. "Sir Patrick Spence", in Thomas Percy, *Reliques of Ancient English Poetry*, 1765.
7. "Fair Helen of Kirconnell", in Sir Walter Scott, *Minstrelsy of the Scottish Border*, 1802–1803.

of discourse is that some of the entailments that belong to other kinds of discourse are, in poetic discourse, cut.

Now, I wish to argue to the impossibility of paraphrase from the fact, if it is a fact, that in poetic discourse the normal entailments are cut. But before I advance what I think to be a persuasive argument, I wish to examine a doctrine that appears to be a presupposition of much criticism : the doctrine that poetic is distinguished from other discourse by certain empirically determinable characteristics, roughly, the presence of paradox and ambiguity. A critic has said that poetry is saying two or more things at once.[8] An example of what is intended would be the last stanza of Blake's moving and beautiful poem, "London".

> But most thro' midnight streets I hear
> How the youthful Harlot's curse
> Blasts the new born Infant's tear,
> And blights with plagues the Marriage hearse.[9]

Ambiguity : we can read "the youthful Harlot's curse" in two ways, as a cry (this would link it with "every infant's cry of fear", "the Chimney-sweeper's cry" and "the hapless Soldier's sigh" of the earlier stanzas), and as the plague of which she is the victim and bearer; and "Blasts the new born Infant's tear" could be read as meaning that the tear is accursed from the beginning and not innocent, and also that it is dried up by the hot breath of the curse. Paradox : this is exemplified by the expression "the Marriage *hearse*". Certainly, paradox and ambiguity can be identified in much of the poetry that moves us most deeply, and the critic can show that the power of such poetry to move us is connected with the successful employment of these devices. But paradox and ambiguity could only be the essentially distinguishing marks of poetry if we did not have a use for paradox and ambiguity in other forms of discourse. This is plainly false.

8. I believe this was Mr. F. W. Bateson. I cannot trace the reference.
9. William Blake, "London", *Songs of Experience*, 1794.

Someone once said to me, perhaps by way of warning, that a professor's life can too easily, through a preoccupation with administrative duties and the work of committees, degenerate into a life of *busy idleness*. We have learned to speak of success as "the bitch-goddess". I need not multiply examples. Even if we were to establish inductively that paradox and ambiguity are much commoner in poetic than in other forms of discourse, this would not affect my conclusion. For we could easily imagine a society where the opposite was true, where the poetry was comparatively limpid and other forms of discourse were crackling with paradox and knotty with ambiguity.

Let me further explain what I mean when I say that in poetic discourse some of the entailments that belong to other kinds of discourse are cut. I have already indicated that it would make no sense to ask a certain range of questions about narrative or descriptive poetry. To return to my earlier example, if Shakespeare tells us that Hamlet studied at Wittenberg it is inappropriate to ask what courses he studied and whether or not his teachers found him an apt pupil. These would be utterly appropriate questions if the statement about Hamlet and Wittenberg were made historically, just as there would be circumstances in which it would be appropriate to point out that Bohemia is land-locked. Again, if I write yet another poem on the *carpe diem* theme and exhort the young and beautiful to take their opportunities, I am not *advising* anybody to behave in a certain way. A final example: it might be poetically defensible to write a poem which had built into its structure some features of the pre-Copernican cosmologies; and to one who objected one would need only to reply that this was not a contribution to *Nature*.

My question now is: Granted that it is an essential characteristic of poetic discourse that the normal entailments, in the sense I have illustrated, are cut, does it follow that how things are said in poetic discourse, and what is said, are in-

separable in ways they are not in other forms of discourse?
(Of course, we cannot even in other forms of discourse
always separate the *how* from the *what*. But this raises other
issues.) My answer is that it does so follow. When we, for
example, describe the world, how we describe it has much to
do with the *force* of our description, very little—provided
we make no syntactical blunders—to do with its *accuracy*.
It has been argued that a true fact-stating sentence is through
its form uniquely fitted to the state of affairs the user of it
asserts to be the case; but no one has ever succeeded in showing that this is true of sentences in a natural language; and if
we could make it true by convention in an artificial language,
as no doubt we could, whatever was said in such a language
could be said otherwise in a natural language; and we could
also explain the convention. Descriptive uses of language,
then, in so far as we are concerned, not with the force and
resonance they have, but with their character as assertions
that such and such is the case, may be translated or para-
phrased. Again, to shift to another kind of discourse, it
seems plain that there is more than one form of words in
which I could state the principle of the Identity of Indiscernibles and that two such forms could be said to have the
same meaning. Finally, it seems, so far as the giving of moral
advice goes, immaterial whether I tell someone that he ought
to pay his debts or whether I tell him that he is obliged to
restore what he has borrowed. What are the features of such
uses of language that make them susceptible of paraphrase?
In the instance of descriptive uses where the intention of the
user is to say that something is the case, what makes a sentence true or false is whether or not what is asserted to be
the case is the case; and the form of the assertion is not
uniquely tied to what is asserted to be the case. If, as I suppose, the principle of the Identity of Indiscernibles lays down
limiting conditions for identification through predication, it
gets its sense, not through the particular linguistic form in
which it is stated, but through its being implicated in the

logical properties of predication in a language. And a piece of moral advice is an exhortation to a certain course of action in the light of an established situation; and once again there is no unique tie between the form of the advice and the description of the action recommended. Briefly, what all these instances have in common, and what makes such uses susceptible of paraphrase, is that in each case the adequacy of what is said is governed by some state of affairs, prior to and independent of what is said. The character of the world, predication, a situation out of which the obligation to pay one's debts arises, these are prior to what may be said about them.

Now, the adequacy of what is said in the form of poetic fiction is not, in any straightforward sense, governed by any state of affairs prior to and independent of what is said. Fictitious descriptions are neither true nor false in the way real descriptions are true or false and this follows from their being fictions. Just as to dream that I make a promise is not to make a promise, for I do not do anything in a dream, I only dream that I do this or that, so to give a fictitious description is not to give a description, though a fictitious description has the form of a description, just as the promise I dream that I make has the form of a promise. It follows from this that I could not give an *alternative* poetic description, for there could be no criterion (as there would be in the case of a real description) for deciding whether or not the alternative description had succeeded. The poetic description has the form of a description; but it exists only as *this* description, these words in this order. What is said and how it is said are thus not distinguishable in the way they are in other forms of discourse.

3

My conclusion is not that truth has no application to poetic discourse but that the way in which it has application remains to be discussed. One pseudo-solution need not trouble us : the view that poetic statements get their sense from, and find their application in, a metaphysical shadow-world which stands to the statements of poetic discourse as the world of nature and human affairs does to the statements of other forms of discourse. There is so constant a witness to the view that in some sense, one yet to be explored, poetic discourse has a relation to the world of nature and human affairs, that a resort to a metaphysical shadow-world would be only a last desperate rescue operation, all other possibilities having been exhausted. When Mr. Graham Hough remarked recently (in *Regina v. Penguin Books Limited*) that "one of the things one would wish to take into account [in assessing the value of a novel] is whether it is a true and sincere representation of an aspect of life",[1] he was enunciating a critical commonplace that goes back to antiquity and has been current in every age. Here romanticism and classicism are at one. "Poetry is the image of man and nature." Thus Wordsworth in the Preface to *Lyrical Ballads*, summing up the whole tradition.

"Image", "representation", these are the central concepts we have to elucidate, together with their many corollaries, "faithfulness", "accuracy", "truth", "sincerity" and so on. If we can know what it is for a poetic fiction to "represent" an aspect of life, to present us with an "image" of man and nature, then we shall know what it is to say of a poetic fiction that it is a faithful representation, a true image.

A representation or image of something will differ in more than one way from what is represented. A "perfect" representation would not be a representation but the thing itself. If I make a noise which is so like the hooting of an owl that it deceives those who hear it, and this includes any owls that may be listening, then I have made the noise an owl makes. If I try to explain to another through bodily gestures, speech and so on what it is for a man to be angry and get so carried

1. *The Trial of Lady Chatterley*, The Transcript of the Trial edited by C. H. Rolph (Penguin Books), 1961, p. 42.

away by my own performance that I try to throttle someone then it is not that I am imitating an angry man—I *am* an angry man. If, being a bachelor, I ask a lady to marry me and put this on paper, saying to myself that I am only playing at making a proposal of marriage, I *have* proposed marriage, and the lady in question will have good grounds for bringing an action for breach of promise should I attempt to extricate myself from the engagement by explaining that I was only playing at making a proposal. These things are not representations: they are the things they declare themselves to be. Of course, we can only fall into the error of thinking there could be, in the sense illustrated, a "perfect" representation where the medium of representation is identical with what is represented. A hoot like the hoot of an owl is a hoot, and so *mutatis mutandis* in the other instances. Then there is the kind of representation which is a trick, ink-blots made of glass and foaming glasses of stout made of rubber that one can buy from joke shops, and *trompe l'œil* painting, like the fiddle on the back of the door at Chatsworth. These really are representations and their "perfection" consists in their tricking us for the time being into thinking they are the real thing. There is something disagreeable in representations of this kind; they arouse the expectations that the real things would arouse; and then we are suddenly let down. We can take pleasure in contemplating things that are not representations; and we can take pleasure in contemplating representations that are plainly such, whether they are representations of things that we like to contemplate or of things that in themselves we find repulsive. We do not take pleasure —or we take only a perverse pleasure—in those representations that are at first taken to be the things they represent.

A representation, then, to count as the kind of representation we are concerned with in the arts, and this is a general point about the arts and is not peculiar to the art of poetry, must be evidently distinct from what is represented. This is indeed a consequence of what I said earlier about its being a characteristic of poetic discourse that in it the normal entailments are cut. When we are in some doubt as to whether or not the normal entailments *are* cut, as in certain ways of presenting the blinding of Gloster in *King Lear*, we are uneasy; and if by some strange chance the actor playing Gloster were to have his eyes put out in reality and not in mime we should say this was not a theatrical performance. And, to reverse the argument, if we suspect that someone is pretending to show emotions, and not feeling them, we say of him that he is being theatrical; and the vice of this lies not in his offering us a representation but in his offering us a representation with the intention of deceiving us.

The possibility, then, is excluded that we should be able to appraise a poetic representation as true or faithful on the ground that we have been tricked into mistaking the representation for the thing represented. Of course, except in theatrical performances, the art of poetry does not lend itself to trickery. A poetic account of a battle cannot be mistaken for a battle. Even in lyric poetry the fictional character of the speaker is indicated by the formal devices, rhyme, metre or other, which are not characteristic of other types of discourse. To make a declaration of war in verse is no doubt possible; but its being in verse would be *prima facie* evidence that the normal entailments were not intended. Equally, my earlier argument has excluded the possibility that a poetic representation may be thought to be true or faithful by reason of its being an accurate account of some happening or some series of events, or an accurate report of a state of mind, or a faithful picture of some natural phenomenon. Poems may be any of these but their character as poems cannot be understood as such accounts, reports or pictures. It is not necessary to visit the Lake District or the valley of the Wye before one can evaluate Wordsworth's nature poetry. Attempts to find the originals of Albertine and Gilberte have a certain interest, of the detective-story kind, but they cannot affect our judgment of Proust's novel.

We may suspect there is self-revelation of a kind in Shake-speare's dark comedies, but whether this is so or not, the critical problems they present remain the same. It is truistic that poetry of some merit can be written only by men who have contemplated the natural and social worlds in a more or less perceptive way, and equally truistic that a minimum of experience has to be had before we are capable of respond-ing to what they write; but no particular poem is related to a particular state of affairs as a map is to a piece of country mapped, or a narrative of events to the events them-selves. We could test the accuracy of the map by going over the piece of country in question; we could test the accuracy of a narrative by questioning witnesses, examining photo-graphs, searching for footprints. There can be no such short and easy way to test the truth or the faithfulness of a poetic fiction.

I hold that when we use such a term as "truth" in the language of poetic appraisal we do so in various ways and employing different criteria in different cases. This would not be an altogether unexpected result, for the same thing holds in other fields. My grounds for asserting that I feel tired, that the blackbirds have begun to nest, that *apartheid* is morally wrong, that the sum of the angles of a Euclidean triangle is equal to two right angles, are very different. Simi-larly, if I wish to maintain the truth of such poetic repre-sentations as *King Lear*, Grimm's fairy story *The Juniper Tree*, the second of Pope's *Moral Essays* ("Of the Characters of Women") and Mr. Allen Tate's *Ode to the Confederate Dead*, it is very unlikely that the same criteria will be usable in each case. But it will not follow from our saying that there is truth in *King Lear* and truth in "Of the Characters of Women", and having quite different grounds for saying so in the two cases, that we are confused, any more than we are confused in saying that the blackbirds are nesting and that *apartheid* is morally wrong and that both statements are true, even though our grounds for saying they are true are not of the same kind in the two cases.

One of the reasons we may have for ascribing truth to a poetic representation is that it reveals to us the character of our inner feelings and dispositions; and by this I do not mean that it describes accurately inner feelings and dispositions of which we could give an account independently of the poetic representation. For reasons I have already given, it will not do to say that the truth of the poem lies in its "matching" a state of affairs of which we have prior and independent knowledge.

We have the idea that the inner life may be described through introspection. We habitually talk of our feelings, passions, dispositions, capacities, in terms that suggest that introspection is to the mind and heart what sight and the other senses are to the world of nature. It is one of the great and, I believe, permanent advances recently made by philosophers in this country to have shown that this account, the monstrous offspring of Cartesian dualism and British empiricism, is impossible. The confusions in the account are legion and they provided the later Wittgenstein with many of the problems that are central to his *Philosophical Investigations*, a rich mine whence many lesser philosophers have carried away their portions of precious ore. I will give an illustrative instance in which the impossibility of our learning to characterize the inner life through introspection may be brought out. It is impossible for me to wonder if I am in pain, though of course I may in a particular instance be in some doubt as to how I should classify a sensation; and pain is certainly something "inward", since it makes no sense to speak of my exhibiting my pain to another. How do I learn to identify one of my sensations as a pain? The force of this question is brought out if we note that it is a prior condition of my applying the concept of pain to my own case that I should already know the meaning of the word "pain". But to say that the word "pain" has a meaning is to imply that it is a unit in the public language and that my uses of the word and the uses of the word by others have the same range. For reasons I have already given, the meanings of words cannot be taught by showing that they "stand for" hidden processes of thought and feeling, since we only have the public language in which to talk about our thoughts and feelings. The conclusion, then, is that just as we can only say that others are in pain by noting their behaviour (and listening to what they say), so in our own case we only learn to characterize our own sensations of pain through learning the behavioural criteria for ascribing pain to others and to ourselves. Sensations, then, do not bear their names on their faces. If we could not learn the criteria for deciding when others are in pain we should be unable to apply the concept of pain to our own case. What holds of sensations such as pain holds also of emotions such as fear and anger, except that in the case of emotions the concepts are linked even more closely and plainly with incipient or actual behaviour than in the case of sensations.

All I have shown so far is that we could not learn to identify and describe our sensations and emotions through introspection alone, that we could not say *what* we were feeling without words that have sense in the public language. It is also true that we could not describe the world of nature and human affairs without the use of language. I now go on to say that understanding what it is we see or feel is necessarily connected with being able to give some account, not always one so adequate or so complete as we would wish, of what this is. It is not that we first understand and then articulate our understanding through a conceptual scheme. Such an articulation *is* understanding. Talk about the inner life is always in terms of concepts made by us as embodied intelligences, not as intelligences contingently and—as has been thought—by misfortune connected with the bodies we happen to have; and even if in one sense each of us has his own private theatre, the performances that go on within the private theatre are not the substance of the life of the mind nor are the various happenings within it the play of jealousy, ambition, desire, love, hate, fear, joy, upon which the poet discourses. When, at the end of "The Waste Land", Mr. Eliot depicted each man as imprisoned within his own consciousness, he gave us an image of man dwelling within the haunted palace of the Cartesians; [2] but the palace is in ruins and the ghosts have departed.

The observation that we should none of us have fallen in love if we had not first read about it is commonly taken to be cynical and to carry the implication that the state of feeling, "being in love", is artificial and silly and is produced in us by an unhealthy diet of poems and romances. It can be understood quite otherwise; and in a sense that brings out the function of the poetic representation in revealing to us the character of our feelings and dispositions. We cannot mistakenly believe we are in love, though we may be quite mistaken in supposing we love the person we are in love with; but the ability to characterize our own state as one of being in love depends upon our having criteria for deciding when others are in love; and these criteria we get from a particular cultural tradition mediated to us in a thousand ways. We could not be in love and not know it, for, as I have already argued, having feelings that can be identified and described is not separable from the conceptual activity of identification and description. If the other animals can be said to have feelings, as they can certainly be said to have

2.        I have heard the key
       Turn in the door once and turn once only
       We think of the key, each in his prison
       Thinking of the key, each confirms a prison.
"The Waste Land", T. S. Eliot, *Collected Poems 1909–1935* (Faber & Faber), 1936, p. 77. It is significant that Mr. Eliot glosses the text with an extract from F. H. Bradley's *Appearance and Reality.* Bradley writes: "My external sensations are no less private to myself than are my thoughts or my feelings. In either case my experience falls within my own circle, a circle closed on the outside; and, with all its elements alike, every sphere is opaque to the others which surround it. . . . In brief, regarded as an existence which appears in a soul, the whole world for each is peculiar and private to that soul."

144

sensations, such feelings must be quite other than ours, and cannot be said to be known in reflection. All we could say would be that in them there is an experienced—though even "experience" may be misleading—unity of inner movement and outward behaviour; for what is characteristically human, the inhibition of the overt manifestation of feeling (striking or embracing or whatever), so that we have the feeling but do not show it in behaviour and may not even betray it in our faces or in our posture, has in them no counterpart.

Characterizing our state of feeling, and so bringing it about that it is *this* state of feeling, is done through the application of concepts that are, so to speak, drawn from the common stock; and thus when we are in love we are in love as others are in love, just as when we suffer pain we suffer as others do. Nevertheless, because each of us is himself and not another, unique in his history and in his relations to others, a characterization of our individual feelings through concepts drawn from the common stock leaves us with a sense of injustice; for the feelings are rendered, not in their particularity, but in respect of their likeness to the feelings of others. There is no complete remedy for this sense of injustice. But it may be diminished and made to seem of no account through the poetic representation (and, no doubt, in other ways too). The consolation of the poetic representation of human love is that it reveals to us that condition of feeling we share with others—it gives us "the image of man and nature"—but not, or not wholly, as articulated in the common run of concepts, but as articulated in a particular concrete representation that speaks to us and for us in our individual situation, and only *through* this to and for our common humanity. It belongs to the poetic representation that it is wholly individual, these words in this order, and that no paraphrase can be given; so that although we know that this poem that speaks to us and for us speaks also to and for others, it is still as though it speaks to us alone. Further, whereas states of feeling characterized through concepts drawn from the common stock may be characterized in mechanical and simple terms, the rendering of a state of feeling through the complexity and inner richness of the poetic representation brings it about that the state of feeling so rendered is itself complex and rich, and valuable on this account; or, for we can place no limit upon the possible achievements of the poetic representation, a state of feeling that is complex and resistant to characterization, and on that account burdensome and frustrating, may be rendered clear and powerful when there is revealed to us a unity in the complexity, a unity we should otherwise have missed.

There is much in our inner life, in our relations with other men, and in that obscure feeling for what is deeply serious which is the ground of our capacity for religious and moral discourse, that we understand fitfully and with difficulty; and steady introspection gets us no farther. But just as we learn what it is to suffer pain, not merely through having pains but also through learning to use the language, so we can learn to understand the inner life in its complexity, and the life of society into which it flows and from which it draws much of its substance, through the poetic representation. A poetic representation is like a concept in that it is something made by man through which we articulate what would otherwise lie beyond our understanding; and just as a concept is not a *picture* of reality which gets its sense from that slice of reality it pictures, but an instrument of understanding, so that truth belongs to the concept only in the act of judgment, in the same way the poetic representation finds its truth in its proved capacity to further our understanding of ourselves and our society. "The image of man and nature" is not a symbolic transcript of something that is merely *there*: it is an instrument of knowledge.

It would be out of place in this essay to attempt a detailed account of how a particular poetic fiction can function as an instrument of knowledge and of how, as thus functioning, it may be accounted "true". This is work for a professional critic and there are many examples readily available. What I will do is to remind you of a crucial instance of the capacity of poetry to do for one man what I have argued it can do for the generality of men. In a dark moment John Stuart Mill came to believe that "the flaw in [his] life, must be a flaw in life itself". From this state of dejection he was rescued by the poetry of Wordsworth. It is worth noticing the precise terms in which Mill describes what Wordsworth's poetry did for him.

> What made Wordsworth's poems a medicine for my state of mind, was that they expressed, not mere outward beauty, but states of feeling, and of thought coloured by feeling, under the excitement of beauty. They seemed to be *the very culture of the feelings* [my italics], which I was in quest of. In them I seemed to draw from a source of inward joy, of sympathetic and imaginative pleasure, which could be shared in by all human beings. . . .[3]

That discipline of the sensibility and the mind to which the art of poetry, largely understood, contributes in a unique fashion enables us not only to understand ourselves; we also learn to look upon the human scene in such a way that, in the degree permitted to us by our talents, we draw from our vision representations which, though their primary and original reference is personal, speak for all men in the same predicament. Nothing could be more personal, more tied to one particular place and time, than Henry James's passionate note on his visit in 1904 to that graveyard in Cambridge, Massachusetts, where the members of his family were buried and where, twelve years later, his own ashes were to be placed. Intensely personal, wholly particular in its reference, it nevertheless displays in a supreme way that combination of consummate artistry with deep and penetrated feeling which makes it a wonderful example, for my purposes, of poetic representation; and of poetic truth, for here James

3. John Stuart Mill, *Autobiography* (World's Classics), 1949, p. 125.

finds in himself "not this or that particular man, but mankind".[4]

Isn't the highest deepest note of the whole thing the never-to-be-lost memory of that evening hour at Mount Auburn—at the Cambridge Cemetery when I took my way alone—after much waiting for the favouring hour—to that unspeakable group of graves. It was late, in November; the trees all bare, the dusk to fall early, the air all still (at Cambridge, in general, *so* still), with the western sky more and more turning to that terrible, deadly, pure polar pink that shows behind American winter woods. But I can't go over this—I can only, oh, so gently, so tenderly, brush it and breathe upon it—breathe upon it and brush it. It was the moment; it was the hour; it was the blessed flood of emotion that broke out at the touch of one's sudden *vision* and carried me away. I seemed then to know why I had done this; I seemed then to know why I had *come* —and to feel how not to have come would have been miserably, horribly to miss it. It made everything right—it made everything priceless. The moon was there, early, white and young, and seemed reflected in the white face of the great empty Stadium, forming one of the boundaries of Soldier's Field, that looked over at me, stared over at me, through the clear twilight, from across the Charles. Everything was there, everything *came*; the recognition, stillness, the strangeness, the pity and the sanctity and the terror, the breath-catching passion and the divine relief of tears. William's inspired transcript, on the exquisite little Florentine urn of Alice's ashes, William's divine gift to us, and to *her*, of the Dantean lines—

*Dopo lungo esilio e martirio*
*Viene a questa pace—*

took me so at the throat by its penetrating *rightness*, that it was as if one sank down on one's knees in a kind of anguish of gratitude before something for which one had waited with a long, deep *ache*. But why do I write of the all unutterable and the all abysmal? Why does my pen not drop from my hand on approaching the infinite pity and tragedy of all the past? It does, poor helpless pen, with what it meets of the ineffable,

4. Thomas Hobbes, *Leviathan*, "The Introduction".

what it meets of the cold Medusa-face of life, of all the life lived, on every side. *Basta, basta!*[5]

I said that in this passage James represents to us "not this or that particular man; but mankind", and in this lies the truth of the representation, in its capacity to increase the understanding of our common nature. Such performances are wonderfully intelligent; but they are so much more than this that one understands why men have so often spoken of the poetic performance as though the words of the poet were not his own but those of the god; or, with Coleridge, of the activity of the poetic imagination as transcendental; or as the expression of an inner glory. It is true that there is in "this life . . . no manifestation of glory coming from human beings except in products of art".[6] But if this is not a manifestation of an inner glory, and it is not, poetry and music, beyond the other arts, show us that there is the transcendent and that human life, that same life which displays "the cold Medusa-face" is open to the altogether beautiful—*tam antiqua et tam nova*[7]—and to the love in whose depths the greatest of the poets saw the scattered leaves of the universe bound together in a single volume.[8]

1961

5. *The Notebooks of Henry James.* Edited by F. O. Matthiessen and Kenneth B. Murdock, New York, 1947, pp. 320, 321. It is worth noting that James prefaces the passage with the remark—he sees the whole scene and mood as standing "in the path like a waiting lion", a challenge, that is, to his art—"that to present these accidents is what it is to be a *master*: that and that only". I would argue that he solves the problem of representation in presenting it.

6. Miss G. E. M. Anscombe has kindly allowed me to make use of this expression from an unpublished paper by her. I also owe to her the idea that the glory of art is not a manifestation of an inner glory in human beings.

7. *Sero te amavi, pulchritudo tam antiqua et tam nova, sero te amavi.* St. Augustine, *Confessions*, X, 27.

8.
    *Nel suo profondo vidi che s' interna,*
      *legato con amore in un volume,*
      *cio che per l' universo si squaderna . . .*
          *Paradiso*, canto xxxiii, lines 85–7.

# 8

# Doctrinal to an Age

### NOTES TOWARDS A REVALUATION OF
### POPE'S *ESSAY ON MAN*

> They support Pope, I see, in the *Quarterly*. Let them
> continue to do so: it is a Sin and a Shame, and a *damna-*
> *tion* to think that *Pope!!* should require it—but he does.
> Those miserable mountebanks of the day, the poets, dis-
> grace themselves and deny God, in running down Pope,
> the most *faultless* of Poets, and almost of men.
>
> BYRON

THE *Essay on Man* is a poem doctrinal to an age and a society
if not to a nation. It is perhaps the most interesting example
in English of a philosophical poem; and as such it has to be
considered in any discussion of the relation between poetic
form and intellectual content. Are we to discuss it as we
should an unornamented philosophical essay, as we should
discuss, say, Locke's *Essay* or Berkeley's *Principles*? It would
plainly be ridiculous so to discuss Lucretius. The *De Rerum*
*Natura* is a deeply moving poem for those who altogether
reject its philosophy and find the argument abstracted from
the poem shoddy. Are we to place it rather with *Paradise*
*Lost* and with *The Prelude*, as a work of the imagination
which touches on philosophical themes but of which it would
not be sensible to demand that it should exhibit logical consistency in a high degree? There is a respectable critical
tradition against so placing this or any other of Pope's works.
Arnold is the most distinguished representative of this tradi-

tion,[1] but it would not be an exaggeration to say that, at least until fairly recently, most English critics later than the Augustan age would have said that to apply the word poetry simultaneously to the work of Pope, and to the work of Shakespeare or Milton or Wordsworth, was almost to equivocate. Agreement with such an assertion would seem to throw us back upon the view that the *Essay* must be judged as rhymed philosophy. Judged in this way, it is not a remarkable piece of philosophy. And yet, after an attentive reading of the *Essay*, it is hard to say without hesitations and involuntary backward glances that the experience has been simply that of reading a poor philosophical essay embellished with rhymes and other ornaments. It is also true that the experience does not seem much to resemble the reading of *Paradise Lost* or of *The Prelude*. It is possible to argue that every poem is such that it differs in kind from every other poem and that it would therefore be unreasonable to approach *An Essay on Man* with expectations prompted by some other poem; but even if we agree that in some sense every poem is *sui generis*, it remains true that some have urged that the word poem cannot be used of the *Essay* except in the most trivial of its meanings. The publication of Mr. Maynard Mack's new edition of *An Essay on Man* in the Twickenham Edition [2] seems to offer an occasion for a reconsideration of the poem and of some of the critical issues thereby revealed.

If we examine Pope's own expressed intentions we find that he saw the *Essay* as "forming a *temperate* yet not *inconsistent*, and a *short* yet not *imperfect* system of Ethics". He continues: "This I might have done in prose; but I chose verse, and even rhyme, for two reasons. The one will appear obvious; that principles, maxims, or precepts so

1. See Geoffrey Tillotson, "Matthew Arnold and Eighteenth-century Poetry", in *Essays on the Eighteenth Century. Presented to David Nichol Smith*, 1945.
2. Alexander Pope, *An Essay on Man*, edited by Maynard Mack, The Twickenham Edition, Vol. III, i, 1950. This is hereafter referred to as Mack.

written, both strike the reader more strongly at first, and are more easily retained by him afterwards: The other may seem odd, but is true, I found I could express them more *shortly* this way than in prose itself; and nothing is more certain, than much of the *force* as well as *grace* of arguments or instructions, depends on their conciseness." [3]

This would seem to suggest that his principal intention was to exhibit a system of ethics and that its being cast in poetic form was a matter of convenience, much as we more readily remember the lengths of the months by reciting to ourselves, "Thirty days hath September . . .". That this was what Pope thought himself to be doing does not tell us that this was what he did. Only from an examination of the poem itself can we decide upon this question. There is evidence that his attitude to the poem was somewhat less decided and more ambiguous than the words quoted above would suggest. When, partly through the influence of the Swiss philosopher Crousaz, the *Essay* began to acquire an evil reputation among the orthodox, Warburton strove to vindicate the orthodoxy of Pope's doctrine in a series of articles in *The Republick of Letters*. Pope was immensely gratified, and wrote that "you have made my system as clear as I ought to have done, and could not. It is indeed the same system as mine, but illustrated with a ray of your own, as they say our natural body is the same still when it is glorified. I am sure I like it better than I did before . . . I know I meant just what you explain; but I did not explain my own meaning so well as you. You understand me as well as I do myself; but you express me better than I could express myself." [4] Even if we allow for an excess of politeness, these admissions surely reveal a radical uncertainty over what exactly he was driving at in the *Essay*.

Pope's method of composing the *Essay*, so far as we can establish it,[5] supports the view that we are concerned with

3. "The Design", Mack, pp. 7, 8.
4. Cited in Samuel Johnson, "Life of Pope", in *Lives of the Poets* (World's Classics, 1906, Vol. II, pp. 289, 290).
5. See George Sherburn, "Pope at Work", in *Essays on the Eighteenth Century*.

philosophy versified. He seems often to have prepared prose statements of arguments later to be turned into verse; and even though there is no longer any very good reason to take seriously the legend that in writing the *Essay* Pope simply cast into verse a prose argument supplied by Bolingbroke, it may be that the argument of the greater part of the *Essay* was first set down in prose. This does not mean that the structure of the *Essay* or of any one Epistle is a prose structure the sequence of which is determined by the development of a continuous argument. The units of which the poem is composed are, as Mr. Sherburn has shown, verse paragraphs, and it is arguable that the order of these paragraphs is up to a point arbitrary.[6] This Johnson perceived. "Almost every poem, consisting of precepts, is so far arbitrary and unmethodical, that many of the paragraphs may change places with no apparent inconvenience; for of two or more positions, depending upon some remote and general principle, there is seldom any cogent reason why one should precede the other."[7] Johnson appears to have thought that this was compatible with a sort of philosophical consistency, and so it may be; but the relevant comparison is with the philosophers of Pope's own day, and it is hard to think of any contemporary work of the first rank of which this would hold good —though it might well be thought to hold good of the work of Shaftesbury or Bolingbroke. In any case, Johnson, in rejecting as improbable the story that Pope had put into verse a systematic argument constructed by Bolingbroke, did so on the ground that "the Essay plainly appears the fabrick of a poet: what Bolingbroke supplied could be only the first principles; the order, illustrations, and embellishments must all be Pope's".[8]

6. "One may well suspect that in later days the *Essay on Man* would have been more favourably regarded by critics if the poet had printed his verse paragraphs frankly as such—if, in the manner of Traherne's *Centuries of Meditations* or of Tennyson's *In Memoriam*, he had been content to leave his verse units as fragmentary reflections on philosophic ideas that are bound to have recurrent interest." Ibid., p. 61.
7. Johnson, op. cit., p. 243.      8. Ibid., p. 287.

It would scarcely be worth while showing that, as philosophy, the *Essay* is an unimpressive performance, unless one had some further purpose in view.[9] But the inadequacies of the poem considered from this standpoint may bring out, by pointing to what Pope has certainly *not* achieved, those characteristics of the poem which may support a claim to another kind of achievement. Two illustrations of what can be taken as incoherences of argument may be offered.

Epistle I is concerned to show that man is necessarily ignorant in two respects. In the first place, the cosmos in its vastness and complexity escapes for the most part man's scrutiny because man's senses and intellectual powers are insufficient for the task.

> But of this frame the bearings, and the ties,
> The strong connections, nice dependencies,
> Gradations just, has thy pervading soul
> Look'd thro'? or can a part contain the whole?
>
> (Epistle I, ll. 29–32.)

In the second place, man is unable to understand the rationale of the cosmos considered as a scheme of things which is, both in its particular operations and as a totality, good. That such is the rationale of the cosmos Pope holds, simply by deduction from the nature of God as infinite wisdom and infinite goodness, to be certain. But *how* this can be is beyond the power of man to determine.

> When the proud steed shall know why Man restrains
> His fiery course, or drives him o'er the plains;
> When the dull Ox, why now he breaks the clod,
> Is now a victim, and now Ægypt's God;
> Then shall Man's pride and dulness comprehend

9. The task of showing how bad as philosophy the *Essay* may be considered has been performed, without much sympathy and with little awareness that this is not the only relevant question, by the late Professor Laird. See John Laird, "Pope's *Essay on Man*", in *Philosophical Incursions into English Literature*, 1946.

His actions', passions', being's, use and end;
Why doing, suff'ring, check'd, impell'd; and why
This hour a slave, the next a deity.

(Epistle I, ll. 61–8.)

Now, the rest of the poem is simply inconsistent with this
contention that man's ignorance is such that he is incapable
of knowing the complex harmonies of the cosmos and of
finding a justification of those detailed cosmic arrangements
which seem inconsistent with the postulated Divine goodness. In the remaining three Epistles we are offered a variety
of arguments designed to show precisely *how* the constitution of human nature and the situation of man vis-à-vis the
forces of nature and the brutes are arranged with a view to
the good of the individual and the whole.

Such appears to be one inconsistency of the poem taken
as a whole. A failure of detail may be illustrated. In Epistle
III Pope employs the conception, derived from Aristotle and
brought home forcibly to the educated public of Pope's day
by Locke, that the best form of State is that possessing a
"mixed constitution". This fits in admirably with the Hera-
clitean thesis, advanced by Pope in several connections, that
order springs from a tension of opposing forces.[1]

... jarring int'rests of themselves create
Th'according music of a well-mix'd State.

(Epistle III, ll. 293, 294.)

---

1. Cf.:   Passions, like Elements, tho' born to fight,
      Yet, mix'd and soften'd, in his work unite:
      These 'tis enough to temper and employ;
      But what composes Man, can Man destroy?
      Suffice that Reason keep to Nature's road,
      Subject, compound them, follow her and God.
      Love, Hope, and Joy, fair pleasure's smiling train,
      Hate, Fear, and Grief, the family of pain;
      These mix'd with art, and to due bounds confin'd,
      Make and maintain the balance of the mind:
      The lights and shades, whose well accorded strife
      Gives all the strength and colour of our life.

(Epistle II, ll. 111–22.)

But within a few lines he can follow this with:

> For Forms of Government let fools contest
> Whate'er is best administer'd is best. . . .
>
> (Epistle III, ll. 303, 304.)

If, then, we expect of the poem a system of ethics and a cosmic scheme notable for their internal coherence and capable of being derived from plausible first principles, we are likely to be disappointed. One has, all the same, to remember that, judged by such tests, there are few philosophical works—perhaps none—that would be thought by all philosophers to be of merit. Thomas Hobbes's *Leviathan* is without doubt a philosophical classic; but the first six chapters do not appear to be coherent with or even relevant to the rest of the argument, which seems to be governed, not by the mechanistic anthropology of the first chapters, but by a quite different anthropology derived from introspection, historical learning, and acquaintance with men and affairs. It is curious, and not altogether irrelevant to our discussion of Pope's *Essay*, that Professor Oakeshott has attempted to account for the distinction of Hobbes's work in terms that in my judgment amount to a defence of the *Leviathan* as an organic whole analogous to a great poem, and not as primarily a work of ratiocination.[2] I do not myself find Pope's argument at all points quite so ludicrously bad as Professor Laird found it.[3] If we are to have an argument for "cosmic Toryism", Pope's is a great deal better than that of

2. Cf.: "The coherence of [Hobbes's] philosophy, the system of it, lies not in an architectonic structure, but in a single 'passionate thought' that pervades its parts. The system is not the plan or key of the labyrinth of the philosophy; it is, rather, a guiding clue, like the thread of Ariadne. It is like the music that gives meaning to the movement of dancers, or the law of evidence that gives coherence to the practice of a court. And the thread, the hidden thought, is the continuous application of a doctrine about the nature of philosophy. Hobbes's philosophy is the world reflected in the mirror of the philosophic eye, each image the representation of a fresh object, but each determined by the character of the mirror itself." Thomas Hobbes, *Leviathan*, edited with an Introduction by Michael Oakeshott, n.d., p. xix.

3. Immanuel Kant greatly esteemed the *Essay*. Cf. Mack, p. xli.

Soame Jenyns, who argues that "our difficulties [with regard to the existence of misery in the universe] arise from our wrong notions of Omnipotence, and forgetting how many difficulties it has to contend with . . . it is obliged either to afflict Innocence, or be the cause of Wickedness; it has plainly no other Option : what then could infinite Wisdom, Justice, and Goodness do in this situation more consistent with itself, than to call into being Creatures formed with such depravity, in their dispositions, as to induce many of them to act in such a manner as to render themselves proper subjects for such necessary sufferings. . . ." [4] Nevertheless, we may agree that if we are to classify Pope as a philosopher he belongs rather with Jenyns than with Locke or Berkeley. Bolingbroke's flashy genius seems greatly to have impressed him. This does not argue philosophic acumen in Pope; but the very qualities which made him respond with such ardour to Bolingbroke, the moving, breathing, eloquent, and fetching man [5]— philosophy, so Pope thought, in the concrete—are qualities which provide a partial explanation of a greatness quite other than philosophical in the *Essay on Man*.

"The great poet, in writing himself, writes his time." So Mr. Eliot in a famous essay. He continues : ". . . it was [Shakespeare's] business to express the greatest emotional intensity of his time, based on whatever his time happened to think. Poetry is not a substitute for philosophy or theology or religion . . . [its] function is not intellectual but emotional, it cannot be defined adequately in intellectual terms." [6] It

4. Soame Jenyns, "A Free Inquiry into the Nature and Origin of Evil", in *Miscellaneous Pieces in Prose and Verse*, third edition, 1770, pp. 306, 307.
5. Cf. : Come then, my Friend, my Genius, come along,
Oh master of the poet, and the song!
And while the Muse now stoops, or now ascends,
To Man's low passions, or their glorious ends,
Teach me, like thee, in various nature wise,
To fall with dignity, with temper rise;
Form'd by thy converse, happily to steer
From grave to gay, from lively to severe;
Correct with spirit, eloquent with ease,
Intent to reason, or polite to please. (Epistle IV, ll. 373–82.)
6. T. S. Eliot, "Shakespeare and the Stoicism of Seneca", in *Elizabethan Essays*, 1934, p. 50.

would be easy wilfully to misunderstand Mr. Eliot. Has "a time" a "greatest emotional intensity"? Are not the greatest emotional intensities of any time precisely those which transcend the time and are human rather than peculiar to a single time and culture? Is not the "function" of poetry too simply and too narrowly defined? These and other objections can be raised to the way in which Mr. Eliot has formulated his thought. If we go behind the formulation we find it suggested (or so I think) that there is an important sense in which, to take examples, Arnold's *Dover Beach* rather than *Locksley Hall*, Mr. Eliot's *The Family Reunion* rather than *The Lady's Not for Burning*, express with some degree of success an "emotional intensity" of their periods. Their importance, the extent to which they do perform their poetic function, lies in an ordering of feeling to expression and of expression to feeling, an ordering which is such that feeling and expression make up an organic rather than a casual and contrived unity. The quality and depth of the reverberation provoked by a reading of them carry with them a suggestion of authenticity that scarcely needs a precautionary analysis of the poem itself.

Such an analysis may all the same be necessary. We know that every culture has certain limitations making it difficult or impossible for those within it to enjoy poems or pictures or buildings which were enjoyed by earlier cultures and which will be enjoyed again by those still to come. These limitations make the distinctive "taste" of a period. The limitations were narrow enough in Pope's own day. The power and charm of the Gothic and of "primitive" art were on the whole inaccessible to the men of the period [7]—even Shakespeare we may suppose to have been less accessible than

7. Cf.: ". . . the grand distinction between Grecian and Gothic architecture, the latter being fantastical, and for the most part founded neither in nature nor in reason, in necessity nor use, the appearance of which accounts for all the beauty, grace, and ornament of the other." George Berkeley, *Alciphron or the Minute Philosopher*, Third Dialogue, in The Works of George Berkeley Bishop of Cloyne, Vol. III, edited by T. E. Jessop, 1950, p. 127. This state of affairs changes later in the century.

he was to the early seventeenth century or than he is to us. Where there was an expressed liking for the Gothic it was on account of its supposed fantasticality and was, so to speak, a species of fooling, resembling in this respect the liking of Mr. Betjeman and his disciples for certain examples of Victorian architecture. What we have to show, if we are to vindicate the claim that *An Essay on Man* is one of our greatest poems, is that an analysis of the poem suggests that the general failure of the nineteenth century—a failure which still overshadows us, making our response to the poetry of Pope an embarrassed one—adequately to respond to the *Essay* is simply a failure of taste, an inability to move outside the narrowness imposed upon our literary culture by the romantic movement. The making of the analysis will, if it does seem to indicate a failure of taste in us, itself be a means of modifying our taste in such a way as to liberate us from our present narrowness.[8]

Mr. Mack's penetrating analysis of the poem is designed to show that it has been enormously undervalued; that in it Pope does "write his time"; and that the achievement in terms of his accomplished union of expression with feeling is great both as a formal structure and as being for us the possible occasion of a deep and rich experience. But before I comment on what Mr. Mack has to say, I should like to show from one example that it is perhaps unjust to deride the failure of the nineteenth century to respond with pleasure to Pope as being simply a failure of taste, a failure unfortified by any serious weighing of the problem.

. . . The relation between the three poems [i.e. *The Faerie Queen*, *Paradise Lost*, and *An Essay on Man*] is, indeed, characteristic. Milton and Spenser could utter their deepest thoughts

8. Two works may be mentioned as having done much to modify our sensibility and make the poetry of Pope more accessible to us: Edith Sitwell, *Alexander Pope*, 1930; and Geoffrey Tillotson, *On the Poetry of Pope*, 1938. Mr. Wilson Knight's "The Vital Flame: An Essay on Pope", in his *The Burning Oracle*, 1939, should also be noted, especially in connection with the *Essay on Man*.

about man's position in the universe and his moral nature by aid of a symbolism intelligible to themselves and their readers. But where was Pope to turn for concrete symbols sufficiently expressive of his thought? The legends of the Bible claimed too little reverence. Even in the majestic poetry of Milton we are unpleasantly reminded of the fact that the mighty ex-pounder of Puritan thought is consciously devising a conven-tional imagery. The old romance which had fed Spenser's imagination was too hopelessly dead to serve the purpose. It had left behind a wearisome spawn of so-called romances; it had been turned into mere ribaldry by Butler; and Pope wisely abandoned his cherished project of an epic poem, though feebler hands attempted the task. The "Essay on Man" is sub-stantially a versification of the most genuine creed of the time; of that Deism which took various shapes. . . . But the thought had generated no concrete imagery. It remained of necessity what it was at first—a mere bare skeleton of logic, never clothed upon by imaginative flesh and blood. As in Clarke's sermons, we have diagrams instead of pictures; a system of axioms, deductions, and corollaries instead of a rich my-thology; a barren metaphysico-mathematical theory of the universe, which might satisfy the intellect, but remained hope-lessly frigid for the emotional nature.

Pope's poetry is thus forced to become didactic, and not only didactic, but ratiocinative. . . .[9]

It may be that in this passage Leslie Stephen betrays a partial failure of taste, a failure which has led him to neglect some of the most striking features of the poem. It is a gross simplification of the *Essay* to describe it as a versification of Deism; this is to neglect the traditional elements that are, as we shall see, both prominent in the poem and necessary to its full effect. (We are not quite sure that Stephen may not also have in mind a curious theory of poetry not at all coherent with his main position; for shortly after the passage quoted above we find him writing: "A consistent pantheism or a consistent scepticism may be made the sources of profoundly

9. Leslie Stephen, *History of English Thought in the Eighteenth Century*, second edition, 1881, Vol. II, p. 351.

impressive poetry. Each of them generates a deep and homo-
geneous sentiment which may utter itself in song. Pope, as
the mouthpiece of Spinoza or of Hobbes, might have written
an impressive poem. . . ." [1]) All the same, his comment is a
shrewd one. He sees that if the *Essay* fails it will be through
the lack of a symbolism that can be used with effect. The
mythological cosmos which earlier poets had used with effect
has at last given way before the attack which has raged with
continual fury from Copernicus to Newton. Poor Pope has
thus no materials to build with: he is reduced to "a barren
metaphysico-mathematical theory of the universe".

Now, I believe there is a perfectly serious and valid point
lying behind and accounting for Stephen's comment. But as
the comment stands it seems to indicate simply a failure on
his part to read the poem with the minimum degree of attention necessary for the understanding of it. Who but Pope has
drawn attention to the bankruptcy of Newtonian physics,
not indeed as *descriptive*, but as *explanatory*?

> Superior beings, when of late they saw
> A mortal Man unfold all Nature's law,
> Admir'd such wisdom in an earthly shape,
> And shew'd a NEWTON as we show an Ape.
> Could he, whose rules the rapid Comet bind,
> Describe or fix one movement of his Mind?
> Who saw its fires here rise, and there descend,
> Explain his own beginning, or his end?
> Alas what wonder! Man's superior part
> Uncheck'd may rise, and climb from art to art:
> But when his own great work is but begun,
> What Reason weaves, by Passion is undone.

> (Epistle II, ll. 31–42.)

Pope here shows that "a . . . metaphysico-mathematical
theory of the universe" does *not* "satisfy the intellect"; and
he is quite consciously setting himself against a prevailing

1. Ibid., p. 352.

climate of thought.[2] If it should be argued that, although he may see the limitation of the Newtonian physics as an explanatory hypothesis, he has nevertheless no other cosmic imagery upon which to draw, and must, if he does so draw, present us with sterile symbols having no power to fructify in the imagination, the answer can only be an appeal to the poem itself.

> Far as Creation's ample range extends,
> The scale of sensual, mental pow'rs ascends:
> Mark how it mounts, to Man's imperial race,
> From the green myriads in the peopled grass:
> What modes of sight betwixt each wide extreme,
> The mole's dim curtain, and the lynx's beam:
> Of smell, the headlong lioness between,
> And hound sagacious on the tainted green:
> Of hearing, from the life that fills the flood,
> To that which warbles thro' the vernal wood:
> The spider's touch, how exquisitely fine!
> Feels at each thread and lives along the line:
> In the nice bee, what sense so subtly true
> From pois'nous herbs extract the healing dew:
> How Instinct varies in the grov'ling swine,
> Compar'd, half-reas'ning elephant, with thine:
> 'Twixt that, and Reason, what a nice barrier;
> For ever sep'rate, yet for ever near!
>
> (Epistle I, ll. 207–24.)

This is surely no "barren metaphysico-mathematical theory of the universe". It is in fact a far more primitive cosmological scheme than Newton's and one imaginatively realized with exquisite grace in these lines. Here Pope shows a fine sense of the connection that must exist for poetry between the experience of living as a concrete process,

> Wild Nature's vigor working at the root[3]

2. Cf.: Marjorie Hope Nicolson, *Newton Demands the Muse*, Princeton, 1946, pp. 135, 136. Pope was by no means alone in this. See R. F. Jones, "The Background of the Attack on Science in the Age of Pope", in *Pope and His Contemporaries*. Essays presented to George Sherburn, 1949.
3. Epistle II, l. 184.

and the conceptual schemes designed to universalize it. The notion of a "scale of being" is here triumphantly shown to be still a valid poetic symbol.

The surface meaning of Stephen's criticism, then, is not altogether supported by an examination of the poem. But I believe there is a point Stephen is trying to make, though he makes it very badly or perhaps not at all. This point, if it can be shown to be valid, by no means disposes of the *Essay* as a poem having pretensions to greatness; but it does suggest that there is a serious failure within it, and one which has to be attributed to a certain superficiality in the theology and philosophy upon which Pope has perforce to rely.

At the beginning of Epistle I Pope summons us to

> Expatiate free o'er all this scene of Man;
> A mighty maze! but not without a plan....
>
> (Epistle I, ll. 5, 6.)

The choice of the word "maze" as the apt symbol of the complex of relations within which man stands is of immense importance in governing our response to the poem as a whole. A maze is a grouping of paths through which it is difficult to find one's way. But every maze is constructed on a plan which can in the end, given patience and ingenuity, be grasped. No doubt many of us, once within a maze, would be unable to find our way to the centre and thence to the point at which we entered, without the help of someone familiar with the construction of the maze. But this failure is not a radical one, springing from the insufficiency of our nature and a mysteriousness intrinsic to mazes; it denotes merely a failure on our part to observe, and to reason correctly. Again, the complexity of a maze exists, as it were, at a single level. It resembles the complexity of a game of chess or of a logical construction. It presents us with a *problem*; whereas, to employ the now familiar distinction of M. Marcel, the poetic cosmos must, if it is to draw from us an adequate response, present itself as *mysterious* rather than *problema-*

*tical*. The *Essay* does not at all points fail to give us a sense of mystery; but the attitude often in control is that suggested by the word "maze".[4]

Again, what weight in reading do we give to "but not without a plan"? I submit that we are compelled to give it a certain lightness, almost jauntiness, indicating some complacency in our contemplation of the maze. It presents us with a teasing problem, certainly: but we are the men to solve it. Thus, although Pope specifically denies that men can do more than apprehend the most general features of the maze, the attitude created in us by the couplet disposes us not to take too seriously his professions of modesty.

In his exposition in Epistle I of "the great scale", "Nature's chain", Pope plays with the supposition—not conceived to be a real possibility—that the cosmic order should break down in one of its parts.

> And if each system in gradation roll,
> Alike essential to th'amazing whole;
> The least confusion but in one, not all
> That system only, but the whole must fall.
> Let Earth unbalanc'd from her orbit fly,
> Planets and Suns run lawless thro' the sky,
> Let ruling Angels from their spheres be hurl'd,
> Being on being wreck'd, and world on world,
> Heav'n's whole foundations to their centre nod,
> And Nature tremble to the throne of God. . . .
>
> (Epistle I, ll. 247–56.)

There is a parallel passage in Hooker.

4. I do not know if it has been noticed that there may be some significance in the professions of K. in Kafka's *The Trial* and *The Castle*. In the former, K. is a bank official, in the latter a surveyor. In both professions we have to do with *measurement*, the criterion of judgment is quantitative. The failure of K. in both instances springs from an inability to see that the relationship between man and the heavenly powers is not problematical but mysterious. A mystery cannot be *solved*: it can only be embraced in humility and love. See my "Theological Fragments", *The Downside Review*, Spring 1949, pp. 144 ff.

. . . Now if nature should intermit her course, and leave altogether though it were but for a while the observation of her
own laws; if those principal and mother elements of the world,
whereof all things in this lower world are made, should lose
the qualities which now they have; if the frame of that
heavenly arch erected over our heads should loosen and dis-
solve itself; if celestial spheres should forget their wonted
motions, and by irregular volubility turn themselves any way
as it might happen; if the prince of the lights of heaven, which
now as a giant doth run his unwearied course, should as it
were through a languishing faintness begin to stand and to
rest himself; if the moon should wander from her beaten way,
the times and seasons of the year blend themselves by disordered and confused mixture, the winds breathe out their last
gasp, the clouds yield no rain, the earth be defeated of heavenly
influence, the fruits of the earth pine away as children at the
withered breasts of their mother no longer able to yield them
relief : what would become of man himself, whom these things
now do all serve? See we not plainly that obedience of creatures unto the law of nature is the stay of the whole world? [5]

If we take into account the advantages and limitations of
the poetic and prose forms—the *intention* in each case seems
much the same—it seems to me plain that we have to say in
the end, not only that Hooker comes off in a way that Pope
does not quite come off, but also that there breathes through
the language and the images employed a different attitude to
the possibility which is being entertained. There is in Hooker
a *serious* attitude to the possibility, the same attitude that is
to be found in the parallel passage on "degree" in *Troilus
and Cressida*,[6] an attitude which (we may conjecture) springs
from a deep feeling of being involved in the strains and conflicts of a revolutionary period. The attitude of Pope remains
that of the spectator. The entities ordered within the cosmos

---

5. Richard Hooker, *Of the Laws of Ecclesiastical Polity*, Book I, Ch. iii,
2, in The Works of Mr. Richard Hooker, arranged by John Keble, seventh
edition, revised by R. W. Church and F. Paget, 1888, Vol. I, pp. 207, 208.
Hooker is here adapting a passage from Arnobius (fl. c. A.D. 305).
6. I, iii.

are *systems*—the choice of the abstract word is significant; I am confident, in face of Mr. Mack's telling us that the "ruling Angels" hurled from their spheres represent "a belief by no means wholly displaced in the Augustan age",[7] that the "ruling Angels" are very far advanced on the way to becoming theatrical properties. Perhaps the notion was not so idle a speculation as it would have seemed to a nineteenth-century agnostic; but there is no conceivable connection with the Newtonian cosmos, which Pope takes perfectly seriously as a *description*, though he properly rejects it as an *explanation*; they are, in short, *ornaments*. This attitude to imagery is strictly incompatible with the seriousness of the theme. That it *is* Pope's conscious attitude, however much he may from time to time rise above it, cannot be doubted. He expresses in "The Design" prefixed to the *Essay*, the hope that "these Epistles in their progress . . . will be less dry, and more susceptible of poetical ornament".[8]

Such, then, are some of the considerations which seem to make it important, for the sake of the credit of the poem itself, not to advance the highest claims for the *Essay on Man*. This granted, it remains to suggest that the unfavourable judgments which have beset the poem from its birth are at least in part misconceived.

Mr. Mack believes that past study of the *Essay* has too often placed the poem against the wrong background: that of the philosophy and natural science of the Enlightenment. We should do better to examine it "in the light of Renaissance thought and literature. Here the ideas . . . can be studied in formulations elaborated and particularized by the literary imagination of centuries, and arranged in a pattern or formed *Weltanschauung* that seeks to take hold of the relations of God and man not through theorem but through symbol." [9] In such a light, we are able to trace the "implicit organization [of the poem], its attitudes, images, emotions,

7. Mack, p. 46.    8. Ibid., p. 8.    9. Ibid., p. xlvii.

and its developing theme"; [1] the "implicit organization" is to be contrasted with the logical meaning and organization of the poem. The latter may be taken as expressing Pope's conscious intention, the former accounts for the impact of the poem, an impact felt in spite of the logical meaning and organization which, abstracted from the concrete *compositum* of words and all they produce in us, and taken too seriously, prevents our receiving the impact of the poem with the greatest effect.

It is possible to show that, seen in this way, the *Essay* has striking affinities with the theme of violated and in the end re-established order which is central in such plays of Shakespeare as *King Lear* and *The Tempest*, which is present (perhaps more at the level of deliberate contrivance) in *Paradise Lost*, and which goes back to the origins of our tragic drama in Greek culture. [2] The "order" of the poem, Mr. Mack is able to demonstrate, is by no means only the order of the Newtonian cosmos, though, of course, it includes this order. Pope's "order" is compounded of many elements: the tradition of Platonic and Aristotelian cosmology; the *concors discordia* of Heraclitus; the hierarchical conception of the pseudo-Dionysius; the Pauline teaching on unity in the Body of Christ; and others. [3]

Pope's anthropology, too, can be traced to more remote and deeper sources than Bolingbroke. He qualifies the murderous simplifications of Montaigne, Hobbes and Mandeville. [4] The conception, Christian at root, of man as a ruined masterpiece is integral to the poem. He is unable (Mr. Mack suggests that the "story had lost, perhaps, its full imagina-

---

1. Mack, p. xlviii.                    2. Ibid., p. liii.
3. Ibid., pp. liv ff. Mr. Wilson Knight has pointed out that Pope in *Windsor Forest* employed the forest as a superb symbol of cosmic order.
    Not Chaos-like together crush'd and bruis'd;
    But, as the world, harmoniously confus'd;
    Where order in variety we see,
    And where, though all things differ, all agree.
G. Wilson Knight, op. cit., p. 131. This seems neither mechanistic nor over-rationalistic.
4. Mack, p. lxvii.

tive availability" [5]) to use the Biblical account of the Fall. He has instead to use the contemporary myth of a "state of nature". But there *is* a Fall—Pope's state of nature is rather Locke's than Hobbes's; and the emphasis on *pride*, often given very nearly its full theological value, is unmistakable throughout the poem. Pride, *hubris*, is for Pope, as it had been for Milton, the source of man's ruin, and humility is among the chief virtues.

In these and in other ways Mr. Mack, whilst admitting that the *Essay* is a "conceptual mutation of a mystic (*sic*) theme [which] perhaps reflects the movement of the modern mind towards its self-extinction",[6] shows that a fresh analysis of the poem and a tracing of it to its authentic sources may go some distance towards making it possible for us to be deeply moved in the reading of it. He does not make extravagant claims; but he does show that, properly approached, *An Essay on Man* may, at least while we remain under the influence of an attentive reading, give us a conviction that "there is a fecundity and comprehensiveness in the Creation and in man himself which man cannot do justice to otherwise than by trusting it for what it is, and simultaneously an ideal order, unity, harmony and purpose which man must both support and help to realize by disciplining himself".[7] All this is not (I would suggest) the argument of the *Essay* reduced to propositional form; such a reduction would produce nothing so consistent; but it is a statement correlative with the experience the poem has within its power to bestow upon the reader.

1951

5. Ibid., p. lxiv.    6. Ibid., p. lxv.    7. Ibid., p. lxxx.

# 9

## Mr. Tillotson and Mr. Pope

NEVER before can there have been so many excellent critics writing in English. If it is hard to be sure that Mr. Eliot, say, and Dr. Leavis are critics of quite the stature of Johnson and Arnold—we are perhaps as yet in no position to judge—the sheer mass of critical work of high quality is all the same impressive. There are what may be called the scholarly critics, those who excel both in the business of establishing and annotating texts and in the analysis and interpretation of the texts. Here I have in mind such scholars as C. S. Lewis, Bonamy Dobrée, Geoffrey Tillotson, John Butt, James Sutherland, to name only a few. Again, we live in a culture which has in a sense rediscovered the theory and the art of criticism, after a period in the doldrums at the end of the nineteenth century and in the first two decades of this. For this rediscovery many critics have been responsible, notably, as well as Eliot and Leavis, Robert Graves and Laura Riding, I. A. Richards, William Empson and Wilson Knight. Then there are those critics who make their point by relating literature to other subject matters, to politics, psychology, natural science and so on. Here the most distinguished work has been done by two Americans, Edmund Wilson and Lionel Trilling. But to mention America suggests a host of other fine critics who are well known and influential here: Wimsatt, Cleanth Brooks, Allen Tate, R. P. Blackmur, Northrop Frye, Fr. Walter Ong and many others.

With all these riches we ought to be happy. But are we? Of course, it is in the nature of the critical pursuit that there should be strong disagreements between critics. Those who are no more than middle-aged have lived through a revolu-

tion in the methods of criticism and have seen the balance of
taste quite reversed. It is not extravagant to say that we have
been given a new Shakespeare, that such writers as Donne
and Marvell who were hard to read a generation ago are
now available on easy terms to the ordinary cultivated
reader, that poets and novelists who not so long ago were
neglected or derided—Hopkins, Eliot, D. H. Lawrence, Henry
James—are now the staple of academic criticism. And there
are already signs of a further shift. The eighteenth century
is going up and the seventeenth perhaps a little down, new
dimensions of the romantics are being explored, the market
for Tennyson may be a little brisker. And so on. All this is to
be expected and is healthy. The notion that criticism is or
can be an exact science, that eternal rules can be discovered
and set out by the critic, is a superstition that—though
prophecy is a chancy business—is unlikely to captivate anyone in the future. Such force as the superstition had was
drawn from a radical misunderstanding of the cautious empiricism of Aristotle in the *Poetics*. As the temporal perspective shifts, as the pressures and interests of civilization
change, as the practice of criticism exercises its pull on the
work of original writers and as the work of these writers
modifies the sensibilities of critics and provides them with
new occasions for reflection, so, inevitably, a battle of the
books is provoked. There follow skirmishes, ambushes,
pitched battles, victories and defeats, revolutions and counter-
revolutions. If one were to suggest, then, that there is a
*malaise* of criticism, and were to explain what he meant by
pointing to ferocious disputes over method and over the
place of this or that writer in the canon, this would indicate
an odd use of the word *malaise*. If this be the sickness of
criticism, criticism can never be healthy.

All the same, when we survey, in all its brilliance and
complexity, the field of criticism written in English, feelings
of anxiety may be provoked that are not altogether neurotic.
The point of criticism—this is surely a truism—is by

analysis, interpretation and comparison to make specific works of literature more luminous and more arresting, and thus more available, to those whose native wit cultivated by education inclines them to the experience of literature. And criticism is an important business, not only because the experience of literature is in itself valuable and needs no extrinsic justification, but also because this experience is one of the sources of spiritual health; it fortifies and illuminates, it is a mark of civilization; and of all the arts literature is the most complete commentary upon the greatness and wretchedness of man.

One source of a certain uneasiness lies in the fact that criticism is so much a vast academic industry eccentric to the main concerns and interests of our civilization. (I am not here concerned with the criticism to be found in the respectable Sunday newspapers and in the weeklies. This is a topic in itself, and an important one, offering rich themes to the sociologist and the moralist. Some of it is of course the work of academics, and some of it is—surprisingly, in view of the conditions under which it has to be done—of a respectable quality; but it is necessarily too hurried and too much played upon by the peculiar influences of political groups, literary cliques and commercial interests to be taken, as criticism, with great seriousness.) To say of criticism that it is academic, and an industry, is not as such to say something disobliging about it; and as to its being eccentric to the main concerns and interests of our civilization, this may be to pass an oblique and damaging comment upon our civilization.

In characterizing criticism as an academic industry I have the following points in mind. Its being academic means that its audience is also very largely academic. Critics are read by other critics or by would-be critics; and a work of criticism, no matter what its merits as a piece of guidance for the reader whose *métier* is not that of a critic, tends to function as a whetstone upon which other critics sharpen their wits. The largest and most horrendous example of what I have in mind is to be found in the United States: the running battle between the "New Critics"—Brooks, Tate, Wimsatt and the rest—and the Chicago critics under the generalship of Professor R. S. Crane. A consequence of this is that criticism becomes enmeshed in an elaborate scholasticism, serpentine, repetitive, fruitful in fine technical distinctions and subtle shifts of ground, something of which only the professional can hope to gain a commanding view; and he may be indisposed to strive after such a view, for there are his own theses to elaborate and defend. All this is much more evident in the United States than in this country; but in this as in other fields it is arguable that the looser and less technically advanced models to be found here will soon be displaced. Its being an industry arises out of its being an academic profession in a period when, in the universities, the study of arts and letters is more and more pursued by the method of specialization; and the production of works of scholarship and criticism is geared to the academic machinery by which reputations are made and professional advancement secured. Given the size of the academic community, and the moral values it sucks in from the society that maintains it, it is hard to see how this could be otherwise. But it does mean that criticism is written for the academic community rather than for the cultivated public, with all the large consequences that this entails.

Critics commonly give us only their finished products, not their working notebooks. Professor Tillotson's work on Pope [1] is something very close to a working notebook, in which he not only sets down a mass of comment upon the text and content of Pope's works and of those of his contemporaries, but also brings in a great deal of related comment upon such nineteenth-century writers as Newman and

1. Geoffrey Tillotson, *Pope and Human Nature*, 1958.

Thackeray whose work Professor Tillotson has been studying in recent years. It has all the interest of such a notebook, with some of its defects. As he is one of our best scholarly critics, it shows us more of the workings of his mind than a more finished work would do. In its candour—which is almost, at times, ingenuousness—it reveals the presuppositions and working methods of a scholarly critic and brings out the strength and the weakness of both. Altogether, the spectacle is both fascinating and instructive: fascinating in its revelation of the depth and spread of a scholarly and sensitive mind: instructive, in so far as some of the virtues and vices of the academic critic are there exemplified. A consideration of it is thus highly relevant to the general points I have advanced concerning the state of criticism. If an excuse has to be offered for treating Tillotson's work as a casebook as well as a notebook, it is that as one of the richest products of scholarly criticism today it illuminates and illustrates the predicaments of the academic study of literature.

Twenty years ago Tillotson published *On the Poetry of Pope*. This was in itself a masterly work, and was of historic importance both as a sign and a cause of that revaluation of the work of Pope which is now pretty well taken for granted and which has its splendid monument in the Twickenham Edition, a venture with which Tillotson has himself been closely connected. In the present work he is concerned, he explains, not so much with Pope's "methods of expression" as with "the material Pope expresses".[2] That is, he is concerned with certain key concepts—"nature", "truth", "the beautiful", "man" and so on—employed or presupposed by Pope and with the moral and social implications of Pope's use of these concepts.[3] This is an inquiry of great interest and importance, and of great difficulty. Pope is so much a

2. Ibid., p. v.
3. Tillotson does in fact concern himself a good deal, especially in the later chapters, with Pope's "methods of expression", and what he has to say on this topic is always happy and instructive.

central figure in the culture of his day that an inquiry into his use of such concepts should tell us quite as much about his period as it does about Pope's mind and should thus enable us to handle more easily a variety of philosophical and religious problems of interest to the student of the English eighteenth century; and in so far as the thought of this period helps to form the thought of the nineteenth century—and that it does so is increasingly recognized—the usefulness of the inquiry has no obviously determinable limits. The difficulty about this inquiry is that it seems to require analytical abilities that are quite other than the analytical abilities of the literary critic and a wide acquaintance with the history of the concepts which are being discussed. Concepts such as those Tillotson is interested in do not have the bound uses of the concepts of mathematics or natural science; their uses are immensely complex and their lines of ancestry run far back; and a part of the understanding of their complexity is the understanding of their ancestry. The ability to use a set of concepts or to understand the use of a set of concepts is not the same thing as the ability to state what these uses are. Speaking a language is itself a highly complex performance; but though it is characteristic of one who speaks a language that he is continually heeding a vast number of rules, it is not a characteristic of the expert user of a language that he is able to state any of the rules he continually heeds. Of course, very useful work can be done—as by Lovejoy, Marjorie Nicolson, Bredvold and others in the United States—in which the main emphasis is laid upon the genealogy and history of ideas, and in which the kind of analysis proper to a philosophical study is eschewed or only lightly touched upon; and such work helps both the philosopher and the critic to avoid anachronistic approaches to particular writers. Philosophers, for example, have too frequently discussed the supposed atheism of Thomas Hobbes without any recognition that he is linked on the one hand with the nominalist theology of the late Middle Ages and on the other with the "mortalist" speculations of the sectarian thinkers of his time. Nineteenth-century Shakespearian criticism was on the whole ignorant of, or set aside as unimportant, the medieval background Shakespeare took for granted, and (for example) manufactured sentimental problems about the attitude of the young Henry V to Falstaff, problems that do not arise in this form if we reckon with Shakespeare's idea of kingship.

Tillotson, then, has taken on a formidable job in attempting to give an account of Pope's use of certain concepts. I shall confine myself to what he has to say about Pope's use of "nature"; and I shall try to show that what he has to say will not do, either as an account of the concept which Pope received or as an account of Pope's use of the concept; and here I shall confine myself to one early work, the *Essay on Criticism*.

Tillotson distinguishes two senses of "nature". First, there is "Nature" defined as follows:

> I am aware of Pope as a poet who subscribed to the old belief that poets put as much human nature as possible into their poems, that they look to mankind—or Nature, as it was called in Pope's day—for their theme. . . . Nature, when it was not human hands and feet, was, and of course is still, that quantum of the mind-and-heart which all men—past, present, and in theory future—hold in common.[4]

This is not very much like a definition, but Tillotson himself says he has in the passage I have quoted "defined" the sense in which he is going to use "Nature". Another sense of "nature" is intended when the capital letter is omitted: this is "nature" as meaning "merely the material universe".[5] Later, Tillotson glances at the history of the term,[6] referring to Aristotle, Cicero, St. Vincent of Lerins (at a further stage of the book he even glides into treating the *quod ubique, quod semper, quod ab omnibus* of St. Vincent as "St. Vincent's

4. *Pope and Human Nature*, p. 1.
5. Ibid., p. v.                    6. Ibid., pp. 19 ff.

definition of Nature" [7]), Quintilian, Longinus, Shakespeare, Dryden, Milton, Davenant, Hobbes, Wordsworth, Johnson, Tennyson, Thackeray, Arnold, George Eliot, Charles Reade and Voltaire. All these writers could certainly with propriety be cited in a history of the concept of nature. What is somewhat puzzling and even alarming is that Tillotson seems to imply that in all these cases "nature" has a roughly similar connotation; equally puzzling and equally alarming, if we were really concerned with the history of the concept, is the omission of any reference to the three writers (in English) whose discussions of the concept are really decisive : Hooker, Locke and Hume. But in fact we are not at all concerned with the history of the concept. If we really were concerned with the history of the concept we should have to bring out that Aristotle's *physis*, for example, is not at all the same concept as Hobbes's "nature" and entails a different and contradictory set of logical consequences. All that Tillotson wishes to say is that the literature which common consent places in the canon is concerned with the exploration and statement of what is common to men considered as desiring and passionate, feeling and rational—he quotes, and this is the heart of his contention, Arnold's tag about "the great primary human affections" which are the subject-matter of great literature. That this is often what writers have meant when they have made use of "nature" as a critical criterion is true; but it is profoundly unilluminating as a comment upon the history of the concept from Aristotle to the nineteenth century; and, as I shall show, it is inadequate as a help to the analysis of Pope's use of the concept.

I shall now examine the *Essay on Criticism*, with the *Essay on Man* perhaps the most "philosophical" of Pope's works, in order to establish two points : that Pope is not relying upon the concept of nature as defined by Tillotson; and that

7. Ibid., p. 72.

Pope *uses* the ambiguities of the concept—ambiguities which arise out of its complex history—in order to frame, not a critical argument [8] in any way to be compared with the critical work of Aristotle or Johnson or Coleridge, but a poem capable of evoking an attitude to criticism and to the subject-matter of criticism.

In so far as we attempt to analyse the *Essay* into its component critical doctrines and arguments, it turns out to be a mosaic of scraps from Aristotle, Horace, Boileau and other critics. An early passage appears to contain advice on the practice of criticism.

> First follow Nature, and your judgment frame
> By her just standard, which is still the same :
> Unerring NATURE, still divinely bright,
> One clear, unchang'd, and universal light,
> Life, force, and beauty, must to all impart,
> At once the source, and end, and test of Art.
> Art from that fund each just supply provides;
> Works without show, and without pomp presides.
> In some fair body thus th' informing soul
> With spirits feeds, with vigor fills the whole,
> Each motion guides, and ev'ry nerve sustains;
> Itself unseen, but in th' effects remains.
>
> (ll. 68–79)

Plainly these lines contain no useful advice : they express, with great vigour and precision, an *attitude*; and it would be a mistake to ask in too peremptory a voice : What does it mean ? i.e. What propositions expressible in other words can be squeezed out of the passage ? It is precisely as the expression of an attitude to poetry and the criticism of poetry that

8. Professor Sutherland seems to me profoundly wrong (about Pope, not perhaps about Dryden) where he writes : "The poetry of Dryden, Pope, Thomson, Johnson, Gray, Goldsmith is not *merely* a poetry of good sense, but good sense it is. The poetical structure is not held together by emotional stresses but by a sort of *steel framework of intellectual argument*." (My italics.) James Sutherland, *A Preface to Eighteenth Century Poetry*, 1948, p. 161. I may add that this is one of the few places where I would venture to disagree with Professor Sutherland.

the *Essay* is impressive, both as illustrating, in action as it were, Pope's sensibility and intelligence, and as illuminating the valuations of the literary society of which Pope was so self-conscious a member.[9]

The attitude Pope seeks to inculcate at the beginning of the poem will be—whatever the superficial *logical* relation of the passage to the rest of the poem—*rhetorically* decisive.

> 'Tis hard to say, if greater want of skill
> Appear in writing or in judging ill;
> But, of the two, less dang'rous is th' offence
> To tire our patience, than mislead our sense.
> Some few in that, but numbers err in this,
> Ten censure wrong for one who writes amiss;
> A fool might once himself alone expose,
> Now one in verse makes many more in prose.

> 'Tis with our judgments as our watches, none
> Go just alike, yet each believes his own.
> In Poets as true Genius is but rare,
> True Taste as seldom is the Critic's share;
> Both must alike from Heav'n derive their light,
> These born to judge, as well as those to write.
> Let such teach others who themselves excel,
> And censure freely who have written well.
> Authors are partial to their wit, 'tis true,
> But are not Critics to their judgment too?

> Yet if we look more closely, we shall find
> Most have the seeds of judgment in their mind :
> Nature affords at least a glimm'ring light;
> The lines, tho' touch'd but faintly, are drawn right.
> But as the slightest sketch, if justly trac'd,
> Is by ill-colouring but the more disgrac'd,
> So by false learning is good sense defac'd :

9. Tillotson makes an excellent point when he observes : "[Pope's] unfolding of a poet's personality is a new thing in English poetry, being completer than that of Donne, who from this point of view is his strongest predecessor." *Pope and Human Nature*, p. 142.

Some are bewilder'd in the maze of schools,
And some made coxcombs Nature meant but fools.
In search of wit these lose their common sense,
And then turn Critics in their own defence:
Each burns alike, who can, or cannot write,
Or with a Rival's, or an Eunuch's spite.
All fools have still an itching to deride,
And fain would be upon the laughing side.
If Maevius scribble in Apollo's spight,
There are, who judge still worse than he can write.

(ll. 1–35)

We are given first a picture of the poet, identifying himself with all reasonable men ("*our* patience . . . *our* sense"),
surrounded by a horde of, in the main, foolish critics. They
are perhaps more than foolish. They may be *dangerous* (l. 3),
even if they are also, and this is stressed in the lines immediately following, obscenely ludicrous.

Some have at first for Wits, then Poets past,
Turn'd critics next, and prov'd plain fools at last.
Some neither can for Wits nor Critics pass,
As heavy mules are neither horse nor ass.
Those half-learn'd witlings, numerous in our isle,
As half-form'd insects on the banks of Nile;
Unfinish'd things, one knows not what to call,
Their generation's so equivocal:
To tell 'em would an hundred tongues require,
Or one vain wit's, that might a hundred tire.

(ll. 36–45)

The " 'Tis hard to say" of the beginning is designed to give
an impression of fair-mindedness; but with the arrival of the
images of the mule and the abortive insects we know that
the poet is taking sides, though the initial assumption of
fairness and Olympian detachment somehow persuades us
that he has a right to bestow praise and blame.

Next: original endowment is not a matter of skill, at least,
not of our skill. The comparison between "judgments" and

"watches" (this figure has an ancestry and a posterity) suggests that "Heaven's" skill is in question, that is, the rules by which human nature has been framed are a *techne* analogous to the art of making clockwork mechanisms.[1] Both the critic and the poet are the creatures of Heaven; and this carries with it the implication that Pope is exploring, and describing in an authoritative way, a providential order; but the whole tone is that of one who surveys the scene rather than that of one who participates in it.

Nature provides for all. But what a botch most make of this provision! No doubt "Most have the seeds of judgment in their mind"; but the impression Pope conveys is of a swarming multitude of malignant fools.

By line 45 Pope has thus created the impression—though this is not what he explicitly *says*—that the true critic, even one who is potentially such, is a rare creature who, no matter now rich his natural endowments, may more easily go wrong than not. There is thus a deliberately created tension between Nature's provision, the providential order expounded with authority by Pope, and the presence everywhere of human perversity. This dramatic tension is commended to us by the double attitude expressed: on the one hand, the poet is, like the rest of us, painstakingly peering through the gloom of a teasingly difficult subject, on the other, he has an Olympian, god-like power of surveying the scene with a penetrating gaze and estimating the capacities and performances of the actors. This is calculated both to reassure us—after all, he is one of us, he has his difficulties too—and impress us—he speaks with authority. And we are disposed (so far as we submit to the mood evoked by the poem) to accept the authority precisely because it seems initially not to be claimed.

The vehicle of the argument is a diagram rather than a

1. This idea is worked out in Hobbes's Introduction to *Leviathan*. "Nature" is here "Art" in the sense of a *techne*, to be understood in the light of the mechanical arts. Nothing could be farther from the Aristotelian *physis*, with its emphasis on the analogy of organism.

picture. The poet of genius is represented as surrounded by a swarm of abortions and monstrosities, the bad critics, those who have choked in themselves "the seeds of judgment". And in spite of its being plainly suggested that the endowments of the poet and the critic are different, the large assumption is made, and enforced upon us by the very fact that this is a poem, that the poet is here competent to establish the rationale, the limitations and the methods of criticism.

An attitude having been established, a mood induced, Pope now advances to an elaborate disquisition on "nature", and this occupies the remainder of the first part of the *Essay*.

"Nature" and "the natural" are among the trickiest of concepts and if Pope were concerned with anything at all resembling a philosophical analysis and account, his first task would be to analyse what is in fact a large and unruly family of concepts into its individual members, lest the discussion should founder upon the ambiguities of the concepts. "Natural", for example, can mean "primitive", "normal", "right", "good", "uncivilized", "civilized", "factual", "existing", and so on. It is pointless to ask what the *real* meaning of the term is: all these meanings are perfectly good since they all represent established uses. Now, Pope's procedure is the direct opposite of the philosophical. He *uses* the ambiguity of the concept, its being capable of suggesting a vast unruly family, to achieve a certain result.

Lines 68–79 have already been quoted on p. 177 above. The poem continues:

> Some, to whom Heav'n in wit has been profuse,
> Want as much more to turn it to its use;
> For wit and judgment often are at strife,
> Tho' meant each other's aid, like man and wife.
> 'Tis more to guide, than spur the Muse's steed;
> Restrain his fury, than provoke his speed;
> The winged courser, like a gen'rous horse,
> Shews most true mettle when you check his course.

Those RULES of old discover'd, not devis'd,
Are Nature still, but Nature methodiz'd;
Nature, like Liberty, is but restrain'd
By the same Laws which first herself ordain'd.

Hear how learn'd Greece her useful rules indites,
When to repress, and when indulge our flights:
High on Parnassus' top her sons she show'd,
And pointed out those arduous paths they trod;
Held from afar, aloft, th' immortal prize,
And urg'd the rest by equal steps to rise.
Just precepts thus from great examples giv'n,
She drew from them what they deriv'd from Heav'n.

(ll. 80–99)

These senses of "nature" may be distinguished. (1) A quasi-deity, infallible, unchanging, illuminating in virtue of its deity ("divinely bright"). (2) A source of power ("Life, force, and beauty"). (3) A repository of criteria for judgment ("your judgment frame/By her just standard"). (4) The *source* of art, perhaps as providing rules for a *techne*, certainly source as a fountain of energy, as the shaper—demiurge—of the world and men: through vagueness we can hold all these ideas as it were in solution. (5) The *end* of art: perhaps no more is suggested than that art has a purpose and that this purpose enjoys cosmic approval. (6) Nature *is* Art and Art *is* Nature; the two concepts are run together in lines 74–9. This is confirmed if we pass on to lines 88–91. Here it is said that the rules of art (to be summarily stated as: Don't let wit and judgment get out of balance—wit being roughly the original energy of the intellect, judgment the capacity to direct the original energy into particular channels) are "Nature ... Nature methodiz'd".

If we want to ask what kind of a noun, here, "Nature" is, what it is used to represent, it is plain that there is more than one answer to the question. But this would surely be an inappropriate question. All the answers are necessary to

Pope. In order to achieve the kind of effect he aims at Nature must simultaneously be God, the world, the soul of the world, the rules for the production of art, the standards of the critic, a reservoir of cosmic energy, the inspiration of the poet; even, as he begins to make clear at the end of the passage cited, and then goes on to elaborate, a particular body of literature, sometimes the work of one author, namely, Homer.

> When first young Maro in his boundless mind
> A work t' outlast immortal Rome design'd,
> Perhaps he seem'd above the Critic's law,
> And but from Nature's fountain scorn'd to draw :
> But when t' examine ev'ry part he came,
> Nature and Homer were, he found, the same.
>
> (ll. 130–5)

An interesting specific use by Pope of one of the ambiguities is provided by the reference to the rules of ancient literature, especially Homer, as providing "natural" guidance for the poet. This must cause difficulties and it is to be expected that Pope will provide himself with an escape-clause. Of course, he does so.

> Some beauties yet no Precepts can declare,
> For there's a happiness as well as care.
> Music resembles Poetry, in each
> Are nameless graces which no methods teach,
> And which a master-hand alone can reach.
> If, where the rules not far enough extend,
> (Since rules were made but to promote their end)
> Some lucky licence answer to the full
> Th' intent propos'd, that Licence is a rule.
> Thus Pegasus, a nearer way to take,
> May boldly deviate from the common track.
> Great wits sometimes may gloriously offend,
> And rise to faults true Critics dare not mend;
> From vulgar bounds with grave disorder part,
> And snatch a grace beyond the reach of art . . .
>
> (ll. 141–55)

Now, the interest of this particular escape-clause is that it doesn't, as one might expect, rend the texture of the poem: for spontaneity, beauty uncovenanted for and uncontrived, that which is, as Pope perceives and states, analogous to Grace in the language of theology, are held within the general scope of the idea of Nature by the particular idea of Nature as a fountain of psychic energy; from such a fountain we should expect to draw spontaneity rather than rules. But the conflation of Nature as infinitely various and as predictably regular enables Pope to overcome what might otherwise be a destructive paradox.

In the last paragraph of the First Part—

> Still green with bays each ancient Altar stands
> Above the reach of sacrilegious hands

—Pope stresses the charm and prestige of classical culture under the image of the supernatural, though it is the supernatural domesticated by centuries of humanistic education in a Christian society. But with this ending, the disorderly junk-shop of concepts he has assembled—it is in fact a résumé of all those traditions in which the words *physis* and *natura* have had a role—is given an appearance of order and a sacred character. And Pope takes the opportunity to give himself a central place in the tradition, and to re-emphasize the combination of humility with authority he has imposed upon us at the beginning of the poem, in the closing lines of the First Part:

> Hail, Bards triumphant! born in happier days;
> Immortal heirs of universal praise!
> Whose honours with increase of ages grow,
> As streams roll down, enlarging as they flow;
> Nations unborn your mighty names shall sound,
> And worlds applaud that must not yet be found!
> O may some spark of your celestial fire,
> The last, the meanest of your sons inspire,
> (That on weak wings, from far, pursues your flights;

Glows while he reads, but trembles as he writes)
To teach vain Wits a science little known,
T' admire superior sense, and doubt their own!

(ll. 189–200)

Pope is "the last, the meanest of your sons"; but he is a *son*, not an interloper in the family; and he prays to be a teacher, for it is he who is to instruct the "vain Wits".

With the Second Part of the *Essay* there is a change of tone and of atmosphere, and a conceptual change as well. One way of putting the change would be to say that there is a shift of level from the *cosmic* to the *moral*, from *natura naturans* and *natura naturata* to Nature as a compendium of the rules of prudence and morality. The shift is not complete; and it is interesting to note that in so far as Nature is still conceived as a creative force she has now a somewhat malign touch.

Of all the causes which conspire to blind
Man's erring judgment, and misguide the mind,
What the weak head with strongest bias rules,
Is *Pride*, the never-failing vice of fools.
Whatever Nature has in worth deny'd,
She gives in large recruits of needful Pride ...

(ll. 201–6)

This is to make Nature a fountain of stupidity.

I shall not offer a detailed analysis of the rest of the poem. My main purposes: to bring out the complexities and ambiguities of the concept of nature; to suggest that these complexities and ambiguities are rooted in the history of the concept; to show that the structure of the poem is not a "steel framework of intellectual argument" but a wonderfully skilful exploitation of the conceptual ambiguities: have been accomplished by the analysis so far given.

We are now in a position to see the inadequacy of Tillotson's definitions and general account of "nature". He selects one use—that which is common to all men at all times—as central and primary, another—"the material universe", *natura naturata*—as the main secondary use; whereas it is clear from an examination of the *Essay on Criticism* alone that Pope's family of concepts is much richer and more various and that from the standpoint of poetic analysis, to say nothing of the history of ideas, Tillotson's account will not do.

Tillotson makes a number of positive mistakes as a consequence of his failure fully to explore the concepts Pope is using. For example, he quotes the famous passage from the sixth of Newman's *Discourses on the Scope and Nature of University Education.*

> Quarry the granite rock with razors, or moor the vessel with a thread of silk; then may you hope with such keen and delicate instruments as human knowledge and human reason to contend against those giants, the passion and the pride of man.

He comments: "Indeed, if pressed, Pope might have agreed with Newman." [2] The fact is that in this matter Pope and Newman belong to two absolutely distinct traditions of thought. For Pope, "reason" exercises a powerful influence upon conduct.

> Two Principles in human nature reign;
> Self-love, to urge, and Reason, to restrain;
>
> .        .        .        .
>
> Self-love, the spring of motion, acts the soul;
> Reason's comparing balance rules the whole. [3]

The moral life is for Pope, as it was for Milton, a battle between "passion" and "reason". Newman, on the contrary, is in the passage cited echoing (whether he is fully conscious of this or not) the doctrine of Hume, who did so much to

2. *Pope and Human Nature*, p. 47.
3. *An Essay on Man*, Epistle II, ll. 53, 54 and 59, 60.

shape his early philosophical development, the doctrine, namely, "that reason alone can never be a motive to any action of the will; and . . . that it can never oppose passion in the direction of the will".[4] It is true, Newman gives the doctrine a new appearance by setting it in a context which is not that of Hume; but the ancestry of Newman's handling of the topic is clear and the logical nuance upon which Newman's point rests was quite unknown to Pope.

Again, he quotes Lovejoy's observation that "the Roman jurists had . . . identified *jus naturale* with *jus gentium*" (in itself a perfectly correct observation), without pointing out —what is crucial for the whole history of Natural Law— that the later Stoics, and later the Fathers and the scholastic theologians, and later still the natural law schools of the seventeenth and eighteenth centuries, had expressly distinguished between the *jus naturale* and the *jus gentium*; arguing that certain institutions and practices that were certainly a part of the *jus gentium* (notably slavery, private property, and the use of coercive power by the State) were contrary to the *jus naturale*. The *jus naturale* is thus conceived as a criterion for distinguishing the good from the bad parts of the *jus gentium*; and the dominant tradition in natural law is delivered, whatever logical difficulties it may encounter, from the vulgarity of "whatever is, is right". In fact, the tension between the Natural conceived as the Ideal and the Natural conceived as the Actual is important even in Pope.[5]

Where Tillotson treats of Pope's "methods of expression" rather than "the material Pope expresses" he is, as in *On the Poetry of Pope*, superb. An especially fine chapter is that on "Man, Poetry, and Pope's Poetry", which contains a penetrating discussion of Pope's language and word-order, use of metre and use of literary forms. He so worships Pope that

4. David Hume, *A Treatise of Human Nature*, Book II, Part III, Section III.

5. Cf. the discussion of the State of Nature in *An Essay on Man*, Epistle III. Here there is little confusion of the brute universality of fact with the universality of the moral order.

he is at times inclined to claim too much for him. He exaggerates unnecessarily, for Pope is great enough not to need this kind of extravagance, when he writes as follows of his satirical verse:

> If he elected to be a satirist, he saw to it that none of his poetic gifts went unemployed; he directed them all into his satire. This is what makes it unique: it is as if a score of poets had written it contributing their individual gifts to it as friends and strangers contributed coloured stones to his grotto: it is as if Virgil and Milton, Marvell, Keats and Tennyson had collaborated with Horace, and Dryden, and Swift.[6]

It is this extravagance in his estimate of Pope's achievement that accounts for his evasion of a problem that must be looked at by anyone who attempts a critical estimate of the poetry. When Matthew Arnold said that Dryden and Pope were "classics of an age of prose" he was wrong, and badly wrong, as a first reading of, say, the second of the *Moral Essays* ("Of the Characters of Women") or of *Eloisa to Abelard* or of the close of *The Dunciad* is enough to show. But wrong as Arnold is, he has a genuine point in mind, though it is not the one he makes. In the last analysis we have to say that Shakespeare and Donne and Marvell, and Wordsworth and Coleridge, are not simply excellent poets in a different mode from that of Pope: they are in a sense more genuinely poetic in a demonstrable sense. When in his essay in *The Rambler* Johnson criticizes Macbeth's speech—

> Come, thick night!
> And pall thee in the dunnest smoke of hell,
> That my keen knife see not the wound it makes;
> Nor heav'n peep through the blanket of the dark,
> To cry, Hold, hold!

—on the ground that "dun", "knife" and "peep through the blanket" are low expressions, he tells us a great deal about the age of Pope and about the limitations of even the greatest

6. *Pope and Human Nature*, p. 237.

poetry of the age, that of Pope himself. The limitations of this poetry are the limitations of an entire culture, limitations which show themselves in politics, philosophy and religion, as well as in poetry: the vital connection between the language of poetry and common speech which is a ground of the vigour and power to move of Shakespeare's verse is almost broken. We may illustrate these limitations by returning to the *Essay on Criticism* which is in the modern jargon something of a cultural manifesto. In the course of a discussion of style and diction Pope writes:

> Expression is the dress of thought, and still
> Appears more decent, as more suitable;
> A vile conceit in pompous words express'd
> Is like a clown in regal purple dress'd:
> For diff'rent styles with different subjects sort,
> As sev'ral garbs with country, town, and court.
>
> (ll. 318–23)

There are two points to notice here. Pope expresses the characteristic theory, influential from at least the time of Hobbes down to our own day, that "thought" is related to "words" as the body to clothes or as (on the Platonic or the Cartesian model) the soul to the body. This is more than a theoretical blunder: it adversely affects poetic practice, since the supposition of the poet is that the distinctive devices of poetry are embellishments of thoughts that could be expressed, with less elegance, it is true, but with no serious diminution of intellectual content, in prose. On all this the most penetrating comment is that contained in Wordsworth's aphorism: "Words are not thought's dress but its incarnation." That is, words are to thought as the body is to the soul, on the Aristotelian and not the Cartesian model. The other point to note is the parallel, drawn by Pope, between "styles" and the clothes appropriate to "country, town and court". These are not three divisions of the nation, but three divisions of polite society. The nation, which talks the language

189

of knives and blankets, bitches, black-puddings and cow-heels,[7] is excluded from the poetic cosmos. English society under the Whig oligarchy was split in a way that the cruder society of Shakespeare's day was not; and the split was not only within society; it was within the cultivated man, too; and the price paid is, as Wordsworth, perhaps more than any other critic, perceived, a loss of depth and imaginative power. We may again illustrate this from the *Essay on Criticism*. Of the unity which the best "work of Wit" will have, Pope writes:

> In Wit, as Nature, what affects our hearts
> Is not th' exactness of peculiar parts;
> 'Tis not a lip, or eye, we beauty call,
> But the joint force and full result of all.
> Thus when we view some well-proportion'd dome,
> (The world's just wonder, and ev'n thine, O Rome!)
> No single parts unequally surprise,
> All comes united to th' admiring eyes;
> No monstrous height, or breadth, or length appear;
> The Whole at once is bold and regular.
>
> (ll. 243–52)

This contempt for York and Canterbury and Chartres and Cologne exactly parallels the contemporary attitude to Chaucer and Shakespeare. Neo-classicism is not seen for what it is, despite its splendid achievements in all the arts: a narrowing and impoverishment of the human spirit.

Earlier I remarked that Tillotson has presented us with what is in effect one of his notebooks, and it may be that some of the criticisms I have pressed are inappropriate to this genre of critical writing. It is nevertheless true that in its unguarded character, in the absence of the caveats that one might have expected to find in a more finished work, some of the difficulties of the academic criticism of literature are betrayed.

7. Cf. the discussion of the difficulties of Fenton (Pope's collaborator in the translation of Homer) over a passage in the *Odyssey*, in Sutherland, op. cit., pp. 88, 89.

It seems evident that in the academic study of literature—as in the academic study of philosophy—the history of ideas is seriously neglected; and that this is a consequence of excessive specialization. I have cited a number of instances in Tillotson's book, where this enormously learned and sensitive scholar fails to handle the *literary* problem well through a failure to grasp the history of the concept of nature. Other illustrations could have been given from works by other men. A trivial instance is provided by Mr. Raymond Williams in his remarkable study, *Culture and Society 1780–1950*. In a discussion of Burke, Williams writes:

> Burke's attack [i.e. upon the Revolution in France] was upon democracy, *as we now commonly understand it*.[8] (My italics.)

If the "we" means, as it surely must, the English and the Americans, the French and the Swiss, this can be seen to be wrong simply by noting that neither the theory nor the practice of democracy as "we" understand it could have been known to Burke or to anyone living at that time. But the important point is a deeper one: that Burke had in mind, just as the Jacobins had in mind, democracy in the classical sense, the democracy of the Greek cities, the democracy for which (or so it was believed) the Roman plebs had struggled. This is democracy understood as direct rule by the poor and its theoretical expression in our own period is the dictatorship of the proletariat. The domination of Burke's mind, and of the European mind in general, by classical discussions and models may be a misfortune; but it is an unmistakable feature of the history of ideas. Later than Burke, in the case of Macaulay (for example, in his speeches on the Reform Bill), even in the case of Bagehot, the extension of the franchise beyond the middle class, that is, an approach towards democracy in "our" sense, was feared because it was thought to carry with it a danger of democracy in the classical sense, and with it the expropriation of the bourgeoisie. Later, Wil-

8. Raymond Williams, *Culture and Society 1780–1950*, 1958, p. 4.

liams notes that Burke "argued that the tendency of democracy was to tyranny";[9] and it is apposite to remark that this is, as well as a sound prediction of the course of the French Revolution, a commonplace of Greek political theory, and that this theory is pretty certainly one of the sources of Burke's confidence.

The moral of this might seem to be that we lack in this country anything like the strenuous pursuit of the history of ideas as this is understood in the United States and finely represented by Lovejoy and others. A centre for the study of the history of ideas would certainly be a good thing and it is immaterial, or so I think, whether this is nurtured in departments of philosophy or history or English literature. But something more modest could accomplish a good deal. Academic persons are always discussing the dangers of specialization, and these dangers are real. The retreat from specialization could, if it ever took place, be just as dangerous; it could lead to no more than *haute vulgarisation* and slipshod syntheses. My argument has been that in the interests of e.g. literary studies quite strictly conceived, the help of other specialists, as fellow teachers and co-operating scholars, is desirable. If we are to discuss the concept of nature in Pope, the relevance of Hartleian psychology to Wordsworth, the use of Scotist concepts by Hopkins, it is essential that this should be done in the light of what the professional scholar has to say, not simply for the sake of accuracy, but for the sake, too, of the interpretative and critical task. It may be that the establishment in university departments of English literature of teaching posts in the history of ideas would be a useful first step.[1]

9. Ibid., p. 8.
1. Of course, much has already been done in a variety of ways. There are Professor Willey's useful *Background* books, very much in the spirit of Leslie Stephen's pioneer and still indispensable works on the thinkers of the eighteenth century and on the English Utilitarians. Such works as D. G. James's *Scepticism and Poetry* and *The Romantic Comedy* represent important work in the exploration of interconnected literary and philosophical themes. Much recent work on Shakespeare—I have in mind, for instance, Miss Parker's *The Slave of Life*—exemplifies the approach I am

## MR. TILLOTSON AND MR. POPE

An apology is perhaps due to Tillotson for making his rich book an occasion for a somewhat carping sermon. Collingwood once said that the only writers he bothered to criticize were those whose names he wished to mention *honoris causa*. This must emphatically be true of any mention of Tillotson. His work, so widely ranging and so informed in the field of eighteenth- and nineteenth-century studies, is a continual rebuke to narrowness and pedantry.

1959

commending. In Miss Elizabeth Sewell's *The Field of Nonsense* we are presented with a mind of rare power in both literary and philosophical analysis. This list could be greatly prolonged. Again, we may expect a great deal of those universities where there are joint schools of philosophy and English literature and philosophy and history, in so far as these schools represent co-operation in scholarly work as well as in teaching.

# 10

## *Alciphron* and Apologetics

SOME Christians in every age have felt a compulsion to engage in apologetics. The mood which persuaded Tertullian to set Athens against Jerusalem, the Academy against the Church, has never persisted for long, though a modern school—the Dialectical Theology—derives from Kierkegaard the conviction that to explain, to defend, and to justify is to offer an insult to the Christian revelation. The very name of the school suggests the inadequacy of their contention. *Dialectic, Logos*; can we ever utter the words without at least an obscure sense of their power to set us in the presence of the subtle and penetrating Greek mind from which St. Augustine himself, so he tells us, learned everything except that the Word became flesh? It is true, the exception is so enormous and so awful that Kierkegaard's repudiation of apologetics has real point, though it is scarcely the point made by the Barthians, for it was Kierkegaard who said that Christianity was the perfection of the truly human.

The paradox of apologetics is that it is precisely in the ages of rationalism that rational explanation and defence seem to have no cutting edge. Butler's *Analogy of Religion* will always have readers; but however much it may have arrested the dissolution of Anglican theology in the eighteenth century into an amiable Deism, perhaps its real force was exercised, not directly, but as it was refined and made more supple by the intellect of John Henry Newman in the romantic nineteenth century. Certainly the works of lesser men than Butler were singularly flat. The apologist who draws a feeling of inner security from his confidence in the power of reason is often deeply influenced by the spirit of rationalism which nourishes his sceptical opponents. He faces the almost impossible task of enticing into a further dimension men who are very well satisfied—odiously so at times—with three. Butler measured the magnitude of the task with great accuracy, and this is one of the reasons for the persisting charm of the *Analogy* and the *Fifteen Sermons Preached at the Rolls Chapel*; but it is Berkeley who, in *Alciphron*, uncovered the roots of the scepticism of the period and indicated the modest though necessary place of the science of apologetics in the scheme of Christian theology.

The long dialogue, set in the landscape, depicted with affectionate care, of Rhode Island, is over. Alciphron and Lysicles, representative men of fashion, wits and sceptics, are gone about their business. Crito and Euphranor, the partisans of orthodoxy, remain and musingly reflect upon the many discussions in which the chief points at issue have been surveyed from every side. They are perhaps a little melancholy, for the sceptics have been unable to meet their arguments, and yet they have been brought no nearer Christianity by the dialectical drubbing administered to them. Crito then remarks that the root difficulty is that the infidelity of the "minute philosophers" is not rationally grounded: rationalism is a practical attitude, a commitment of the feelings and the will governed by other than rational considerations.

> Had men reasoned themselves into a wrong opinion, one might hope to reason them out of it. But this is not the case; the infidelity of minute philosophers seeming an effect of very different motives from thought and reason. Little incidents, vanity, disgust, humour, inclination, without the least assistance from reason, are often known to make infidels. Where the general tendency of a doctrine is disagreeable, the mind is prepared to relish and improve everything that with the least pretence seems to make against it. Hence the coarse manners of a country curate, the polite manners of a chaplain, the wit of a minute philosopher, a jest, a song, a tale, can serve instead

of a reason for infidelity. Bupalus preferred a rake in the church, and then made use of him as an argument against it. Vice, indolence, faction, and fashion produce minute philosophers, and mere petulancy not a few. Who then can expect a thing so irrational and capricious should yield to reason? [1]

Does this mean, then, that in disputing with the sceptics Crito and Euphranor have been engaged in a foolish and unfruitful enterprise? By no means.

It may, nevertheless, be worth while to argue against such men and expose their fallacies, if not for their own sake, yet for the sake of others; as it may lessen their credit, and prevent the growth of their sect, by removing a prejudice in their favour, which sometimes inclines others as well as themselves to think they have made a monopoly of human reason. [2]

Judgments on *Alciphron* have varied a good deal. For Professor Jessop, "as a work of art it stands supreme in the whole body of our English literature of philosophy, and perhaps supreme also in our literature of religious apologetics". [3] In the view of Professor Luce "it ranks with Hooker's *Ecclesiastical Polity*". [4] G. A. Johnston, on the other hand, considered that in *Alciphron* Berkeley's attitude (in so far as the dialogue is a polemic against Shaftesbury) was "unworthy of a moral philosopher", and was "that of the man whose prejudices make him incapable of appreciating whatever truth may exist in the opinions of those with whom he does not see eye to eye". [5] Professor John Wild, in his vast and curious work on Berkeley, even denies what is taken for granted by other commentators, namely, that *Alciphron* is a piece of apologetic. "No greater mistake", he

1. The Works of George Berkeley Bishop of Cloyne. Edited by A. A. Luce and T. E. Jessop. Volume Three. *Alciphron or the Minute Philosopher.* Edited by T. E. Jessop, 1950, p. 326.
2. Ibid.
3. Ibid., p. 2.
4. A. A. Luce, *The Life of George Berkeley Bishop of Cloyne,* 1949, p. 132.
5. G. A. Johnston, *The Development of Berkeley's Philosophy,* 1923, p. 314.

writes, "could be made than to think of the *Alciphron* as religious 'Apologetic' "; and he argues that a contemporary attack (by Benjamin Hoadly) gives a more accurate character-ization of the work than do the plaudits of its admirers.[6] Hoadly had described it as "the most plain attempt to bring obscurity and darkness into all science, as well as to make nonsense essential to religion, that the last age has produced".

Two questions seem worth consideration: how far *Alci-phron* is to be described correctly as Christian apologetic; and what the relation is between the doctrine, explicit and implicit, of *Alciphron* and the doctrine of the *Principles*— the question, that is, of the place of the work in the com-pleted structure of Berkeley's thought. Until the latter ques-tion is settled, the former cannot be answered with any assur-ance. Professor Wild's contention, for example, that the dialogue cannot properly be classified as apologetic, rests upon his argument that Berkeley's whole philosophy is a dialectical development which passes through a moment of absolute scepticism (*Alciphron* belongs to this "moment") to the transcendental philosophy which, like a vein of precious ore, lies hidden in the drossy bulk of *Siris*. However this may be—and perhaps the material upon which we must rely for a sound judgment in the matter is too exiguous ever to make possible a perfectly confident judgment—*Alciphron* offers a problem fascinating not only to the student of Berkeley's philosophy but also to those with a lively concern for the perennial task of justifying to the lazy, the indifferent and the hostile the deadly seriousness of religion. The Lenin of *Materialism and Empirio-Criticism* considered Berkeley the ancestor of all philosophical blockheads, the most subtle and sophistical defender of reactionary clericalism. To speak candidly, Lenin did not understand Berkeley very well and contraposed to Berkeley's epistemology a crude and fallacious theory of knowledge extracted from *Anti-Duehring*, and, more remotely, from Locke. But he was not wrong in think-

6. John Wild, *George Berkeley*, Cambridge, Mass., 1936, pp. 360. 361.

ing that any philosophy which saw in the world of nature a language that, deciphered, spoke of a creative and loving mind sustaining all things was a more dangerous threat to his own passionately nursed convictions than counter-revolutionary violence.

*Esse* is *percipi*, or *percipere*, does not as an explicit doctrine appear in *Alciphron*. The reader already familiar with the *Principles* and the *Three Dialogues* will see that there are places where its absence yet contrives to suggest its presence, as an empty room may retain the presence—the curtains still tremble, the looking-glass is still reflective—of the one who has just quitted it. Immaterialism breathes, as it were, through the prose, though it never speaks out. As a matter of tactics, Berkeley is in the right. To have bound his apologetic to the doctrine of immaterialism would have been to present his opponents with a perfect opportunity to divert the whole discussion from the main issues and to dismay most of the orthodox to whom immaterialism appeared as itself a form of scepticism. Experience has taught him that here even the most sympathetic grow uneasy. He does, however, carry over from his earlier work the view that all ideas are concrete and that an abstract idea is a contradiction in terms; and that which is an object for thought but lacks the concreteness of an idea is termed a notion. The explicit epistemological doctrine of *Alciphron* is that of the *New Theory of Vision*: "that the great Mover and Author of Nature constantly explaineth Himself to the eyes of men by the sensible intervention of arbitrary signs, which have no similitude or connection with the things signified".[7] That in sense-experience we are confronted with a language testifying to the existence, the activity, and the providential care of God he argues vehemently in the fourth of the dialogues. He bemuses the minute philosophers by persuading them to admit that our knowledge of other minds is inferential. "I do not see Alciphron, i.e. that individual thinking thing,

7. *Alciphron*, p. 157.

but only such visible signs and tokens as suggest and infer the being of that invisible thinking principle or soul." [8] If this be granted—Professor Ryle had not yet risen up to exorcize the Ghost in the Machine—then the visible universe, understood as a systematic whole composed of lesser systematic wholes (this ground is common to Berkeley and to his opponents and is of course emphasized by Shaftesbury, for Berkeley the type of all minute philosophers), "suggests and infers" the being of God, and with the greatest force and certainty.

"Some of its arguments," writes Professor Jessop in the introduction to his edition of *Alciphron*, "and perhaps all the principles of the argument, could be honestly reaffirmed today." [9] If among "the principles of the arguments" he includes the argument from design which *begins* with the postulate of a cosmic order, and the contention that our knowledge of other minds is inferential—a piece of vicious abstraction curious in one with so much feeling for the concrete as Berkeley, though it is forced upon him by his doctrine of ideas—he will find few other philosophers to agree with him. Indeed, setting aside the ethical content of the work and the practical rather than speculative concern, which is, as we have seen, fundamental for Berkeley, we may even agree with Professor Wild that in a sense *Alciphron* represents a moment of scepticism. This seems evident when Berkeley has to defend such mysteries as the Trinity and Incarnation. He sees that such mysteries cannot be reduced to clear and distinct ideas. Equally, he rejects the classic theory of analogical predication as it had been restated by his contemporary, Peter Browne. (Professor Jessop seems to think, though he is not perfectly explicit, that Berkeley was in the right as against Browne and that Browne did not understand the Schoolmen on the subject of the *analogia entis*. This seems doubtful; in particular, as Browne pointed out in the reply which Berkeley ignored, he seems not to

8. Ibid., p. 147.    9. Ibid., p. 8.

have grasped the crucial importance of the dictum that God is *extra omne genus*.) He comes in the end to explain the Christian mysteries in terms of the theory of signs which elsewhere he uses to show that mathematics and the natural sciences are not bodies of knowledge about abstract ideas and their relations, for there are no such things and there can therefore be no such relations, but systems of signs which we manipulate for predictive and practical ends. The verbal signs which we employ to designate the Christian mysteries can be used to encourage the life of virtue. They are directed primarily to the will and the test of their truth is a pragmatic one. Christianity and the vague Deism of the minute philosophers are to be judged by their respective fruits.

Not everyone may agree that Berkeley keeps his balance on this particular knife-edge. Having regard to the prejudices of the age, the veneration of a spurious clarity and the contempt and fear of the mysterious, it is remarkable that he should have made the attempt. It is the making of the attempt which discloses his philosophical magnanimity, a magnanimity which may appear rashness if we fasten upon particular Berkeleian contentions and then reject them as unsound; but it is all the same a true greatness of soul. Even if we judge, as perhaps we must, that simply as apologetic *Alciphron* is a relative failure and that to compare it with Butler's *Analogy* or with *Ecclesiastical Polity* is to do the book a poor service, it has rare qualities that spring in part from the passion with which Berkeley felt the pressure of his own genius as a philosopher. The settings and even the characters of the dialogues are perceived with a remarkable intensity, the dialectical exchanges are contrived with exquisite ease and grace, the rapid alternations of comedy and deep feeling give the whole work a certain richness of texture. These qualities are not only and not chiefly the fruits of calculation. They are not *arranged*, as so much in Shaftesbury is arranged. They spring from the effort to fuse the philosopher with the man, the fine critical intellect with the believer's simplicity.

It may seem an extravagance, but it is hard to think of any instances of the philosophical dialogue with which *Alciphron* can be compared in respect of general excellence, except the dialogues of Plato. In both instances strong feelings are dammed back, to be released, now into this channel, now into that; only the power of intelligence could master such feelings; and yet, although the intellect is master, it draws its authentic energies from feeling, intellect and feeling in the end seek the *same* object and satisfaction. Men, not discarnate minds, are philosophers; and to philosophize is to realize at the level of intellect, reflectively and at the same time with passion, what it is to be human.

> It seems an invincible proof of the power and excellency of the Christian religion that, without the help of those civil institutions and incentives to glory [Berkeley has been referring to the external rewards of virtue in classical antiquity], it should be able to inspire a phlegmatic people with the noblest sentiments, and soften the rugged manners of northern boors into gentleness and humanity....[1]

So Crito in the fifth dialogue of *Alciphron*. It is easy to smile and to think this a childish simplicity it would be cruel to deride. But such a passage represents well enough Berkeley's conviction that either religion is central, a controlling and shaping energy, or it is nothing. This energy he sees, with an awareness, rare in his age, of history as a concrete process, as having given the culture and institutions of Europe their peculiar character. He has an intuition that the sour rationalism of his own day offers a more radical challenge to Christian manners than others are willing to admit. That which for Berkeley was only a shadow of coming evils has for us grown immensely solid. The minute philosophers of our day are no longer the slightly ridiculous fops

1. Ibid., pp. 184, 185.

pilloried in *Alciphron*; today they stiffen their dialectic with
machine-guns. If most of the arguments provided by Berkeley
are obsolete as weapons, the temper of his work may still do
something to raise our spirits.

1950

# 11

## The Logic of the Heart

ALL his life John Henry Newman was concerned with how one ought to speak of knowing and believing, reason and faith. As a young don in Oxford, as Vicar of St. Mary's and leader of the Tractarians, in the years of seclusion at the Birmingham Oratory, in his old age, he returned again and again to this question: How—and how far—is Christian faith to be justified intellectually? This is still a living question and Newman's way of handling the question is perhaps of special interest to us today. By this I mean that he felt with passion some among the difficulties that press hard upon us too, in an intellectual climate formed by positivism and by the logical empiricism of the philosophical schools. It is as though he saw beyond the preoccupations of his own day to the problems of the coming age, just as, in different ways, Kierkegaard did, and Dostoevsky.

In what I have to say about Newman's ideas I shall keep to the Anglican period and I shall draw my illustrations from the *University Sermons*. The first of these was preached in 1826, when he was a young man in his twenties; its title, "The Philosophical Temper first enjoined by the Gospel", seems a faint echo of the Age of Reason. The last, preached in 1843 when the mutterings of the impending earthquake are already to be heard, is entitled "The Theory of Developments in Religious Doctrine", and is perhaps rather a foreshadowing of the age of Darwin.

First, let me note something about his method. It is useless to look in his work for the precisions of another kind of theology. His approach is Biblical and Patristic, not scholastic. His language is that of the ordinary educated persons of his day. He does, of course, employ terms which have a quasi-technical use in philosophy; but these—terms such as "the moral sense", "moral perceptions", "the passions", "nature", "the heart"—are drawn from the tradition of British empiricism. They had become so much a part of educated speech that it is a nice question whether they ought to be considered technical terms at all.

Newman is very self-conscious about language and has a severe view of its functions. "Moral truth" (by which he means truth in religion as well as in morals), he argues, "cannot be adequately explained and defended in words at all".

> Its views and human language are incommensurable, for, after all, what *is* language but an artificial system adapted for particular purposes, which have been determined by our wants? And here, even at first sight, can we imagine that it has been framed with a view to ideas so refined, so foreign to the whole course of the world, as those which (as Scripture expresses it) "no man can learn", but the select remnant who are "redeemed from the earth", and in whose mouth "is found no guile"? Nor is it this heavenly language alone which is without its intellectual counterpart. Moral character in itself, whether good or bad, as exhibited in thought and conduct, surely cannot be duly represented in words. We may, indeed, by an effort, reduce it in a certain degree to this arbitrary medium; but in its combined dimensions it is as impossible to write and read a man . . . as to give literal depth to a painted tablet.[1]

Language, then, for Newman is a set of tools well enough adapted to the furthering of particular practical or even speculative purposes, but compelled to strain itself to breaking point when it attempts to speak of God or the soul or faith. Language is framed to deal with our ordinary commerce with the world of things and persons, not with the

1. J. H. Newman. *Sermons, chiefly on the Theory of Religious Belief, preached before the University of Oxford,* 1843, pp. 70, 71.

subject-matter of theology. It is the tragedy of the vocation of the theologian—or the philosopher—that he must proceed by way of analysis and definition; but the nature of language is such that every comment he makes is an oblique one, every description a travesty, every definition a mutilation. Emphatically Newman does not suffer from what a modern philosopher has called a "clarity neurosis", nor does he think that everything that can be said can be said clearly. He does not hesitate to say—and this in a period when the words of the Authorized Version of the Bible were superstitiously venerated—that "even the words of inspired Scripture [are] imperfect and defective . . . in consequence of the medium it uses and the beings it addresses. It uses human language, and it addresses man; and neither can man compass, nor can his hundred tongues utter, the mysteries of the spiritual world, and God's dealings in this." [2]

There is no doubt a certain amount of confusion in some of this. Newman has the view of language as a set of tools the functions of which are determined by needs arising out of the way of life of those who use the language, and this view is close to that elaborated by Wittgenstein in his later work. But he does not face all the implications of this view of language and is inclined to think it a *defect* of language that it is unable to give a complete and detailed picture of situations and states of affairs; and this is like thinking it a defect in a painter of landscapes that he does not deceive us into trying to walk into his landscapes. All the same, there is a kind of sense in saying that we strive to communicate more than can be said and that in the sphere of faith we feel with peculiar poignancy the burdens imposed upon us by the ordinary functions of language when we strain this language for the purposes of another kind of discourse.

Nevertheless, Newman thought one could do a good deal with words. In particular, he thought it was possible to make clear the distinction between Christianity as he understood

2. Ibid., p. 264.

it and what he took to be its chief intellectual rivals, rationalism and scepticism. Indeed, he thought that in a way one could not argue for Christianity: one could only make it clear what Christianity was and in what ways it differed from its rivals for men's attention; and then leave the issue to Divine Grace and human freedom. There is a remarkable passage in the ninth of the *University Sermons*:

> Half the controversies in the world are verbal ones; and, could they be brought to a plain issue, they would be brought to a prompt termination. Parties engaged in them would then perceive, either that in substance they agreed together, or that their difference was one of first principles. This is the great object to be aimed at in the present age, though confessedly a very arduous one. We need not dispute, we need not prove, we need but define. At all events, let us, if we can, do this first of all; and then see who are left for us to dispute with, what is left for us to prove. Controversy, at least in this age, does not lie between the hosts of heaven, Michael and his Angels on the one side, and the powers of evil on the other; but it is a sort of night battle, where each fights for himself, and friend and foe stand together. When men understand what each other mean, they see, for the most part, that controversy is either superfluous or hopeless.[3]

It is impossible not to be reminded of the concluding lines of Matthew Arnold's poem, *Dover Beach*. Arnold writes that

> the world which seems
> To lie before us like a land of dreams,
> So various, so beautiful, so new,
> Hath really neither joy, nor love, nor light,
> Nor certitude, nor peace, nor help for pain;
> And we are here as on a darkling plain
> Swept with confused alarms of struggle and flight,
> Where ignorant armies clash by night.

3. Ibid., pp. 192, 193.

It is of course possible that there is in Arnold's poem a reminiscence of the passage from Newman's sermon—we know he was a student and admirer of Newman. However this may be, there is a kinship of mood between the two passages. Both feel the intellectual pressures of the age as a kind of agony. Newman is singular among the men of faith of this period in so feeling. But it is precisely here that he awakens our sympathy and understanding. For us he is a living figure where so many of his contemporaries—Keble and Pusey, Faber and Ward—are inconceivably remote, thin as ghosts.

Newman knew quite well that the most serious challenge to the Christian is not that of a rival religion, not even so elegant and economical a religion as the Deism touched with Christian feeling which was the staple of so many Broad Church divines when he was a young man; the serious challenge is that of scepticism. He had a lively appreciation of Hume's arguments, and he knew that the arguments with which many Christians met the attacks of the sceptic—arguments drawn for the most part from the writings of such rationalistic theologians as Paley—were in practice ineffective and (he suspected) contained hidden sophistries. For example, he speaks of the "proofs" and "evidences" employed in these arguments as

> satisfying, indeed, the liberal curiosity of the mind, and giving scope for a devotional temper to admire the manifold wisdom of God, but doing comparatively little towards keeping men from infidelity, or turning them to a religious life. The same remark applies to such works on Natural Theology as treat of the marks of design in the creation, which are beautiful and interesting to the believer in a God; but, where men have not already recognized God's voice within them, ineffective, and this moreover possibly from some unsoundness in the intellectual basis of the argument.[4]

If this kind of apologetic is ineffective and logically un-

4. Ibid., p. 55.

sound, we are not however to conclude that reason gives sentence for scepticism in religious matters. Newman commonly uses "reason" in the sense given to it in his own day, that is, as the faculty employed in formal reasoning of a mathematical and logical kind and in scientific and historical investigation. Such investigation employs "certain scientific rules and fixed standards for weighing testimony, and examining facts". It presupposes a public world all the features of which can be sufficiently described by means of a commonly understood language. "Nothing can be urged or made to tell, but what all feel, all comprehend, all can put into words . . . only such reasons are in point as can be exhibited in simple propositions; the multiform and intricate assemblage of considerations, which really lead to judgment and action, must be attenuated or mutilated into a major and a minor premiss." [5]

Now faith, Newman argues, goes far beyond what can be shown by reason to the common satisfaction. It rests upon what he calls an antecedent judgment or presumption, that is, we approach (for instance) historical evidence with some notion already in our minds as to what to expect and hope for. To take one of Newman's favourite examples. If there is God and if man is estranged from Him, there will very likely be a means of salvation; here is what claims to be a means of salvation; the man of faith will then run forward with eagerness and without suspicion to embrace this means and will be satisfied with evidences that, judged by the standards of historical or scientific investigation, are slender and incomplete.

But if faith goes beyond reason (in this sense of reason), so, equally, Newman argues, does scepticism.

> As Faith may be viewed as opposed to Reason, in the popular sense of the latter word, it must not be overlooked that Unbelief is opposed to Reason also. Unbelief, indeed, considers itself especially rational, or critical of evidence; but it criticizes

5. Ibid., p. 223.

the evidence of Religion, only because it does not like it, and really goes upon presumptions and prejudices as much as Faith does, only presumptions of an opposite nature. . . . It considers a religious system so improbable, that it will not listen to the evidence of it; or, if it listens, it employs itself in doing what a believer could do, if he chose, quite as well, what he is quite as well aware can be done; viz., in showing that the evidence might be more complete and unexceptionable than it is. On this account it is that unbelievers call themselves rational; not because they decide by evidence, but because, after they had [sic] made their decision, they merely occupy themselves in sifting it. This surely is quite plain, even in the case of Hume, who first asks, "What have we to oppose to such a cloud of witnesses," in favour of certain alleged miracles he mentions, "but the absolute impossibility or miraculous nature of the events which they relate? And this surely," he adds, "in the eyes of all reasonable people, will alone be regarded as a sufficient refutation"; that is, the antecedent improbability is a sufficient refutation of the evidence. And next, he scoffingly observes, that "our most holy Religion is founded on Faith, not on Reason"; and that "mere Reason is insufficient to convince us of its veracity". As if his infidelity were "founded on Reason", in any more exact sense; or presumptions on the side of Faith could not have, and presumptions on the side of unbelief might have, the nature of proof.[6]

We may put Newman's point in this way. Unbelief and faith are, logically speaking, counterparts one of the other. If this is so, we must then ask, if both believer and sceptic view evidence in the light of an antecedent presumption, what could be a respectable reason for choosing one of these positions rather than the other? Perhaps whether we are believers or unbelievers is a matter of temperament about which there is no more arguing than there is about questions of taste. Perhaps the only thing to do, if we feel compelled to choose, is to bet, as Pascal had urged long before.

Newman's dialectic may have confused the sceptic. But

6. Ibid., pp. 223, 224.

has it not intensified the darkness of the night battle? If belief and unbelief are indistinguishable from the standpoint of logic, how are we to distinguish between friend and foe? Newman was very well aware of all these difficulties and thought he saw how to meet them.

2

Newman argues, then, that belief and unbelief are logical counterparts. Both go beyond reason and beyond the evidence in the sense that they have antecedent presumptions as to what is possible and impossible, what may be expected or feared. How one reads the evidence depends upon the presumption one brings to it. But is not this to reduce religious faith to wishful thinking or to a choice for which no adequate reason can be given?

Newman in the *University Sermons* gives two different kinds of answer to this difficulty. The first kind of answer has a good deal in common with Hume in his less sceptical moods. One of the philosophical questions discussed by Hume is whether or not we have any reason to believe in the existence of bodies external to ourselves. His answer is that there are no convincing arguments for this belief; nevertheless, we do believe quite firmly in the existence of such bodies, and no philosophical reasoning to the contrary produces any lasting conviction. Nature, not reason, gives sentence against scepticism, Nature, in Hume's words, "has doubtless esteemed it an affair of too great importance, to be entrusted to our uncertain reasonings and speculations". Newman, perhaps with Hume in mind, makes a similar point when he casts about for an analogy to show the reasonableness—not the rationality—of faith. He remarks that

> we trust our senses, and that in spite of their often deceiving us. They even contradict each other at times, yet we trust them. But even were they ever consistent, never unfaithful, yet their fidelity would not be thereby proved. We consider that there is so strong an antecedent probability that they are

faithful that we dispense with proof. We take the point for granted; or, if we have grounds for it, these either lie in our secret belief in the stability of nature, or in the preserving presence and uniformity of Divine Providence—which, again, are points assumed. As, then, the senses may and do deceive us, and yet we trust them from a secret instinct, so it need not be weakness or rashness, if upon a certain presentiment of mind we trust to the fidelity of testimony offered for a revelation.[7]

Newman is here arguing that what can be rationally demonstrated is insufficient even for the purposes of common living. We have to make assumptions, to trust the general tendencies of our nature, to make anything of the world at all. Scepticism is a mood engendered by the study; it is not and cannot be the attitude of the whole man, man the agent, man the maker, the investigator, the moral being. Scepticism is a malaise peculiar to the sophisticated; but even the sophisticated shed their scepticism when they turn from speculation to practice. This may be all very well so far as philosophical absurdities are concerned. But how does it help us with regard to religious faith in general, Christian faith in particular? Our tendency to believe the evidence of our senses is, so far as we know, common to all persons in good health; but in matters of religion some of us are natural believers, have "a certain presentiment of mind", others are sceptical by nature; and this is to make the difference between the believer and the unbeliever in the end one between two temperaments, two psychological types.

Newman is, I think, aware of this difficulty, and his awareness of it drives him into offering a second solution to the general problem. I have suggested that the analogy between trusting our senses and trusting our tendency to religious faith breaks down because there is no general human tendency to religious faith, at least not in any form which would have satisfied Newman, whereas we all trust our

7. Ibid., p. 206.

senses. Philosophers may have discussed in what tone of voice we ought to speak of oranges as coloured and round; but if we are to talk about oranges at all, this is how we must talk about them. Is there anything which can plausibly be said to belong to human nature in as universal a sense as our disposition to trust our senses, to believe that they give us authentic information about the world, and which provides a justification—or the beginnings of a justification—of religious belief? Newman believes there is. He points to conscience.

By conscience he understands very much what Bishop Butler understood by it, that is, a faculty by which "we naturally and unavoidably approve some actions, under the peculiar view of their being virtuous and of good desert; and disapprove others, as vicious and of ill desert". For Butler, and Newman follows him, conscience witnesses to its own authority. "Conscience does not only offer itself to show us the way we should walk in, but it likewise carries its own authority with it, that it is our natural guide; the guide assigned us by the Author of our nature. . . ." [8]

It is through an analysis of conscience—what it implies and what it commits us to asserting—that Newman hopes to show the reasonableness of faith. In the second of the *University Sermons* he maintains

that Conscience is the essential principle and sanction of Religion in the mind. Conscience implies a relation between the soul and a something exterior, and that moreover superior, to itself; a relation to an excellence which it does not possess, and to a tribunal over which it has no power. And since the more closely this inward monitor is respected and followed, the clearer, the more exalted, and the more varied its dictates become, and the standard of excellence is ever outstripping, while it guides, our obedience, a moral conviction is thus at length obtained of the unapproachable nature as well as the

8. Joseph Butler, *Fifteen Sermons preached at the Rolls Chapel*, in *Sermons by Joseph Butler*, edited by W. E. Gladstone, 1897, Sermon III, pp. 60, 61.

supreme authority of That, whatever it is, which is the object of the mind's contemplation. Here, then, at once, we have the elements of a religious system; for what is Religion but the system of relations existing between us and a Supreme Power, claiming our habitual obedience . . .? [9]

Newman's argument is that if we attend to conscience, as an "original existence", in Hume's sense, something that presents itself to us with all the denseness and weight of an ineluctable fact, and as that which in its growth becomes more powerful and more subtle, we are led to affirm the existence of a transcendent judge; and once brought to this point we cannot stop short, we have to go on to trace all the consequences of this affirmation; and this is the life of faith.

Moreover, obedience to conscience is itself the beginning of faith. Shortly after the passage I have just quoted Newman has this to say :

. . . since the inward law of Conscience brings with it no proof of its truth, and commands attention to it on its own authority, all obedience to it is of the nature of Faith; and habitual obedience implies the direct exercise of a clear and vigorous faith in the truth of its suggestions, triumphing over opposition both from within and without; quieting the murmurs of Reason, perplexed with the disorders of the present scheme of things, and subduing the appetites, clamorous for goods which promise an immediate and keen gratification.[1]

Reflection upon conscience, then, and especially upon a developed conscience, leads us to affirm the existence of a transcendent judge; and this is the first step, and it is unlikely to be the last, in the life of faith. Obedience to conscience, appearing as in itself an absolute authority, is a first exercise of faith. In so far as we are moral beings, we are committed to belief in God; and we know what it is to believe without asking for proof. Here, then, is something which purports to be natural to all men; for the capacity to make moral judgments was, for Newman, as much a defining characteristic of man as the capacity for sense experience.

9. Newman, op. cit., pp. 19, 20.     1. Ibid., pp. 20, 21.

So far I have spoken of Newman's argument as being that reflection upon conscience *leads* us to this or that conclusion. I have deliberately used this ambiguous way of speaking. To say that x leads us to assert y does not make it clear what kind of a connection between x and y is being spoken about. We can say that examination of the anatomy and habits of lions leads us to the conclusion that they are carnivorous. Equally, education and upbringing may lead us to adopt certain views, for example, that Negroes are intellectually inferior to Europeans. In the first instance, the connection between what we come to know about lions and the conclusion that they are carnivorous is a logical one. In the second instance, the connection is merely psychological. That John Smith has been brought up in such a way that he believes Negroes to be intellectually inferior to Europeans has no bearing on the truth or falsity of his belief; whereas what we come to know about the anatomy and habits of lions *does* have a bearing on the truth or falsity of the statement that lions are carnivorous. My question, then, about what Newman has to say about reflection upon conscience is this. When he speaks of our coming, by means of reflection upon conscience, to a belief in God's existence and a knowledge of his relation to us, is he speaking simply of what very often happens as a matter of fact? If this should be what he means, then clearly his second argument is no better than his first, for we can still ask if the belief is true or probable or well grounded. That many people do come to a belief in God in this way does not answer this question. Perhaps, though, he is saying that the connection is a logical, not simply a psychological and factual, one; in which case what he has to say must be taken seriously. I think he certainly intends us to take the connection as being in some sense a logical one. He uses the language of logic when he says, for example, that conscience "*implies* a relation between the soul and a something exterior . . . to itself". He wishes, I think, to say that there is a sense in which a candid scrutiny of conscience brings with it certain intellectual commitments, not just that brooding upon conscience has commonly certain pyscho-logical effects.

The question then becomes this. What kind of logical con-nection does Newman believe he is directing our attention to? It is hard to think that Newman supposed that he had discovered an instance of entailment in the strict sense; for there seems to be no *logical* absurdity, nothing *self-contra-dictory*, in asserting the existence of conscience as a supreme authority and denying the existence of God. I agree that it may be absurd to acknowledge the authority of conscience and deny the existence of God; if it is, then the absurdity will be more like the absurdity of admitting that the continent of Africa is mentioned in all the books and figures in all the atlases and at the same time denying that there is such a place. In this case, while it is silly to deny the existence of Africa, there is nothing self-contradictory about it.

Newman's position must, then, be that conscience is evi-dence, possibly very good or the best possible evidence, for God's existence and his peculiar relation to ourselves. It can-not be evidence of the kind which satisfies the historian or the natural scientist—Newman has already made it plain that there is no question of this. It is evidence for the man who has already come to believe, in at least a rudimentary sense. But isn't this to beg the question, to argue in a circle?

I do not think Newman's case is quite so desperate as this. He wishes, I think, to mark a distinction between two kinds of intellectual capacity, two modes of reasoning: one is reason in the solid and narrow eighteenth-century sense already discussed—*esprit de géométrie*, to use Pascal's phrase, together with the inductive reasoning of the his-torian and the scientist; the other a way of thinking—per-haps *esprit de finesse*, to quote Pascal again, comes as near as anything to naming it—the nature of which can only be shown by pointing to particular instances. What should we say, for example, to a man who evinced no disapproval of wanton cruelty but, on the contrary, approved of it? He has committed no logical absurdity. The act of cruelty in question being what it is is not evidence for its being morally bad in the way in which a document is evidence for the historian, an observed chemical change evidence for the scientist. If the man continues to approve of cruelty no matter what considerations we may urge, then there is no logical procedure, no experiment, to which we can appeal in order to *prove* to him that he is in the wrong. But quite certainly such a man is in error, and in saying he is in error we are not simply expressing our own moral disapproval of him. He has failed to see, I suggest, that the act in question being what it is *is* evidence for its moral badness, though, of course, we only see it is this if we already see the act as morally bad. Considered as an argument, this too is circular, just as Newman's argument from conscience to God is circular.

The solution to the difficulty is, I believe, this. In neither case are we faced with an *argument* in the usual sense. In neither case is there a movement from premises to conclusion. We are faced rather with an insight or an intuition—these are unfortunate and much-abused words but I can think of no better ones—which can indeed be *analysed*, and this is what we do if we say that a scrutiny of conscience leads us to a belief in God or that an act of cruelty being what it is is evidence for its being morally bad. Such an analysis has meaning and carries conviction only to those who share the insight or intuition and *recognize* the analysis as a true explication of what they already possess. This is why in the field of ethics and religion, the field of what Newman calls "moral truth", we tend to use the ambiguous language of feeling and to suppose that in this field a different mode of reasoning is appropriate, a different logic; perhaps, to echo Pascal yet again, a "logic of the heart".

To say all this is, I am well aware, to set problems rather than to solve them. And this is what Newman does. The question is whether, in the context of the philosophy of religion, Newman sets the fruitful problems, asks the right questions. I think he saw very clearly that religious apologetics in his own day were concerned with the wrong problems; that the argument from design in the form given to it by Paley and others was fallacious and—apart from this—had no power to move men and convert them to a living belief in God. He even goes so far as to admit that "it is indeed a great question whether atheism is not as philosophically consistent with the phenomena of the physical world, taken by themselves, as the doctrine of a creative and governing Power". He goes on to argue that "the practical safeguard against atheism in the case of scientific inquirers is the inward need and desire, the inward experience, of that Power, existing in the mind antecedent and independent of their examination of His material world".[2] It is vain to hope that a more strenuous examination of the world or a stricter attention to the requirements of formal logic will issue in faith or strengthen faith where it is weak.

> What, then [Newman asks], is the safeguard [of Faith], if Reason is not? I shall give an answer, which may seem at once common-place and paradoxical; yet I believe is the true one. The safeguard of Faith is a right state of heart. This it is that gives it birth; it also disciplines it. This is what protects it from bigotry, credulity, and fanaticism. It is holiness, or dutifulness, or the new creation, or the spiritual mind, however we word it, which is the quickening and illuminating principle of true Faith, giving it eyes, hands, and feet. It is Love which forms it out of the rude chaos into an image of Christ. . . .[3]

To be a reasonable being, for Newman, is not only to employ those capacities to be seen at work in the historian and the natural scientist and the mathematician; it is also to respond to the claims of morality and religion. To suppose that in the fields of morality and religion we can use the same criteria as those we use in history, natural science and

2. *University Sermons*, p. 186.  3. *Ibid.*, pp. 227, 228.

mathematics is as absurd as to suppose that we can employ moral and religious criteria to determine questions of science or formal logic. Such a mistake springs from our failure to recognize that religious utterances have (to use the terminology of some philosophers of today) their own logical grammar.

1957

# 12

## Newman and Empiricism

### I

THERE is a curious remark in Mark Pattison's *Memoirs*. He writes that after Newman's secession from the Church of England in 1845 "Oxford repudiated at once sacerdotal principles and Kantian logic [and] for more than a quarter of this century Mill and nominalist views reigned in the schools".[1] The implication of Pattison's remark is that there was some kind of connection between the sacerdotal principles of the Tractarians and "Kantian logic". (By "Kantian logic" Pattison almost certainly does not mean "logic" in the technical sense, for in this sense Kant's logic is substantially that of Aristotle, as this logic was understood—or misunderstood—in the eighteenth century; but rather Kant's epistemological and metaphysical views.[2]) Further, the implication is that Mill's empiricist and nominalist views came to prevail over those of Kant in the University of Oxford as a consequence of there being some kind of relation, causal or logical, between the collapse of that phase of the Tractarian movement which relied upon the leadership of Newman and the alleged change in the philosophical climate of Oxford.

The general point lying behind Pattison's remark is a sound one: that there was a connection, no doubt a very complex one and certainly not a simple relation of cause and effect, or ground and consequent, between the failure of Tractarianism to capture either the University of Oxford or the mind of England and the rise of secularism and utilitar-

1. Mark Pattison, *Memoirs*, 1885, p. 166.
2. There is a confused but interesting account of the views of Kant in Charles P. Chretien, *An Essay on Logical Method*, 1848, p. 87, pp. 122–4. Chretien was Fellow and Tutor of Oriel.

ianism in the educated world. But this story can be confused
with a different one, that overlaps with it only in part, the
story of the relations between the empiricist and the idealist
schools in British philosophy. It is no doubt tempting to
suppose, as perhaps Pattison did, that there is an affinity between idealist metaphysics and the sacerdotal mind; and
that empiricism in philosophy is logically implicated with
hard-headedness, agnosticism, the movement for social reform and what have you. Many as well as Pattison have encountered this temptation and have succumbed to it. In
general the supposition is absurd; and it is especially absurd
in the case of the man Pattison has chiefly in mind as the
typical embodiment of Tractarian sacerdotalism : John Henry
Newman. There is nothing to suggest that Newman's philosophical culture differed in any radical way from that of his
fellow-members of the Oriel Common Room of whom Professor Dwight Culler justly remarks that "they had not read
the writings of Rousseau and Voltaire and they knew nothing
of Kant. British philosophy they did know, especially Locke,
Hume, Paley and Adam Smith, but the thinker to whom
they were most deeply indebted was Aristotle." [3] (Perhaps
Dwight Culler should have added the name of Butler to his
catalogue.) And, as I shall argue, the philosophical affinities
of Newman are peculiarly with one philosopher in the British
empiricist tradition, namely, David Hume; and in more
general terms it can be said that Newman's cast of mind and
intellectual sympathies are, in philosophical matters, always
with the empiricist school. It is not accidental that we find
in the unpublished material at the Birmingham Oratory ap-
preciative notes, written in 1857, on Mill's *Logic*; or that in
this material we find such remarks as: "The logical evolu-
tions of science (induction &c.), are a rule of the game, not in
the nature of things" (note of 16th November 1861); ". . . the
soul would not think without some external stimulus [but]

3. A. Dwight Culler, *The Imperial Intellect*, New Haven and London,
1955, p. 36.

our experience is not so much of external things, but of our own minds" (24th February 1859); "In most departments of writing to speak of self is egotistical : not so in metaphysics. In it the writer cannot propose to do more than record his own opinions, the phenomena to which he appeals and the principles which he assumes being within his own breast. . . . His hermit spirit dwells in his own sphere" (1st December 1859).[4] There is no mistaking the company these remarks keep. And if Newman wrote in this strain when he had been more than ten years a Catholic and had thus become even more *sacerdotal* in Pattison's sense of term than when he was a Tractarian, *a fortiori* we should expect his mind to have had the cast of empiricism when he was still the leader of the Oxford counter-reformation.

My intention here is only in a minimal sense to write, or rewrite, a chapter in the intellectual history of the nineteenth century. My primary concern is with the intellectual structure and the tone of Newman's thought. In so far as I show that much of what he writes consists of variations, often beautiful and ingenious, on philosophical themes that are commonplaces of British empiricism, I do so with three aims in mind. First, I wish to show that reflection upon the case of Newman brings out one of the peculiar perils that lie in wait for the historian of ideas. In surveying the Victorian period from the standpoint of the history of ideas we incline to emphasize what is novel and to forget or under-emphasize deep currents of thought, springing from an earlier period, that still run powerfully beneath the surface. Part of what is novel in Newman is a relatively fresh ap-

4. Unpublished papers at the Birmingham Oratory. All modern students of Newman are indebted to the Fathers of the Oratory for their generosity in placing the rich store of unpublished material in the Birmingham archives at their disposal; and I should like to express my own gratitude to them for their kindness to me. Newman's philosophical remarks should be read in the light of this statement to be found in "Newman's Philosophical Papers", Sundries: A.46.3, at the Birmingham Oratory: "What I write, I do not state dogmatically, but categorically, that is, in investigation, nor have I confidence enough in what I have advanced to warrant publication."

proach to certain central theological problems; and there may therefore be a failure to note the deep continuity between his thought and that of the English eighteenth century. Secondly, I wish to bring out (as against those who have argued, usually from the Anglican side—though sometimes, in the nineteenth century, from the Ultramontane side too —that Newman was temperamentally and intellectually a sceptic who used the sceptical arguments to press men into faith) that Newman at certain points deepened the empiricist position to show that the logical issues were more complex than Hume, for example, had supposed, and that here the strongest currents in his thought make against scepticism. And thirdly, I wish to show that here and there Newman transcends the common empiricist position and reaches forward to new philosophical insights that link him on the one hand with Kierkegaard and the existentialist critique of traditional accounts of, for instance, judgment and belief and on the other hand with our own inclination to think that the analysis of philosophical problems goes together with sustained reflection on the function of language.

(Questions about the *literary* dependence of one writer upon another are notoriously difficult to answer where there is no plain independent testimony to be had. The thesis I want here to maintain, namely, that there are many striking parallelisms between the thought of Newman and that of Hume, and that this far-reaching similarity represents a certain affinity in spirit and method—though not in conclusions —between the two writers, is not a thesis which is in any way tied to the possibility of demonstrating the literary dependence of Newman upon Hume. This question is in any case peculiarly hard to answer in the case of Newman. He absorbed from other men what nourished his own thought; but in the process of absorption what had been taken from others was so transformed, not so much in its logical content as in its logical role, that he himself saw what was initially the thought of another as most intimately and organically his own. That he was a close student of Hume is certain.[5] It is also clear that at one level he adopted what was in his period the conventional view of Hume, at least among Christian believers, as the great infidel philosopher, the most subtly dangerous of the adversaries of the Christian religion; and that if, at a deeper level, he was on some issues philosophically close to Hume, this was something he scarcely suspected, so different were for him the consequences even of those premises he shared with Hume. In general, what I show is that he shares with Hume a dramatic and paradoxical interpretation of that empiricist tradition of which they are both ornaments. In both, a destructive philosophical analysis is a moment in an argument designed to show that we have no alternative to putting our trust in "nature". But as to what putting our trust in "nature" commits us to, here the two men could scarcely be more different.)

If I am right, Newman's *philosophical* originality has been underestimated. (Of course, no reader of the *Essay on Development* or of *The Idea of a University* is likely to be unaware of his intellectual freshness and energy, no reader of the *Parochial Sermons* is likely to miss the note of spiritual genius.) For this there are many reasons. There is the natural assumption that what of philosophical interest Newman had to say will be found in the *Grammar of Assent*, a work overvalued somewhat by both admirers and critics.[6] Then there is the difficulty that much of what is most interesting and original from the standpoint of philosophy has to be dug for, sifted out from a mass of work concerned with matters not philosophical at all. But the greatest difficulty is that New-

---

5. See *Two Essays on Biblical and Ecclesiastical Miracles*, 1870; *Apologia pro Vita Sua*, London and New York, 1955, p. 31; *On The Scope and Nature of University Education*, London and New York, 1915, p. 31 (Hume is here described as "this acute, though most low-minded of speculators"); and elsewhere.
6. Father Stephen Dessain may be right in saying that "the first piece of advice . . . to be tendered to any reader of the *Grammar* is not to embark on it as though it were a philosophical treatise". "Cardinal Newman on the Theory and Practice of Knowledge", *Downside Review*, 76, 1957, p. 9.

man was a stumbling-block, an offence, in his lifetime, both to the Anglicans he left and to the Catholics among whom he made his spiritual home; and posterity has found him no less a divisive figure. Anglicans and other Protestants have ever charged him with sophistry and many among his Catholic contemporaries at bottom sympathized with those who brought the charge. Later generations of Catholic commentators, the question of Newman's theological orthodoxy having been settled by the conspicuous judgment of the Church in elevating him to the cardinalate, have thought it a duty to rebut charges of sophistry and scepticism; and such rebuttals have too often taken the sad form of arguing that since Newman is theologically orthodox, and since (so it is commonly believed) there is a necessary connection between theological orthodoxy and the belief in "thomist" metaphysics, then it must be possible to show that *au fond* Newman is not far from the "thomist" position; and that those expressions that—it cannot be denied—are both frequent in his writing and in appearance highly unthomistic which constitute a difficulty in linking the thought of Newman with "thomism", are to be explained either as the products of a lack of philosophical sophistication (common enough in this period even among princes of the Church) or as expressions that don't *really* mean what they are most naturally taken to mean.[7] It is thus hard to get a straight look at Newman; and of course I make no claim to have done more than show that a correction of our vision is needed; and that, our vision having been corrected, there is much of interest to see that has hitherto been neglected.[8]

7. Dr. Boekraad is to the point when he observes: "That three Popes approved of Newman and his teaching does not prove that Newman was an Aristotelian." A. J. Boekraad, Review of *Cardinal Newman Studien Dritte Folge, Philosophical Studies*, VIII (Maynooth, 1958), p. 142. I may add, too, that when I speak of "thomism", it is the "thomism" of the textbooks, not the philosophy of Aquinas, I have in mind.

8. It should be said that while what I have written is sound enough as a generalization, there have in recent years been great changes in the approach to Newman. These changes are well represented by D. G. James, *The Romantic Comedy*, 1948, and above all by Dwight Culler's *Imperial Intellect* referred to above. Of recent European studies of Newman which

Such terms as empiricism and idealism are notoriously difficult to handle. The sense in which I shall employ the term empiricism will become plainer as I go along. It may be useful, however, to attempt here a rude sketch of what might almost be called the myth—in somewhat the Sorelian sense—of empiricism; for its perennial fascination springs as much from the power of its myth as from the intellectual cogency of its particular arguments and analyses. I shall give the myth a sharpness of outline and a stridency of colour that it may never in fact display in the work of any one empiricist (though it is above all Hume that is before my mind); but in dealing with an empiricist so unsystematic, so mercurial, so passionate, so poetic, as Newman, this may be no disadvantage; for it is in its *piercing* character, the extent to which it seems to press us to the edge of an abyss in which the solidities of common prejudice fall away from us, that the myth of empiricism haunts Newman.

Under one of its aspects empiricism is a thesis about priorities in the enterprise of stating what is or can be known; and as such a thesis it entails doctrines which stand in more or less dramatic contrast with those beliefs which seem to be embedded in our discourse about the world as this discourse is commonly taken. The foundation upon which all our knowledge of matters of fact is held to rest consists of "those *impressions*, which arise from the *senses*" (to choose the terminology of Hume); and Hume goes on to say of these

bear upon the problems under consideration here, A. J. Boekraad, *The Personal Conquest of Truth according to J. H. Newman*, Louvain, 1955, deserves to be singled out. I should add that in this essay I am not concerned to give a balanced picture of Newman's thought; and I must make it especially clear that I am not concerned except peripherally with Newman as a theologian. In any complete account of Newman as a religious thinker, the Scriptures and the Christian Platonism of some of the Fathers would be more important, as sources, than what I have called "empiricism". I should also emphasize that although I have occasionally cited post-1845 material, I am concerned with Newman's thought in the period before 1845. By the time of the *Essay on Development* Newman has reached his intellectual maturity, a maturity represented by *Discourses on the Scope and Nature of University Education*, Dublin, 1852, *Apologia pro Vita Sud*, 1864, and *A Letter Addressed to His Grace the Duke of Norfolk*, 1875.

"impressions" that "their ultimate cause is, in my opinion, perfectly inexplicable by human reason, and 'twill always be impossible to decide with certainty, whether they arise immediately from the object, or are produc'd by the creative power of the mind, or are deriv'd from the author of our being".[9] So that when Hume writes: "Original impressions, or impressions of sensation, are such as . . . arise in the soul, from the constitution of the body, from the animal spirits, or from the application of objects to the external organs":[1] what he writes is analysable into terms used to refer to what is given and cannot with reason be doubted (that is, "impressions of sensation") and those used to refer to an hypothesis for which no compelling reason can be given (that these impressions "arise in the soul, from the constitution of the body, from the animal spirits, or from the application of objects to the external organs"). Now, it is equally characteristic of empiricism, in the sense in which I take it, that self-scrutiny should be held to disclose powerful and ordinarily irresistible impulses to believe certain hypotheses; and that the felt energy of these impulses should in all matters of practice overcome, and rightly overcome, the uncertainties that belong to these hypotheses so long as they are treated as making claims to be rationally demonstrable. "Where reason is lively, and mixes itself with some propensity, it ought to be assented to";[2] but not otherwise. This trust in our steady impulses and propensities is represented as a life lived under the guidance of Nature. When Newman writes in *Tract 85* that "Nature certainly does give sentence against scepticism",[3] he echoes the teaching of Hume where in the *Treatise* he writes of "the sceptic" that "he must assent to the principle concerning the existence of body, tho' he cannot pretend by any arguments of philosophy to maintain its

9. David Hume, *A Treatise of Human Nature*, ed. L. A. Selby-Bigge, Oxford, 1896, p. 84. (Referred to as *Treatise*.)
1. *Treatise*, p. 275.
2. Ibid., p. 270.
3. "Lectures on the Scripture Proof of the Doctrines of the Church", *Tracts for the Times*, No. 85, Second Edition, 1840, p. 72.

veracity. Nature has not left this to his choice, and has doubt-less esteem'd it an affair of too great importance to be trusted to our uncertain reasonings and speculations." [4] The calmness, good-humour and brisk assurance with which Hume picks his way through the republic of letters reflect the pupil of Nature; but there is also the Hume of whom Boswell remarked that he had been "tortured on the meta-physical rack", who could write, no doubt with a hint of melodrama, for all its portrayal of a condition of meta-physical anxiety:

> Where am I, or what? From what causes do I derive my existence, and to what condition shall I return? Whose favour shall I court, and whose anger must I dread? What beings sur-round me? and on whom have I any influence, or who have any influence on me? I am confounded with all these ques-tions, and begin to fancy myself in the most deplorable condi-tion imaginable, inviron'd with the deepest darkness, and utterly depriv'd of the use of every member and faculty. [5]

For thinkers in the empiricist tradition the question: *Have I a soul?* is scarcely worth asking, for it is of the soul and its states that I am immediately aware. The hard ques-tion is: *Have I a body?* An affirmative answer here is linked with a causal hypothesis that is indeed defensible, though not demonstrable: the hypothesis that our perceptions "arise in the soul, from the constitution of the body, from the animal spirits, or from the application of objects to the external organs". It is as though we are at a luminous centre; beyond this centre is a region of shadow deepening towards the limit of vision into impenetrable darkness. We can indeed be content with this darkness, which is only that of a neces-sary (granted the force of the argument) ignorance; but the assumption behind the picture is so violently different from the assumption upon which our common beliefs about the world rest, namely, that we gaze upon the public theatre of the world, not the private theatre of the soul, that it is

4. *Treatise*, p. 187.     5. Ibid., p. 269.

natural that our peering into the darkness should be attended with anxiety and distress. Further, when the empiricist comes to explore the structure of the private theatre, as distinct from the performances that go on within it, when he attempts a phenomenology of the soul, the darkness is now as much an interior as an exterior darkness. It will not be surprising if the sensitive or the melancholy should find that the argument has cast them "into a wild deserted hopeless region".[6]

Such a region is not permanently habitable. And it is therefore a part of the empiricist myth that there are means of dispelling the darkness created by uninhibited philosophical argument. Broadly speaking, the means are to be found in a more exact psychology. It is the restriction of our knowledge to an awareness of the contents of the soul that has produced the horrid predicament; perhaps we can escape from it through a stricter attention to the contents of the soul and to their interconnections. This is in fact, as we have seen, Hume's way of ridding himself of the burden of metaphysical anxiety. We mark out those impulses of our nature that are strong and persistent; and where a tenable hypothesis, for example, that there are bodies, points in the same direction as natural propensity, then the problem of how we are to take the world and ourselves in order that we may live, and live well, is soluble in the only sense possible : by uniting reason with natural propensity.

All the same, it remains unforgettable that this procedure, to which there is no alternative, has come under suspicion. And even though we may frame, as Hume does, a variety of psychological theories to account for the principles of the imagination, the role of causal reasoning in human affairs, demonstration and belief, and so on, the strictly philoso-

6. Compare "To attempt to go beyond [the province of faith] by our reason is like a schoolboy going out of bounds; it is going into a wild deserted hopeless region, ad terram tenebrosam et opertam mortis caligine; terram miseriae et tenebrarum, ubi umbra mortis, et nullus ordo, sed sempiternus horror inhabitat." To A. B. (August 20th 1887), in unpublished papers at the Birmingham Oratory.

phical doubt dwells in the background. In Hume the presence of this doubt is shown in a reluctance to extend the frontiers of belief farther than seems absolutely necessary to the secular spirit, free thinking or deistical, of his age. It is frivolous to raise doubts about the validity of the methods of the natural sciences; here the "experimental philosophy" [7] shows its worth by its power to unify within a consistent scheme the world of our perceptions and to make the natural world serve our purposes. It is equally frivolous to raise doubts as to the claims of the *consensus humani* in questions of morals. But there are, for Hume, no such good reasons, there is no happy coincidence of natural propensity and rational hypothesis, when questions connected with philosophical theology come to be considered. In these cases the destructive process of philosophical analysis is not inhibited: here we can face without too much anxiety, and with a certain satisfaction that no rational human interests are put in peril, the results of such an analysis. "The whole is a riddle, an enigma, an inexplicable mystery. Doubt, uncertainty, suspense of judgment, appear the only result of our most accurate scrutiny concerning this subject." [8]

This distinction between those beliefs which can, and those which cannot, be safely or seriously put to the question, is drawn by Hume in one place rather than another for reasons that are respectable but not coercive. He can find in his philosophy no cogent argument against one who distinguishes differently between what is seriously questionable and what is not. Where and how the distinction is drawn rests upon an antecedent prejudice or presumption. We may guess that in Hume's case (and no doubt in Newman's too) the antecedent prejudice is at least in part shaped by temperament and by the cultural milieu within which he moved most happily. It seems quite plain that unless some quite

7. *Treatise*, p. xx.
8. David Hume, "The Natural History of Religion", *Essays and Treatises on Several Subjects*. A New Edition, 1822, Vol. II, p. 449.

unexpected turn in the argument is made the antecedent prejudice is as it were external to the argument upon which the need for *some* antecedent prejudice rests. What, granted the felt necessity to avoid the inconveniences of a radical scepticism, is taken as given no longer belongs, as it does at that stage of the argument where it is our primary perceptions—"impressions of sensation"—that are taken as given, to the logical structure of empiricism; it is brought to empiricism from without.

## 2

Coleridge's saying that we are all born Aristotelians or Platonists has in it a quantum of truth. There are philosophical doctrines that will strike one man, and not another, as confirming what he has believed and loved prior to philosophical reflection; and he will therefore be inclined to accept —almost, he will run to meet and embrace—philosophical doctrines that seem an echo of his earliest and deepest convictions.

> I used to wish the Arabian Tales were true; my imagination ran on unknown influences, on magical powers, and talismans. . . . I thought life might be a dream, or I an Angel, and all this world a deception, my fellow-angels by a playful device concealing themselves from me, and deceiving me with the semblance of a material world.[9]

Thus Newman on his schooldays. Again (in connection with his "inward conversion" at the age of fifteen):

> . . . I believe that it had some influence on my opinions, in the direction of those childish imaginations which I have already mentioned, viz. in isolating me from the objects which surrounded me, in confirming me in my mistrust of the reality of material phenomena, and making me rest in the thought of

9. J. H. Newman, *Apologia pro Vita Sua*, London and New York, 1955, p. 29.

two and two only supreme and luminously self-evident beings, myself and my Creator. . . .[1]

It is surely not extravagant to see some of the characteristic statements of his mature position as continuous with these accounts of his "childish imaginations". The following sufficiently represent a numerous class of such statements.

> . . . a belief in our Lord's divinity is closely connected . . . with deep religious feeling generally—involving a sense both of our need and of the value of the blessing which He has procured for us, and *an emanicipation from the tyranny of the visible world*. . . . [My italics.] [2]

> . . . faith, without asking for one ray of light more than is given, muses over the wonderful system of Providence, as seen in this world, which is ever connecting events, between which man sees no necessary bond. The whole system of what is called cause and effect, is one of mystery. . . .[3]

We are then in a world of spirits, as well as in a world of sense, and we hold communion with it, and take part in it, though we are not conscious of doing so. If this seems strange to any one, let him reflect that we are undeniably taking part in a third world . . . the world of brute animals. Can any thing be more marvellous or startling, unless we were used to it, than that we should have a race of beings about us whom we do but see, and as little know their state, or can describe their interests, or their destiny as we can tell of the inhabitants of the sun and moon. It is indeed a very overpowering thought, when we get to fix our minds on it, that we familiarly use, I may say hold intercourse with creatures who are as much strangers to us, as mysterious, as if they were the fabulous, un-

1. *Apologia*, p. 31. Tolstoy's childhood offers a partial parallel. "I imagined that besides myself nothing and nobody existed in the universe, that objects were not objects at all, but images which appeared only when I paid attention to them, and as soon as I left off thinking of them, these images immediately disappeared." Cited in Aylmer Maude, *The Life of Tolstoy*, 1930, Vol. I, p. 33.
2. J. H. Newman, *The Arians of the Fourth Century*, fifth edition, 1883, p. 273.
3. J. H. Newman, *Parochial Sermons*, fourth edition, 1843, Vol. II, p. 237.

earthly beings, more powerful than man, yet his slaves, which Eastern superstitions have invented. We have more real knowledge about the Angels than about the brutes.[4]

Perhaps it will be urged that there does seem an antecedent improbability in any alleged fact [the reference is to the doctrine of the Real Presence in the Eucharist which Froude has characterized as a "double miracle"], which undermines our reliance upon our senses. Considering how entirely our reliance is built upon instinct and prejudice not on reason, it might appear that God would not so appoint things as to bring objections to a medium of knowledge which we are accustomed to receive implicitly as His own impression upon our minds. To this it may be replied that the separate senses themselves sometimes contradict each other.[5]

Just as, according to the maxim of Aquinas, Grace completes Nature and does not overthrow it, so, here, we encounter a mind that comes to maturity by cherishing rather than abandoning the predilections of childhood. Newman's case is as good an example as we could find of Hume's principle, that "where reason is lively, and mixes itself with some propensity, it ought to be assented to". Of course, Hume would probably have thought the reasoning sluggish and the propensity a monkish quirk rather than one belonging to human nature as such.

The propensity with which Newman mixes his very lively reason is a propensity to believe in God and in the Christian Revelation. He first encountered the problem as to the justification of Christian faith in a complex situation that, here, I can do no more than sketch. The Evangelical tradition within which he had been brought up considered any kind of intellectual inquiry into the fundamentals of faith a species of infidelity. The old "high and dry" party in the Church of England was often satisfied with the rationalistic apologetic

4. *Parochial Sermons*, Vol. IV, pp. 233, 234.
5. Unsigned footnote to *Remains of the Late Reverend Richard Hurrell Froude*, Part the Second, Vol. I, 1839, p. 66. There can be no doubt that this footnote is by Newman.

and the reliance upon "evidences" well represented by the work of Paley. The classical Anglican theology of the seventeenth century, dear as it was to Newman in his Tractarian period, did not, however much it supplied him with a norm of orthodoxy, provide material with which to come to terms with the intellectual problems of the nineteenth century. Of these three traditions only that of rationalism professed to meet the intellectual problems; and Newman found this tradition theologically defective (he speaks in the *University Sermons* of the age of evidences as "a time when love was cold" [6]) and in tendency making for the elegant and economical religion of too many Broad Church divines, a kind of Deism touched with Christian feeling; and in any case he had learned the lesson of Hume and suspected that the head and centre of Paley's natural theology, the Argument from Design, was logically unsound. It is true, there was one thinker of genius within that element in the Anglican tradition which Newman found sympathetic, Joseph Butler; and it is roughly true that Newman at times saw himself, and rightly, as continuing and deepening Butler's apologetic, dark and inconclusive as compared with the specious clarity of Paley, but massive and humane, with a proper sense of the mystery of revelation. But although there is much of Butler in Newman, they are men of very different temperaments and, more importantly, of very different intellectual climates. Newman is the author of the *Essay on the Development of Christian Doctrine* and is himself one of the makers of an age which took history seriously and saw the rise of scientific biology; and deep though his roots may be in the empiricism of the eighteenth century, his affinities are also with the romantics. In a situation of this kind, then, it is likely that a man of powerful mind will try to work out a line of his own; and this Newman essayed to do in a series of remarkable works, from *The Arians of the Fourth Century* (1833)

6. J. H. Newman, *Sermons Chiefly on the Theory of Religious Belief Preached before the University of Oxford*, 1843, p. 189.

down to the *Essay on Development* (1845). Nothing that came from his pen during these creative twelve years can safely be neglected. Newman had the least compartmentalized of minds. We are as likely to find a remark on epistemology or on the relations between reason and feeling in one of the *Tracts for the Times* or in one of the *Parochial Sermons* as in a work such as the *University Sermons* which is mainly concerned with the philosophy of religion. It is as though he felt his intellectual problems like a passion, so that they forced their way to the surface no matter what the ostensible topic of discourse.

The "given" for Newman, from the time when, under the influence of Hurrell, Froude and Keble, he abandoned the gush of the Evangelicals and the cheerful worldliness of Whateley and essayed to construct, at first almost single-handed, the *via media*, consists of the Christian revelation, understood as the Scriptures interpreted in the light of the dogmatic teaching of the Fathers and the Councils. It was only as summing up and restating (as he then thought they did) this teaching that he valued the classic theologians of the Anglican tradition. It is, of course, in some ways a mistake to date his reception of this "given" too precisely. As we have already noticed, he early rested "in the thought of two and two only supreme and luminously self-evident beings, myself and my Creator". In one form "the given" is there from childhood; but it is only with his conversion to a patristic and dogmatic religion that it becomes firmly articulate. The formula, "two and two only supreme and luminously self-evident beings", does nevertheless give us a principle of interpretation. Many for whom the Christian revelation is "given" in the sense of being not seriously questionable, have found very little else seriously questionable. The Christian revelation has consisted of a collection of solid facts; but there are also the facts of history, of the natural sciences, of human psychology; and there is the commonsense world of pleasure and money, chairs and tables, battle, murder and sudden death : a great, solid, indubitable and intelligible world; of which religion is a constituent part. For Newman this is a delusion of the imagination. We live in the midst of uncertainties. If religion offers us a certainty, it is not certainty as the world understands it, but a certainty which is a mysterious fact to be taken far otherwise than the man of the world takes *his* certainties; as not certain at all by his criteria; as certainty only to those who find the certainties of the world uncertain. Newman ingeniously conflates in his apologetic "the world" as the term is used in the Gospels with "the world", uncertain in its outlines and in its operating principles, of an empiricism of sceptical mood.[7] If and in so far as we take the world seriously (as apologists of the school of Paley did), it is far from certain that we can find in it evidence for its Creator and for its being subject to the rule of Providence and the dispensation of Grace.

> The natural man has no heart for the promises of the Gospel, and dissects its evidence without reverence, without hope, without suspense, without misgivings; and, while he analyzes it perhaps more philosophically than another, and treats it more luminously, and sums up its result with the precision and propriety of a legal tribunal, he rests in it as an end, and neither attains the further truths at which it points, nor inhales the spirit which it breathes.
>
> And this remark bears upon a fact which has sometimes perplexed Christians—that those philosophers, ancient and modern, who have been eminent in physical science, have not infrequently shown a tendency to infidelity. The system of physical causes is so much more tangible and satisfying than that of final, that unless there be a pre-existent and independent interest in the inquirer's mind, leading him to dwell on the phenomena which betoken an Intelligent Creator, he will certainly follow out those which terminate in the hypothesis of a settled order of nature and self-sustained laws. *It is indeed a great question whether atheism is not as philosophically consistent with the phenomena of the physical world,*

7. See, for example, Sermon VI, *University Sermons*, pp. 108 ff.

*taken by themselves, as the doctrine of a creative and govern-ing Power.* [My italics.] [8]

The pattern of argument strikingly resembles that of Hume. We may take the world of things as in its structure an hypothesis to account for the world of our perceptions. But if we take the hypothesis seriously, as we are entitled to do if we unite reason with natural propensity, then we cannot argue from the world so taken to one rather than another metaphysical view. Here no marriage of reason and natural propensity is possible.

Newman's design is not a rhetorical one: to use the weapons of empiricism to frighten men into the world of faith understood as being, in contrast with the visible and tangible world, a world of exquisite clarity. Far from it. Such clarity as we find in the world of things and of society is a consequence of rational reflection and criticism, though even here it is only in so far as we have confidence in "nature" and curb the wild ranging of the intellect that we can take this world as being clear in its outlines. A similar clarity *can* be achieved in the world of faith, and by the use of the same intellectual powers; but the cost is high: that of evacuating the world of faith of its supernatural and mysterious content, a content which can be grasped only by faith and which is in its structure "foolishness to the Greeks", scandalous and paradoxical to the natural man. Newman, therefore, is not contradicting Hume, arguing that a dispassionate survey of the natural world brings us to one certain metaphysical con-clusion. He accepts the incapacity of reason to frame such an argument. If he has reasons, nevertheless, which are in a sense prolegomena to faith, they are of another order.

The strict definition of terms is not a part of Newman's method. He inherits a number of terms from the eighteenth-century writers—"reason", "feeling", "the passions", "the moral sense", "moral perceptions", "nature", "the heart"—and employs them in the then received sense, a sense not

8. Ibid., pp. 185, 186.

very strictly determined, and perhaps incapable of being strictly determined, if these terms are to be adequate to the many uses to which they are put. By "reason" he commonly means the faculty employed in formal argument of a mathematical and logical kind and in investigations in history and the natural sciences. The method of the natural sciences, understood as finding its paradigm in the writings of Bacon and the practice of Newton (this is Hume's paradigm as well), seems very often to make its presence felt when there is talk of the role of reason and where this role is contrasted with that of faith or feeling. Investigation in history or the natural sciences employs "certain scientific rules and fixed standards for weighing testimony, and examining facts".[9] He also sees that the operations of reason in this sense presuppose a public world, a common language and a set of accepted rules.

> Nothing can be urged or made to tell, but what all feel, all comprehend, all can put into words . . . only such reasons are in point as can be exhibited in simple propositions; the multiform and intricate assemblage of considerations which really lead to judgment and action, must be attenuated or mutilated into a major and a minor premiss.[1]

He wishes to emphasize a certain artificiality in the procedures of reason in this sense. These procedures are not those which lead to judgment and decision. Quite apart from faith, and much more so where faith is in question, we judge and decide not in accordance with the scientific paradigm but in response to a multitude of considerations we are quite incapable of itemizing and the connections between which cannot be exhibited in formal patterns satisfying to the logician. Our belief in the applicability in the fields of history and the natural sciences of the paradigm rests upon an antecedent judgment that cannot itself be justified by reasons that measure up to the paradigm; and where we are concerned with moral truths (when Newman speaks of "moral truth" he has in mind truth both in ethics and religion) the paradigm cannot be employed, not because it is impossible to apply it in practice, but because it is in this field logically inappropriate. By definition faith goes beyond what can be shown by reason to the common satisfaction; and in matters of morality, even though Newman would no doubt have avoided the bluntness, the desire *épater les philosophes*, of Hume's "Reason is, and ought only to be the slave of the passions, and can never pretend to any other office than to serve and obey them",[2] the ends of human action are for him determined by desire and not by reason, by passion or by a moral perception refined by Grace. Questions in faith and morals are, he writes, "addressed to the cultivated moral perception, or, what is sometimes improperly termed, '*feeling*'; improperly, because feeling comes and goes, and, having no root in our nature [i.e. because feeling cannot strictly be said to be a natural propensity], speaks with no divine authority; but the moral perception, though varying in the mass of men, is fixed in each individual, and is an original element within us".[3]

There is some variation in Newman's view of reason, even within the same work and at the same time. The view of reason, and of its relation to faith and moral perception, that I have expounded is substantially that to be found in, for example, the *University Sermons*. Sometimes he wishes to argue for a less restricted use of the term; and there is a certain development in his view of reason and in his view of the paradigm of rational discourse between the earlier and the later of the *University Sermons*. (This is scarcely surprising: the first of these was preached in 1826 and the last in 1843.) In the second sermon, preached in 1830, he is completely a disciple of Butler, and of a Butler with some of the roughnesses taken out. He argues, for example, that "the whole revealed scheme rests on nature for the validity of its evidence"; that "the two systems [of Natural and Revealed

<hr />

2. *Treatise*, p. 415.     3. *University Sermons*, pp. 44, 45.

Religion] coincide in declaring the same substantial doctrines"; that "Scripture completes the very deficiency of nature"; and he echoes a famous passage in St. Augustine's *Confessions* when he declares that he finds in Scripture "one solitary doctrine, which from its nature has no parallel in this world, an Incarnation of the Divine Essence".[4] Even in the third sermon, preached eighteen months later, there is a sign of a shift in position. After remarking that "evidences" do "comparatively little towards keeping men from infidelity, or turning them to a religious life", he adds:

> The same remark applies to such works on Natural Theology as treat of the marks of design in the creation, which are beautiful and interesting to the believer in a God; but, where men have not already recognized God's voice within them, ineffective, and this moreover possibly *from some unsoundness in the intellectual basis of the argument.* [My italics.][5]

Later still, in the eleventh sermon, preached in 1839, he dares to make his own Hume's ironical conclusion to Section X of the *Enquiry* ("Of Miracles"): "Our most holy religion is founded on *Faith*, not on reason";[6] and by a turn of the wrist argues that in this respect Faith and Unbelief are, logically speaking, counterparts one of the other. He writes, with Hume's argument on miracles in mind:

> As Faith may be viewed as opposed to Reason, in the popular sense of the latter word, it must not be overlooked that Unbelief is opposed to Reason also. Unbelief, indeed, considers itself especially rational, or critical of evidence; but it criticizes the evidence of Religion, only because it does not like it, and really goes upon presumptions and prejudices as much as Faith does, only presumptions of an opposite nature.[7]

This leaves us of course with a problem: What could be a respectable reason for choosing between Faith and Unbelief,

4. Ibid., pp. 32–34.    5. Ibid., p. 55.
6. David Hume, *Enquiries Concerning the Human Understanding and Concerning the Principles of Morals*, ed. L. A. Selby-Bigge, second edition, Oxford, 1902, p. 130.
7. *University Sermons*, pp. 223, 224.

supposing such a choice to be possible? Newman had more than one answer to this question. That he found it a question that gave him a stomach-ache (as did Wiseman's article in the *Dublin Review*) is plain from his desperate resort on occasion to Pascal's expedient of supposing that in this matter *il faut parier*. There are two passages in the *Parochial Sermons* that bear this out.

> If it is but slightly probable that rejection of the Gospel will involve [a man's] eternal ruin, it is safest and wisest to act as if it were certain.[8]

> And when Christ comes at last, blessed indeed will be [the true Christian's] lot. He has joined himself from the first to the conquering side; he has *risked the present against the future, preferring the chance of eternity to the certainty of time.* . . . [My italics.] [9]

Newman could do much better than this. I quote these instances of his reliance upon the wager of Pascal to bring out his decisive break with the rationalism to which he sat loosely even in his earlier days but from which, following the same pattern of argument as Hume and with an appreciation of the logical nuances of Hume rare in his own time, he swiftly freed himself. In what ways Newman may be said to have done better than this I leave aside, so far as this essay is concerned.[1]

## 3

I have now shown in what sense Newman stands within the empiricist tradition; that in a number of ways his thought and imagination are nourished by the myth of empiricism; that he succeeded in showing that the logical issues were more complex than the subtlest and deepest of the empiricists, Hume, had supposed. I now wish to point to particular instances where the thought of Newman runs forward

8. *Parochial Sermons*, Vol. II, p. 23.
9. *Parochial Sermons*, Vol. IV, p. 271.
1. See "The Logic of the Heart", *supra*.

to suggest problems and approaches in philosophy that belong to our own period rather than to the English nineteenth century.

The concepts of knowledge and belief are not easy to elucidate. Within the empiricist tradition there is a general tendency to try to elucidate them in terms of inner states such as can be described by an accurate psychology. The dilemmas into which philosophers have been forced by this procedure are notorious. If knowing or believing is an inner state having determinate characteristics, we are then faced with the difficulty that there seems nothing self-contradictory in the supposition that my inner state has these determinate characteristics, but that what I judge to be the case is not the case. If this is so, there are obvious logical objections to counting this as an instance of knowing. Similarly, if my inner state has the characteristics of belief, then it seems not self-contradictory to suppose that I may have such an inner state and yet have no grounds for belief. Would this then count as an instance of belief? Again, if my believing or my knowing is an inner state it is in principle not such that it can be inspected by another; and yet we seem able, even where verbal avowals of knowledge or belief are absent, to say something about what others know and believe by watching what they do. And if a man *says* that he believes p and offers as evidence that he does so an introspective report, and yet at the same time his behaviour is altogether what we should expect of one who disbelieves p, then we are inclined to suppose that he disbelieves p without necessarily concluding that he has given a false introspective report.

Newman, certainly, is by no means clear about the difficulties of all such accounts of what it is to know and to believe. But there are, here and there in his work, remarkable instances of his power to transcend the limitations of the empiricist analysis. I choose two instances.

In his *Lectures on the Prophetical Office* he wishes at one point to maintain that Anglicans have the right to say that faith is possible within their Church, despite their disbelief in the Roman doctrine of the Church's infallibility. Concerning the difference between faith and opinion he writes:

> This indeed is [faith's] trial and its praise, so to hang upon the thought of Him, and desire Him, as not to wait till it knows for certain from infallible informants whether or no He has spoken, but to act in the way which seems on the whole most likely to please Him. If we are asked, how Faith differs from Opinion, we reply, in its considering His being, governance, and will as a matter of personal interest and importance to us, not in the degree of light or darkness under which it perceives the truth concerning them. When we are not personally concerned, even the highest evidence does not move us; when we are concerned, the very slightest is enough. Though we knew for certain that the planet Jupiter were in flames, we should go on as usual; whereas even the confused cry of fire at night rouses us from our beds. Action is the criterion of true faith, as determining accurately whether we connect the thought of God with the thought of ourselves, whether we love Him, or regard Him otherwise than we regard the existence of the solar system.[2]

Again, in a sermon on the theme of the immortality of the soul, he asks what it is to know or feel or realize that we have souls. Is it, he asks, a sufficient condition for saying that a man knows he has a soul that he should be able to say that he has or to assent to the doctrine that he has a soul? He continues:

> And yet, in spite of our being able to speak about it . . . there seems scarcely room to doubt, that the greater number of those who are called Christians in no true sense realize it in their own minds at all. Indeed it is a very difficult thing to bring home to us; and to feel that we have souls; and there cannot be a more fatal mistake than to suppose we see what the

2. J. H. Newman, *Lectures on the Prophetical Office of the Church, viewed relatively to Romanism and Popular Protestantism,* second edition, 1838, pp. 105, 106.

doctrine means, as soon as we can use the words which signify it. So great a thing is it to understand that we have souls, that the knowing it, taken in connexion with its results, is all one with *being serious*, i.e. truly religious. *To discern our immortality is necessarily connected with fear and trembling and repentance, in the case of every Christian.* [Italics in the last sentence mine.] [3]

Two fundamental points come out of these passages. First, his awareness, not indeed fully worked out, that while it may be a *necessary* condition for saying that a man knows *p* or believes *p* that he should be in a certain mental state or say that he knows or believes *p*, it is never a *sufficient* condition by itself. The criterion of behaviour or practice is always needed. Secondly, there are strong similarities between Newman's position in these instances and the position of Kierkegaard and later existentialists in precisely this field. To believe is to commit oneself. A merely speculative conclusion, no doubt appropriate in, say, astronomy, is, where matters of faith are in question, a sign that one remains at the level of the aesthetic. The first point represents an anticipation of contemporary philosophical analysis. As to the second, isn't it plain that a modish student, faced with the task of giving the author of "To discern our immortality is necessarily connected with fear and trembling and repentance, in the case of every Christian" (supposing the sentence not to have been identified), would without much hesitation plump for Kierkegaard? Kierkegaard, too, is in a sense "a great Victorian"; but Newman and Kierkegaard are alike in that much in their work that slipped past their contemporaries finds a place in the debates of our own day.

1960

3. *Parochial Sermons*, Vol. I, pp. 19, 20.